Serverless Integration Patterns with Azure

Build powerful cloud solutions that sustain next-generation products

Abhishek Kumar
Srinivasa Mahendrakar

BIRMINGHAM - MUMBAI

Serverless Integration Design Patterns with Azure

Commissioning Editor: Vijin Boricha
Acquisition Editor: Prachi Bisht
Content Development Editor: Roshan Kumar
Technical Editor: Snehal Dalmet
Copy Editor: Safis Editing
Language Support Editor: Mary McGowan, Storm Mann
Project Coordinator: Namrata Swetta
Proofreader: Safis Editing
Indexer: Priyanka Dhadke
Graphics: Jisha Chirayil
Production Coordinator: Saili Kale

First published: February 2019

Production reference: 1120219

Published by Packt Publishing Ltd.
Livery Place
35 Livery Street
Birmingham
B3 2PB, UK.

ISBN 978-1-78839-923-4

www.packtpub.com

`mapt.io`

Mapt is an online digital library that gives you full access to over 5,000 books and videos, as well as industry leading tools to help you plan your personal development and advance your career. For more information, please visit our website.

Why subscribe?

- Spend less time learning and more time coding with practical eBooks and Videos from over 4,000 industry professionals

- Improve your learning with Skill Plans built especially for you

- Get a free eBook or video every month

- Mapt is fully searchable

- Copy and paste, print, and bookmark content

Packt.com

Did you know that Packt offers eBook versions of every book published, with PDF and ePub files available? You can upgrade to the eBook version at `www.packt.com` and as a print book customer, you are entitled to a discount on the eBook copy. Get in touch with us at `customercare@packtpub.com` for more details.

At `www.packt.com`, you can also read a collection of free technical articles, sign up for a range of free newsletters, and receive exclusive discounts and offers on Packt books and eBooks.

Contributors

About the authors

Abhishek Kumar works with New Zealand Trade and Enterprise as an integration and data specialist. He is a Microsoft Azure MVP with deep expertise in software development and design. He is a co-author of Robust Cloud Integration and a seasoned contributor to Microsoft blogs, forums, and events. As a technological evangelist, he is specialized in cloud-based technologies such as Azure Functions, Microsoft Graph, Logic Apps, Web API, and Cosmos DB, along with various Software-as-a-Service (SaaS) such as Salesforce, Office 365, and ServiceNow. As a technology advocate, he promotes loosely coupled solution design along with event-based programming.

Srinivasa Mahendrakar has more than 13 years' experience in the IT industry in building applications and data integration solutions using Microsoft technologies including BizTalk, SSIS, Azure Integration Services, and Azure Functions. His career roles included developer, technical lead, solution architect, and product owner, and he has been involved in building highly regarded solutions in industries such as finance, healthcare, retail, energy, and utilities. For the past three years, he has been working at BizTalk360, to build tools for modern integration solutions. Currently, he is a product director, heading up the Atomic Scope product team. He has also hosted Integration Monday and Global Integration Boot camp sessions.

About the reviewers

Lex Hegt lives with his wife Odette and two kids, Denise and Casper, near The Hague in the Netherlands. His first steps in IT date back to the mid-1980s; in 2004, he started with Microsoft Integration. Lex has worked at consultancy companies such as Ordina and Axon Olympus (now Codit NL), and all his assignments shaped him into an experienced BizTalk administrator, developer, and trainer. In 2016, Lex joined BizTalk360 as a Technical Lead for the BizTalk360 and Atomic Scope products. He also runs the Integration Monday community initiative and some community-oriented newsletters. In his spare time, Lex enjoys spending time with his family, listening to music, playing piano, goal-keeping at field hockey, and dining with good company.

Wagner Silveira is the Principal Integration Architect at Theta. Originally from Brazil, he started his IT career as a class-led instructor of Microsoft products, coming to New Zealand in 2002, where he has been working on Microsoft Integration Technologies ever since, using the Microsoft stack and technologies such as BizTalk Server, Azure Integration Services, and Azure Function to create award-winning solutions. Wagner is one of the organizers of the Auckland Connected Systems User Group (ACSUG) and Integration Downunder webcast, and member of the Global Integration Bootcamp board, helping to organize the event across the globe and in New Zealand.

Mayank Sharma is Senior Program Manager for Azure Commerce and Ecosystems at Microsoft, Redmond, with more than 15 years of industry experience. He has been with Microsoft for 5 years, worked as Project Manager for Azure Integration Services, PaaS offering integration landscape, partnering with Azure Logic Apps group. Earlier, he worked on Microsoft's platform modernization programs, focused around cloud adoption, Hybrid integration patterns, and migration tools. Being a passionate presenter, he has also shares Microsoft's integration case study at various conferences and events around the world. He also worked with other industry leaders including Accenture, HCL Technologies, and Fidelity, on various business transformation programs.

Packt is searching for authors like you

If you're interested in becoming an author for Packt, please visit authors.packtpub.com and apply today. We have worked with thousands of developers and tech professionals, just like you, to help them share their insight with the global tech community. You can make a general application, apply for a specific hot topic that we are recruiting an author for, or submit your own idea.

Table of Contents

Preface

With the surge in cloud adoption, serverless integration has gained popularity, as have Microsoft Azure's offerings, such as Azure Logic Apps, Functions, API Management, Event Grid, and Service Bus. These serverless platforms allow enterprises to build powerful, secure, and scalable integration solutions in the cloud. The primary goal of *Serverless Integration Design Patterns with Azure* is to teach you how to work with enterprise design patterns, and how to connect services and platforms hosted in the cloud or on premises.

This book builds your understanding of Azure Integration Services by providing you with hands-on labs to test and improve your skills and knowledge of cloud integration and the different connecting platforms in Azure. As well as Azure, you'll also learn about the Microsoft Cloud Platform Integration Framework, along with various other architecture design principles that can be applied when connecting systems.

Who this book is for

Serverless Integration Design Patterns with Azure is intended for solution architects and integration professionals aiming to build complex cloud solutions and next-generation integration patterns using the Microsoft Azure platform. This books covers cloud and hybrid integration patterns using serverless platforms such as Logic Apps, Azure Functions, API Management, Event Grid, and Service Bus.

What this book covers

Chapter 1, *Serverless Integration with Microsoft Azure*, provides an overview of Azure Integration Services and what this means for organizations in terms of their digital transformation roadmap. This chapter introduces serverless platforms and outlines the key advantages and benefits for organization moving their enterprise IT workload's into the cloud. We have also given brief introduction to Integration services, such as Logic Apps, API Management, Service Bus, Event Grid, and Azure Functions.

Chapter 2, *Azure Functions and Enterprise Integration*, looks at Azure Functions. They are the linchpin in Azure's serverless offerings. With a range of triggers and bindings available, developers will see how quick and easy it is to spin up Azure Functions for given problems or APIs. Microsoft has made it possible for users to either use the Azure portal, Visual Studio, or Visual Studio Code for development.

Chapter 3, *Introduction to Azure Event Grid*, closely examines the capabilities of Azure Event Grid and considers how we can utilize Event Grid features in a modern integration framework. We cover multiple routing options with Event Grid and experiment with a few sample exercises for Event Grid topics and domains.

Chapter 4, *Azure API Management*, looks at how Azure API Management fits into the overall enterprise application landscape and can help to secure APIs and Logic Apps.

Chapter 5, *Azure Service Bus with Integration Services*, introduces Azure Service Bus and explains how we can use code, along with Logic Apps and Azure Functions bindings, to create an integration layer in Microsoft Azure. We also cover some design patterns, focusing on parameters and priority queues.

Chapter 6, *Introduction to Logic Apps*, introduces Logic Apps and demonstrates applications of the different types of triggers and actions that are available through the designer and code views. You'll learn how to implement some complex design patterns with Logic Apps and associated software and services. This chapter has also highlights aspects of the Cosmos graph database.

Chapter 7, *Control Flow Actions and Custom Connectors*, discusses the different control flow actions available in Logic Apps to create robust workflows to connect disparate systems. You'll learn how to write with the Logic Apps expression language, using Logic Apps designer and with code editor. Finally, we discuss how you can leverage your existing API as a custom connector in Logic Apps, and how to build your own custom connector for Logic Apps.

Chapter 8, *Patterns with Azure Integration Services*, covers how you can perform exception handling in Logic Apps, along with multiple design patterns such as sequential message flow, webhooks for event-based architecture patterns, and simple batching with Logic Apps.

Chapter 9, *B2B/EDI Solutions for Enterprise Integration with Azure Logic Apps*, explains how creating B2B flows is easy when using Logic Apps and an integration account. In the world of Microsoft integration, customers are slowly but steadily moving from BizTalk-based on-premises integrations to Logic Apps-based integrations. EDI/AS2-based integrations are moving fastest to the cloud out of all integrations out there.

Chapter 10, *Hybrid Integration Using BizTalk Server 2016 and an On-Premises Data Gateway*, explores the capabilities of Logic Apps and how they can be applied to typical hybrid integration scenarios using Logic Apps adapters. Logic Apps provide connectivity to on-premises applications. We have shown how we can connect on-premises BizTalk and a wide variety of services, such as SQL and WCF services, hosted within corporate networks with no access to the cloud.

Chapter 11, *Intelligence in Integration Using Azure Cognitive Services*, explains terminology related to artificial intelligence, machine learning, and neural networks. We look at Microsoft and the democratization of AI, the Microsoft AI platform, and applications of AI in serverless integration. We also examine a case study on sentiment analysis.

Chapter 12, *DevOps for Azure Integration*, considers DevOps practices in Azure Integration. We list why DevOps processes are necessary for modern integration, along with how you can automate Azure Integration Services using a DevOps pipeline.

Chapter 13, *Monitoring for Azure Integration*, discusses enabling monitoring for Azure Integration Services. We walk through the process of enabling monitoring for Logic Apps, API Management, Azure Functions, and Service Bus. In this chapter, we also cover how you can use a third-party product, Serverless360, to effectively monitor the messaging layer for your entire enterprise.

To get the most out of this book

To get the most out of this book, we assume that you have the prerequisite knowledge of Visual Studio and Visual Studio Code, along with prior programming experience with C# and JSON.

Download the example code files

You can download the example code files for this book from your account at www.packt.com. If you purchased this book elsewhere, you can visit www.packt.com/support and register to have the files emailed directly to you.

You can download the code files by following these steps:

1. Log in or register at www.packt.com.
2. Select the **SUPPORT** tab.
3. Click on **Code Downloads & Errata**.
4. Enter the name of the book in the **Search** box and follow the onscreen instructions.

Once the file is downloaded, please make sure that you unzip or extract the folder using the latest version of:

- WinRAR/7-Zip for Windows
- Zipeg/iZip/UnRarX for Mac
- 7-Zip/PeaZip for Linux

The code bundle for the book is also hosted on GitHub at `https://github.com/ PacktPublishing/Serverless-Integration-Design-patterns-with-Azure`. In case there's an update to the code, it will be updated on the existing GitHub repository.

We also have other code bundles from our rich catalog of books and videos available at `https://github.com/PacktPublishing/`. Check them out!

Download the color images

We also provide a PDF file that has color images of the screenshots/diagrams used in this book. You can download it here: `http://www.packtpub.com/sites/default/files/ downloads/9781788399234_ColorImages.pdf`.

Conventions used

There are a number of text conventions used throughout this book.

`CodeInText`: Indicates code words in text, database table names, folder names, filenames, file extensions, pathnames, dummy URLs, user input, and Twitter handles. Here is an example: "Mount the downloaded `WebStorm-10*.dmg` disk image file as another disk in your system."

A block of code is set as follows:

```
[CosmosDB(databaseName:"Sales",
        collectionName:"Orders",
        ConnectionStringSetting ="dbConnectionString")]
        IAsyncCollector<PurchaseOrder> writeResultsToCosmos
```

When we wish to draw your attention to a particular part of a code block, the relevant lines or items are set in bold:

```
[CosmosDB(databaseName:"Sales", collectionName:"Orders",
ConnectionStringSetting ="dbConnectionString")]
IAsyncCollector<PurchaseOrder> writeResultsToCosmos
```

Bold: Indicates a new term, an important word, or words that you see onscreen. For example, words in menus or dialog boxes appear in the text like this. Here is an example: "Select **System info** from the **Administration** panel."

Warnings or important notes appear like this.

Tips and tricks appear like this.

Get in touch

Feedback from our readers is always welcome.

General feedback: If you have questions about any aspect of this book, mention the book title in the subject of your message and email us at customercare@packtpub.com.

Errata: Although we have taken every care to ensure the accuracy of our content, mistakes do happen. If you have found a mistake in this book, we would be grateful if you would report this to us. Please visit www.packt.com/submit-errata, selecting your book, clicking on the Errata Submission Form link, and entering the details.

Piracy: If you come across any illegal copies of our works in any form on the Internet, we would be grateful if you would provide us with the location address or website name. Please contact us at copyright@packt.com with a link to the material.

If you are interested in becoming an author: If there is a topic that you have expertise in and you are interested in either writing or contributing to a book, please visit authors.packtpub.com.

Reviews

Please leave a review. Once you have read and used this book, why not leave a review on the site that you purchased it from? Potential readers can then see and use your unbiased opinion to make purchase decisions, we at Packt can understand what you think about our products, and our authors can see your feedback on their book. Thank you!

For more information about Packt, please visit packt.com.

1
Serverless Integration with Microsoft Azure

In the current era of cloud adoption, enterprises are heavily investing in new platforms, services, and frameworks. They are also moving closer to a customer-focused approach with new offerings to new customers in a geographically extended customer base. Gone are the days of queuing outside of shops in order to get a new device or standing in line to perform a single bank transaction. With new business models and technological innovation, everything is now available at our fingertips. We have witnessed this with the rise of endless online platforms such as LinkedIn, Netflix, Google, Facebook, and Twitter.

This book will explain how integration has changed across different industries, with more cloud adoption and innovation occurring in the software sector. Throughout this book, we will use step-by-step processes to explain key integration concepts, and each chapter will dive into the details of the individual service components of the Microsoft Azure Integration stack. Whether you are new to integration or are experienced in the integration field, each chapter will provide you with valuable technical information that can be implemented within your enterprise solutions.

As the title suggests, this chapter will give a basic overview of Microsoft Azure Integration Services and how it has evolved from being an on-premises integration stack to a cloud-first integration framework. So, fasten your seatbelt and join us on this great journey of integration!

In this chapter, we will cover the following topics:

- Introduction to serverless platforms
- Advantages and disadvantages of serverless architecture
- Introduction to Azure Integration Services
- Components of Azure Integration Services

Introduction to serverless in the cloud

You might have heard the buzzword **serverless** previously, perhaps through your colleagues or cloud advocate. You must have wondered what this means for your enterprise or for you as developer, architect, or DevOps associate. However, do not get confused by the word serverless; it does not refer to the process of running your code without servers.

For an enterprise, serverless actually means managing the enterprise's IT workload in cloud without having to make vast investments in setting up an infrastructure to run products and services. For new and existing organizations, a serverless platform means that an enterprise need only be billed for consumed resources.

For developers, serverless means writing efficient code that makes the most of the resources available. Cloud computing has evolved over time, and we need to appreciate this when making applications for the cloud. The following diagram describes the journey of cloud computing:

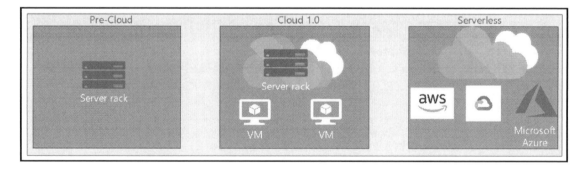

Throughout this journey, Microsoft has invested heavily in making its infrastructure more suited to customer requirements in a much more efficient manner. With Azure, Microsoft's own cloud service, there are numerous platforms and services that let you get started without having to consider the internal infrastructure and any starting costs. These platforms include Azure Functions, Logic Apps, Cosmos DB, Data Factory, API Management, and many more. In this book, we will concentrate on Microsoft's serverless integration stack and how you can take advantage of these serverless platforms in the real world.

Benefits and disadvantages of serverless architecture

In this section, we will discuss the advantages and disadvantages of having a serverless environment in your organization. As the name suggests, a serverless environment provides you with abstraction from operating systems, servers, and infrastructure. This comes with its own set of advantages and disadvantages. For example, if you are using **Function as Service (FaaS)** or an **integration workflow**, you only need to concern yourself with development implementation rather than with procurement of hardware and the building of infrastructure to run functions or integration workflows. This allows an organization to concentrate more on business requirements and innovation in the sector, rather than external factors such as infrastructure setup, firewalls, hardware procurement, and networking.

The following diagram is a representation of a serverless FaaS environment in the cloud, where auto scaling is catered for through multiple execution runtime environments:

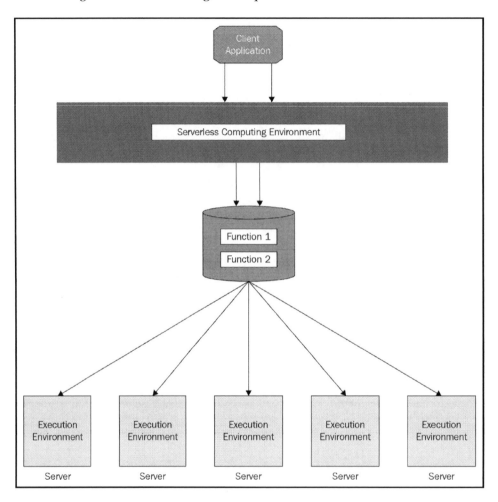

As there are multiple layers to this discussion, let's discuss how you and your organization benefit from a serverless application architecture:

- **Event-driven architecture**: As we move closer to a serverless architecture, we also move closer to reactive asynchronous design patterns. For example, think of your application reacting to an event of your choice instead of polling for all events and then filtering for the required data. This has huge benefits for your organization in terms of the optimization of available resources and minimizing the overall application running cost in the cloud.

- **Language of your choice**: Organizations often struggle to find the right set of development resources that work for their business requirements. You might be a .NET developer or Node.js expert; these serverless platforms provide us with a platform in which language and framework are not constraints and you can write your own code with the language of your choice. This is one of the amazing benefits of utilizing serverless environments for your organization.

- **Microbilling**: A business cares about expenditure and innovation. When you think about a business owner's prospective costs, optimization is one of the biggest challenges in today's world. Most cloud vendors have worked through this challenge to provide better experiences to businesses by introducing a consumption-based pricing model. As more and more organizations are moving to the cloud, there has been a huge reduction in consumption across all cloud vendors. This helps cloud vendors to maximize their resource utilization.

- **Scale on demand**: Serverless environments are highly flexible in terms of scaling. As each serverless platform runs on a separate container, it is easy for cloud vendors to scale services as per demand. With auto scaling enabled, we need only worry about the best implementation of our applications and software, rather than about making applications to suit infrastructural requirements.

- **Geolocation**: Most serverless platforms can run across multiple regions. This is another key advantage when moving to the cloud. With geolocation features, businesses can meet customer requirements across different regions the world over without experiencing any latency or user experience problems.

- **Better monitoring and priorities**: With great monitoring capabilities in serverless environments, the DevOps team can now concentrate more on best practices for application development, deployment, and innovation, rather than spending endless nights supporting the infrastructure. This has benefited organizations in remaining competitive against market changes and innovation in their respective sectors.

We just covered some of the benefits of serverless environments – those were just a few of the many that there are. Now, let's discuss some disadvantages of serverless platforms:

- **Vendor-specific resources**: Most serverless platforms are managed and controlled by specified cloud vendors. This has potential drawbacks if you think of moving your resources to different hosting platforms or different cloud vendors. When using serverless platforms, you are locked into a specific implementation design that may not allow for your organization's flexibility requirements, and there may also be compatibility issues regarding business regions and changing pricing models.

- **Governance**: Most serverless platforms provide you with frameworks with easy startup, but there is a potential drawback to this. If you do not follow the right practices from the start, then you can put your business at risk. An example of this would be storing your database connection in your configuration file rather than using secure configuration storage or not implementing security for your outbound APIs. Though these are considered best practices, sometimes teams tend to move toward unsecured architecture patterns to meet business requirements.

- **Monitoring across different cloud platforms**: If your organization uses multiple cloud platforms, then each vendor will likely have a different set of monitoring implementations. This drawback means it can be harder for enterprises to maintain cross-cloud platform resources.

- **Infrastructure insights**: With serverless solution patterns, you can lose insights into the overall infrastructure setup. To gain maximum resource utilization, most cloud vendors share resources across multiple application implementations. This has the potential drawback of you not being aware of neighboring systems or encountering application noise, which might hinder the performance of your application.

So, we have given you a glimpse of the pros and cons of serverless environments. These are what you need to consider when you port your new services to serverless environments. In the following sections, we will concentrate on Microsoft's serverless offerings, discussing their concepts before moving on to their implementation logic.

Azure Integration Services

In the current era of digital transformation and cloud-first strategy, organizations host their applications both in the cloud and in on-premises environments in a hybrid model. These organizations often struggle to find the right platform to connect these disparate systems.

To address this problem, Microsoft has heavily invested in building an integration framework to run in Azure; it is called Azure Integration Services. Azure Integration Services comprises a set of different services and platforms in Azure, such as Azure Logic Apps, Service Bus, Azure Event Grid, and API Management. Taking the capabilities and power of multiple serverless platforms, Azure Integration Services now serves a variety of customer sectors, ranging from healthcare and the automobile industry to governmental organizations and insurance companies.

Before we dive into a detailed explanation, let's understand what Azure Integration Services is and why you should bother with it. As we've already explained, Azure Integration Services is an umbrella for a number of Azure serverless integration platforms, and you will be surprised at how well these offerings work in harmony; for instance, by how well Azure Functions integrates with Azure Logic Apps to improve an organization's workflow. In the coming chapters, we'll get into more detail about all this, but for now, we'll just concentrate on familiarizing ourselves with the basics of these individual offerings, including what they are and a bit about how they work together to form a cloud-first integration solution.

Granular integration design and microservice patterns have changed the face of modern integration. Now, modern integration is not about learning a specific platform or mastering a product, but is more about getting the best out of connecting platforms. For example, if you want to automate your business workflow, then you can use Azure Logic Apps to build workflows in the cloud by utilizing a reactive programming model along with Azure Event Grid capabilities. Another example might be securing your external-facing endpoint. In that case, API Management is for you. If this confuses you, do not worry; we will learn all of these techniques and best practices throughout this book.

The following diagram describes what you are going to master in this book. We also urge you to go through the Microsoft Azure Integration Services whitepaper at `https://azure.`
`microsoft.com/en-au/resources/azure-integration-services/en-us/`:

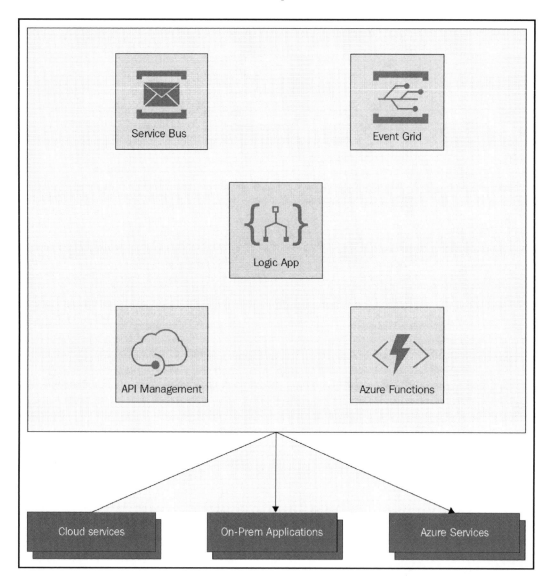

Since we have now looked at an overview of Azure Integration Services, let's discuss the individual offerings separately. We will start with **Azure Logic Apps** and then move on to other services such as **API Management**, **Service Bus**, **Azure Functions**, and **Azure Event Grid**.

If you are already familiar with integration frameworks in the cloud, then we urge you to read these about services' individual capabilities in this chapter. This will help you to get a broader overview of the different platforms and services available within the Azure Integration Services umbrella for connecting enterprise-wide applications with better design patterns.

Azure Logic Apps – cloud workflow engine

Azure Logic Apps is part of the Azure Integration Services family and is an integration workflow engine in the cloud. With Azure Logic Apps, you can get started in no time and automate your workflows as required. With Azure Logic Apps, you can build highly scalable workflows in the cloud by taking advantage of more than 200 connectors (more than 200 were available at the time of writing):

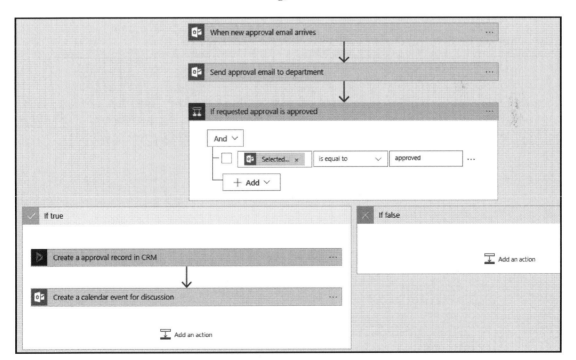

Logic Apps works natively in a serverless fashion. What this means is that, like other serverless platforms, Logic Apps is also highly extensible in terms of micro-billing, scaling on demand, no infrastructure cost, a high level of monitoring, and the ability to bring your own APIs into Logic Apps and use it as a standard connector for building your integration solution.

Organizations are also reaping the benefits of flexible pricing models for Logic Apps. With Logic Apps, you are only charged for your usage (consumption-based pricing model); alternatively, you can opt for the **Integration Service Environment** (**ISE**) and pay a fixed price for your enterprise integration environment. ISE is a great step toward running an enterprise integration environment within a client's own virtual network, while still enjoying all the benefits of the cloud. We will learn more about ISE capabilities in later chapters.

Azure Service Bus – cloud messaging service

Azure Service Bus is a multi-tenant, cloud-based service that sends and receives information between application and services. It is the oldest and most widely used member of Azure Integration Services.

As Azure Service Bus promotes asynchronous programming and works in a publish-subscribe model, various enterprises use its capability for message routing to provide decoupling for their existing solution. Azure Service Bus has grown over the years, experiencing success stories and supporting multiple languages for developers. With Azure Service Bus, you can either use queues for **First-In-First-Out** (**FIFO**) messaging or use topics to work with a publish-subscribe model.

Some of the languages that are supported for sending and receiving messages from a Service Bus queue are listed here:

- .NET
- Java
- Node.js
- Python
- Ruby
- The Azure portal
- The Azure CLI
- Azure PowerShell

The following list notes the languages supported for communication with Service Bus topics/subscriptions:

- .NET
- Java
- Node.js
- PHP
- Python
- Ruby
- The Azure portal
- The Azure CLI
- Azure PowerShell

Azure API Management – API gateway

Azure API Management is a **Platform-as-a-Service (PaaS)** framework for publishing an organization's internal and external APIs. With Azure API Management, you can secure your internal or external APIs, or compose your own API that talks to your backend system to cater to the needs of client applications.

Like other serverless platforms, API Management also comes with a variety of pricing models. For example, you can run an instance of API Management with a consumption plan, or you can pay a fixed price to utilize services in both the standard and premium plans. You can integrate API Management as part of your ISE:

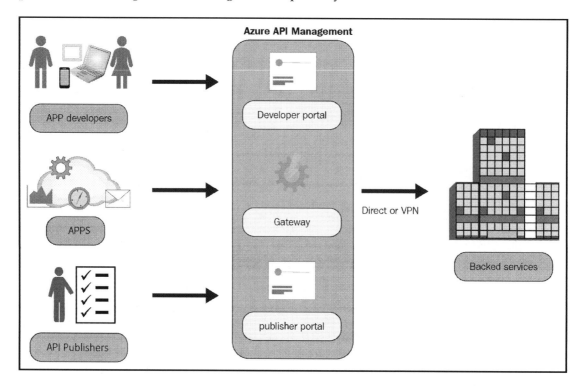

People are often confused by the role of API Management. API Management is not only the façade layer preceding your APIs, but also a security door to your enterprise data. A better solution design should also cater to the security aspect of talking to internal or external services.

We have seen stories where organizations continue creating a plethora of APIs to connect their internal or external business partners, without paying much attention to security, content-type handling, caching, and so on. Often, these service behaviors are managed on an individual basis, which is not suited to a highly scalable infrastructure.

In Chapter 4, *Azure API Management*, we will discuss these aspects in more detail, along with industry best practices, so that you can get the most out of your investment and make your organization more agile and secure.

Azure Functions

Azure Functions embraces a code-first approach to developing enterprise-grade solutions in Azure. Like other serverless platforms, Azure Functions is a powerful framework available in Microsoft Azure, where you can run your code on demand and pay only for your resource consumption.

The Azure Functions runtime supports multiple languages. When developing custom code for integration, developers can use the language of their choice, such as .NET, Node.js, Java, PowerShell, and more. When it comes to hosting, you can host your Azure Functions in any environment, such as Kubernetes, Windows, or a Linux environment. With various available application bindings, Azure Functions also follow a reactive programming model and can be used in a plethora of use cases. On the development front, you can either use the Azure portal to develop your Azure Function, or you can embrace development environments such as Microsoft **Visual Studio** or **Visual Studio Code**:

Visual Studio   Visual Studio Code

You can combine the workflow capabilities of Logic Apps and the code-first execution of Azure Functions to develop enterprise-grade integration solutions without worrying about the infrastructure implementation. Alternatively, you can develop your lightweight API though Azure Functions and leverage the capabilities of API Management to expose your API to the outside world.

When you have a huge workload running on an Azure Functions runtime, you can concern yourself with latency rather than changing your design patterns. There are also various pricing models for Azure Functions, such as fixed-price application plans or the premium runtime environment. All of these considerations are essential architecture decisions, and this book will help you to get the most out of Azure Functions through a chapter dedicated entirely to it.

We also suggest that as you go through this book, you keep yourself informed by reading the Azure Functions documentation: `https://docs.microsoft.com/en-au/azure/azure-functions/`.

The Azure Functions runtime is a great platform for processing data, offering capabilities to integrate systems through input and output bindings, while also suiting big data ingestion use cases such as the **Internet of Things (IoT)** and **Azure Data Factory**.

Azure Event Grid – event-handling platform

Azure Event Grid is a fully managed, intelligent event-routing service. With Azure Event Grid, enterprise applications can leverage an event-driven programming model to build reactive interfaces that can be used to connect external or internal applications. Using Azure Event Grid as a middleware messaging layer for application and interface integration helps organizations to optimize the performance of their software resources with a notification push design pattern, rather than a data pull operation model. Azure Event Grid works with a publish-subscribe mechanism, where you can have one or more event publishers and with each event, there can be one or more subscribers consuming the events.

In the following example, Logic Apps acts as a subscriber to the event published to Azure Event Grid. Events are routed to a Logic Apps endpoint in real time, and once an event is posted to the Logic App endpoint, a Logic Apps workflow sends an auto-triggered email using a Logic Apps-managed API connector for Office 365:

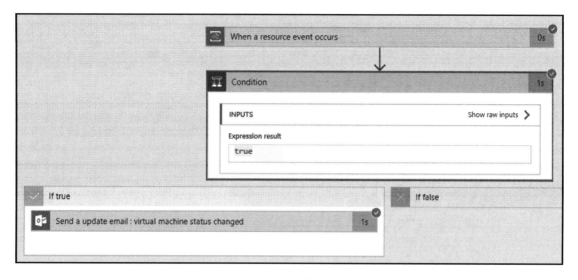

Azure Event Grid is the perfect match for Logic Apps and Azure Functions, and you can leverage events emitted from your environment or external resources to react in real time, instead of consuming resources through a polling-based mechanism. Various blogs and articles have been written on how to use the capabilities of Azure Event Grid, along with other connecting Azure resources such as Data Factory, blob storage, Service Bus, and external services.

This book has dedicated a chapter to the use of Azure Event Grid within enterprise applications, and how you can connect Event Grid services to an application of your choice and reap the benefits of the event-based messaging pattern.

We've now covered the basics of all the services that constitute Azure Integration Services. In the coming chapters, we will discuss each of these services separately, looking at their various architecture design patterns along with the code that can be implemented within your enterprise integration framework.

Summary

In this chapter, we looked at an overview of Azure Integration Services and what it means for an organization's digital transformation roadmap. We also covered an introduction to serverless platforms and their advantages and disadvantages, and we briefly described some individual product offerings, such as Logic Apps, API Management, Service Bus, Event Grid, and Azure Functions.

In next chapter, we will discuss Azure Functions in more detail, learning about some of the advanced capabilities of Azure Functions for building robust solutions and secure frameworks in the cloud.

Azure Functions and Enterprise Integration
2

In the previous chapter, we looked at how serverless computing helps organizations to build applications without worrying about infrastructure. Serverless computing eliminates the operational overhead, brings agility into application development, and allows teams to spend more time on innovation.

Function-as-a-Service (FaaS) is a concept in serverless computing that helps developers to deploy an individual piece of code in the form of a function for executing business logic. Serverless functions have the following benefits:

- Developers can focus purely on the code needed to solve the problem instead of worrying about infrastructure
- They bring consumption-based hosting plans, which allow users to pay only for the time spent running the code
- They integrate well with other cloud services, which ensures that they are responsive to other cloud-based events

Azure Functions is Microsoft's response to FaaS in Azure. Apart from providing the standard features of a FaaS, it also brings the following benefits:

- Users are able to create functions in languages of their choice, such as C#, F#, and JavaScript
- Users are able to add dependencies using NuGet and NPM
- Azure Functions are very well integrated with OAuth providers such as Azure Active Directory, Facebook, Google, and Twitter
- Azure Functions are very well integrated with other Azure services and **Software-as-a-Service (SaaS)** offerings
- Azure Functions can be created in the Azure portal or deployed through **continuous integration (CI)**/**continuous delivery (CD)** pipelines using GitHub or Azure DevOps services

In this chapter, we are going to cover the following topics:

- Understanding the Azure Functions hosting architecture
- Creating a sample Azure Function using Visual Studio Code
- Understanding the components of an Azure Function
- Understanding Azure Function use cases
- Considerations when building Azure Functions
- Understanding durable functions

Azure Functions hosting architecture

In the Azure portal, we need to create a function app for creating Azure Functions. A function app provides the execution context for individual functions. All configuration done at the function-app level will be applied to all Azure Functions. The following is an example of an Azure Function app named **ShipAnyWhere-AzureFunction** and a function called **UpdateInventory**:

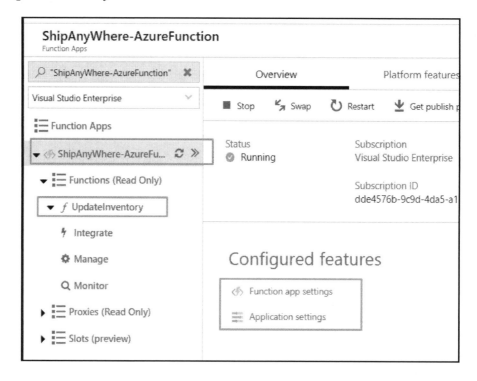

These function apps are run and maintained by the Azure App Service platform, which is an Azure service used for hosting web applications, REST APIs, and mobile backends. The following is a layer diagram showing the dependencies of an Azure Functions runtime over other Azure technologies:

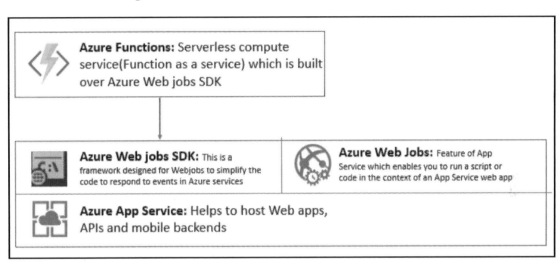

From the preceding diagram, it is clear that the root of **Azure Functions** is the **Azure App Service** platform, which brings following core capabilities to **Azure Functions**:

- It provides the ability to configure the application settings used across Functions in a function app
- It provides a console to navigate through all the files in a function app
- Kudu or advanced tools for app services provides access to administrative features of function apps
- It provides built-in authentication capability to use Azure Active Directory and other social providers

The Azure App Service platform was mainly used for web applications, REST APIs, and mobile backends. However, there will always be some background tasks that need to be executed. These background tasks can be achieved by another service called WebJobs, which runs under the context of the same web application. The WebJobs SDK was designed for Azure WebJobs to help them to integrate easily with other Azure services such as Azure Storage, Service Bus, Event Hub, and so on.

Though it was built for Azure WebJobs, the WebJobs SDK can also work independently.

The Azure Function runtime, also called the Azure Function host, can be built from the ground up using the WebJobs SDK. As such, Azure Functions make use of the Azure Function runtime, which is a `Webjob.Script` (`https://github.com/Azure/azure-functions-host`) library leveraging the power of the Azure WebJobs SDK and is hosted on the Azure App service platform.

Sample Azure Function

To explain the concepts of Azure Functions, we'll make use of a fictional company, ShipAnyWhere. ShipAnyWhere is a large logistical company that is specialized in commerce and fulfillment. ShipAnyWhere provides solutions for e-commerce businesses across the world. It has got more than 100 distribution centers across more than 30 countries. It provides B2B, e-commerce, and multi-channel fulfillment solutions to its customers using cutting-edge technologies.

ShipAnyWhere has a web application that allows orders to be submitted by customers. When an order is submitted, the following takes place:

1. The web application puts the **Order** message in a **Service Bus queue**
2. An Azure Function receives the **Order** messages from the **Service Bus queue**
3. The availability of the products being ordered is checked with **Inventory DB**, which is a Cosmos DB database collection
4. Based on the availability of the products, the status of the order is updated to either "accepted" or "rejected" in **Sales DB**, which is also a Cosmos DB collection:

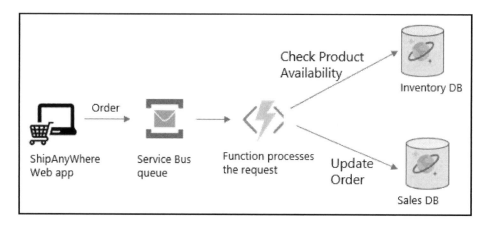

There are two approaches we can take to create an Azure Function:

- **Using the Azure portal**: The Azure portal provides a quick and easy way to create Azure Functions by making use of built-in templates.

 Please refer to `https://docs.microsoft.com/en-us/azure/azure-functions/functions-create-first-azure-function` to find out how to create your first Azure Function in the Azure portal.

- **Using Visual Studio or Visual Studio Code**: In real-world development scenarios, it is best practice to use Visual Studio or Visual Studio Code to build Azure Functions rather than create them in the Azure portal directly. This approach helps in reusing the existing libraries and aligning with DevOps practices.

Since this book tries to faithfully recreate the real-world experience for you, we will create an Azure Function using Visual Studio Code.

Prerequisites for using Visual Studio

The prerequisites for using Visual Studio are listed here:

- **Installing Visual Studio Code**: Install the latest version of Visual Studio Code from `https://code.visualstudio.com/Download`.
- **Installing .NET Core 2.x**: The latest version of the Azure runtime, which is 2.x (at the time of writing), depends on .NET Core 2. Install this version of .NET Core from `https://dotnet.microsoft.com/download`.
- **Installing Node.js**: Install Node.js from `https://docs.npmjs.com/downloading-and-installing-node-js-and-npm`. This is mainly to install Node Package Manager.
- **Installing Azure Functions Core Tools**: Azure Functions Core Tools helps you to develop, debug, and test Azure Functions locally on development machines.
- Open the command terminal in Visual Studio Code (*Ctrl* + *Shift* + '). Run the following command to install Azure Functions Core Tools:

```
npm install -g azure-functions-core-tools
```

- **Installing the Azure Function extension to Visual Studio:** Install the Azure Function by searching for it in the Azure Functions extensions marketplace and restart Visual Studio Code once installed:

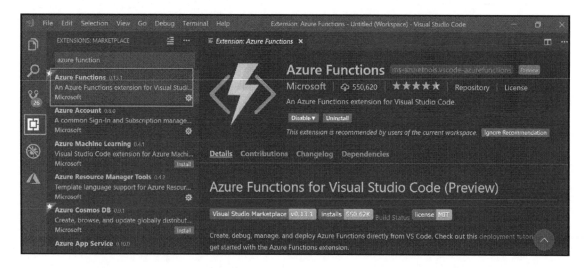

- **Sign into an Azure account:** From Visual Studio Code, you need to sign into an Azure account. Press *Ctrl + Shift + P* in Visual Studio Code. This opens up a command pallet. Select **Azure: Sign In::**

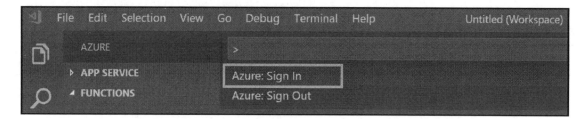

Creating dependent Azure services

For this example, we need a Service Bus queue and a Cosmos DB collection. Here we are assuming that you have knowledge of how to create these artifacts from the Azure portal.

Step 1 – Creating a Service Bus queue

In our scenario, the Azure Function picks up the order message from the Service Bus queue. To create a Service Bus queue, you need to do the following:

1. Log into the Azure portal and create a Service Bus namespace called **ShipAnyWhere**:

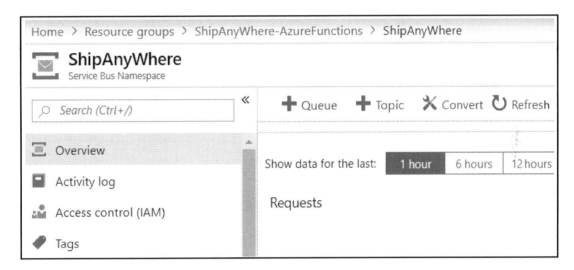

2. Create a queue named **orders**.

Step 2 – Creating a Cosmos DB account and a collection

Our Azure Function processes the order, finds the products, and updates the inventory collection in Cosmos DB. To create a Cosmos DB account, you need to do the following:

1. Create a Cosmos DB account named **shipanywhere:**

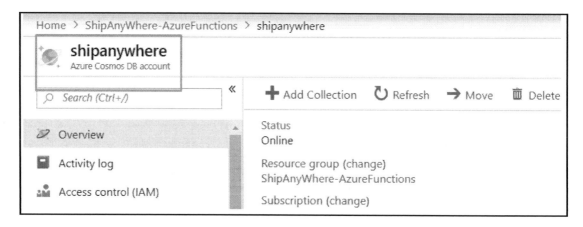

2. Create a collection named **Products:**

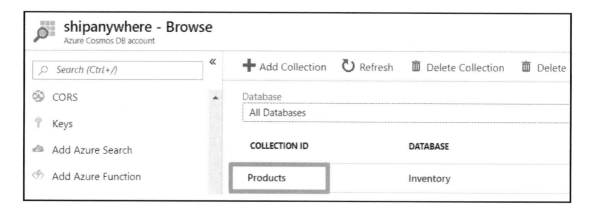

3. Similarly, create another database called **Sales** and a collection called **Orders** under that, as shown:

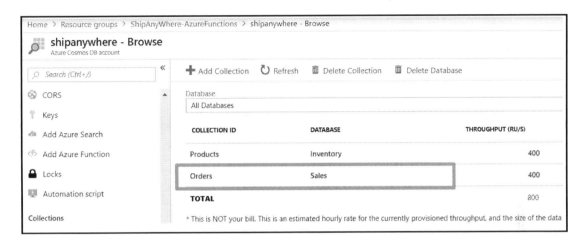

Step 3 – Creating a storage account

Azure Functions make use of a Storage account for its internal purposes and for all triggers except HTTP triggers. Hence, we should have a Storage account ready when creating Azure Functions. Create a Storage account with the name **shipanywherestorage**:

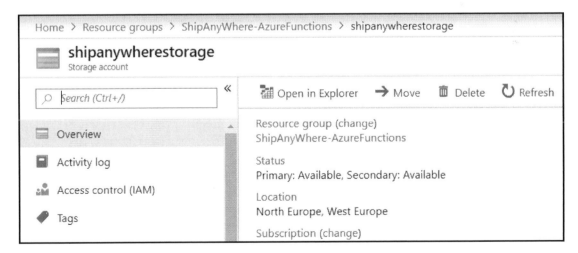

Creating a function app project

Azure Functions run in the App Service environment. The first step for creating an Azure Function is to create a function app that will be deployed as an App Service. In Visual Studio Code, we need to create a new Azure Functions project, which will be equivalent to a function app:

1. In the Visual Studio Code activity bar, click on the **Azure** icon. This opens the section for Azure Functions. Click on the Create New Project... icon as shown. **Browse** to a folder location called `ShipAnyWhere-AzureFunctions`:

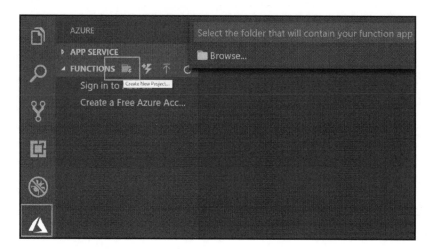

2. Select C# as the language of choice.

Note: In Azure Functions runtime version 1.0, a single function app was able to accommodate functions with different languages. From version 2.0, it is mandatory to select a language for a function app and all the functions must be created in the same language.

3. Select the option to add the project to the workspace.

Creating a function

We can add one or more Azure Functions in a single function app:

1. In the Azure Function section, click on the Create Function... icon:

2. Select the folder location of the function app that we created previously:

3. Now we will have to choose the type of trigger for the function. In our sample scenario, we would like our function to pick up messages from a Service Bus queue. Select **ServiceBusQueueTrigger** from the dropdown:

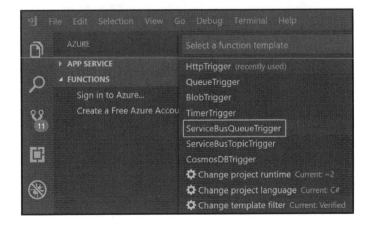

4. Give `UpdateInventory` as the name of the Azure Function. Use `ShipAnyWhere` as the namespace when prompted:

5. We need to specify the application setting field, which will contain the connection string to Service Bus. Select **New App Setting**:

6. Select the **ShipAnyWhere** Service Bus namespace and the **Orders** queue created previously. This creates a function named **UpdateInventory** in the project as shown:

7. In the Visual Studio notifications area, when prompted, choose to **Restore** unresolved dependencies:

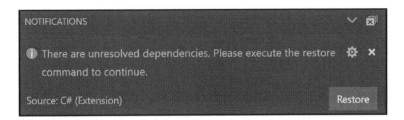

8. Open the `local.settings.json` file and update `AzureWebJobsStorage` with the ShipAnyWhere Storage account connection string:

```
{} local.settings.json
1  {
2      "IsEncrypted": false,
3      "Values": {
4          "AzureWebJobsStorage": "DefaultEndpointsProtocol=https;AccountName=shipanywherestorage;AccountKey=NX9E5g"
5          "FUNCTIONS_WORKER_RUNTIME": "dotnet",
6          "ShipAnyWhere_SERVICEBUS": "Endpoint=sb://shipanywhere.servicebus.windows.net/;SharedAccessKeyName=RootM
7      }
8  }
9
```

Running and debugging functions locally

Once the function is created, Visual Studio Code makes running it very convenient:

1. Press the *F5* key. The function host will be initiated and the Azure Function starts listening to the **Orders** queue for any new orders:

```
PROBLEMS   OUTPUT   DEBUG CONSOLE   TERMINAL              2: Task - runFunctionsH

[13/01/2019 15:11:28] Starting JobHost
[13/01/2019 15:11:28] Starting Host (HostId=lenovopc-77734798, InstanceI
7c-3c7d0c192218, Version=2.0.12246.0, ProcessId=24536, AppDomainId=1, In
nosticMode=False, FunctionsExtensionVersion=)
[13/01/2019 15:11:28] Loading functions metadata
[13/01/2019 15:11:29] 1 functions loaded
[13/01/2019 15:11:29] WorkerRuntime: dotnet. Will shutdown other standby
[13/01/2019 15:11:29] Generating 1 job function(s)
[13/01/2019 15:11:29] Found the following functions:
[13/01/2019 15:11:29] ShipAnyWhere.UpdateInventory.Run
[13/01/2019 15:11:29]
[13/01/2019 15:11:29] Host initialized (459ms)
[13/01/2019 15:11:29] Host started (642ms)
[13/01/2019 15:11:29] Job host started
```

2. The following is the sample file, which contains `sku`, `quantity`, and `location`. These will be used for updating the product inventory:

```json
{

        "ponumber": "10001",
        "name": "John Smith",
        "sku": "111",
        "location": "New York",
        "price": 23.95,
        "quantity": 10,
        "messagetype": "Purchase Order",
        "status": "New",
  "shipTo": {
                        "name": "Jane Smith",
                        "address": "123 Maple Street",
                        "city": "Pretendville",
                        "state": "NY",
                        "zip": "12345",
        },
        "billTo": {
                                "name": "John Smith",
                                "address": "123 Maple Street",
                                "city": "Pretendville",
                                "state": "NY",
                                "zip": "12345",

        }
}
```

3. Open the Service Bus Explorer and send the message to our **Orders** queue:

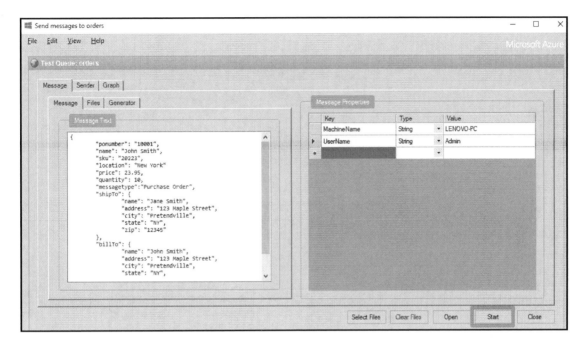

 The Service Bus Explorer is a free tool that can be used for exploring Service Bus entities and sending messages to queues and topics. Please refer to the GitHub page of this tool: `https://github.com/paolosalvatori/ServiceBusExplorer`. You can also make use of Serverless360 for this purpose: `https://www.serverless360.com/`.

4. At a breakpoint, you can see that any message received from the **Orders** queue will be printed in the terminal window:

```
namespace ShipAnywhere
{
    0 references
    public static class UpdateInventory
    {
        [FunctionName("UpdateInventory")]
        0 references
        public static void Run([ServiceBusTrigger("orders", Connection = "ShipAnywhere_SERVICEBUS")]string m
        {
            log.LogInformation($"C# ServiceBus queue trigger function processed message: {myQueueItem}");
        }
    }
}
```

```
PROBLEMS    OUTPUT    DEBUG CONSOLE    TERMINAL          2: Task - runFunctionsH ▼    ✚  ▥  🗑  ∧  ✕

Application started. Press Ctrl+C to shut down.
[13/01/2019 16:02:18] Executing 'UpdateInventory' (Reason='New ServiceBus message detected on '
orders'.', Id=f345465a-9780-4ed6-bf73-0d22eb50a267)
[13/01/2019 16:02:18] C# ServiceBus queue trigger function processed message: {
[13/01/2019 16:02:18]     "ponumber": "10001",
[13/01/2019 16:02:18]     "name": "John Smith",
[13/01/2019 16:02:18]     "sku": "20223",
[13/01/2019 16:02:18]         "location": "New York"
[13/01/2019 16:02:18]     "price": 23.95,
[13/01/2019 16:02:18]     "quantity": 10,
[13/01/2019 16:02:18]     "messagetype":"Purchase Order".
```

Publishing Azure Functions

Once the Azure Function is tested locally, we can publish it to Azure. This can be done directly from Visual Studio Code:

1. In the **FUNCTIONS** menu, click on the Deploy to Azure App... option as shown:

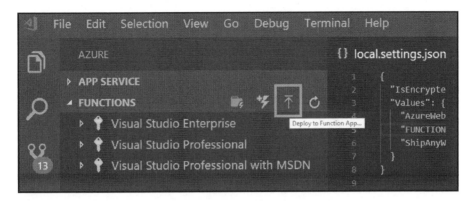

2. When prompted, specify the name of the new function app that will be created in Azure. In our case, we will name it `ShipAnyWhere-AzureFunction`:

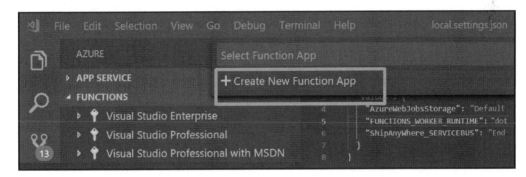

3. Select the `ShipAnyWhere-AzureFunction` resource group that we created previously:

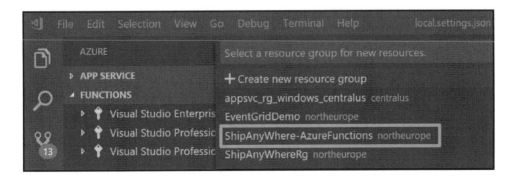

4. Select the `shipanywherestorage` Storage account that we created earlier:

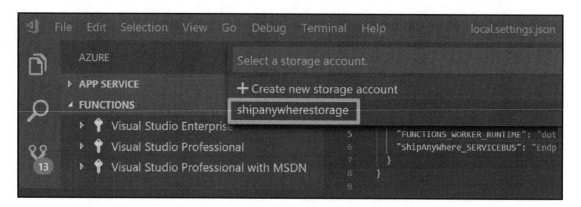

5. Once deployment is finished, add a new **ShipAnyWhere-SERVICEBUS** app setting with the connection string details for the ShipAnyWhere Service Bus we created earlier:

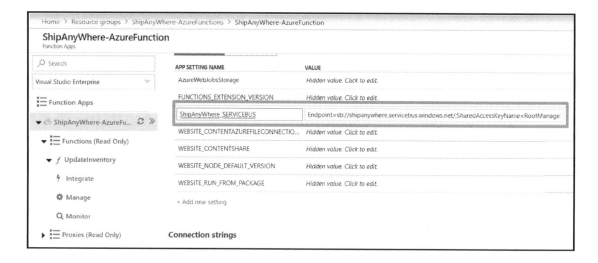

6. After publishing, Visual Studio Code prompts you to start streaming the Azure Function output. Select this option and send a message from the Service Bus Explorer. You will be able to see the output stream in the **OUTPUT** window as follows:

```
PROBLEMS    OUTPUT    DEBUG CONSOLE    TERMINAL        ShipAnyWhere-AzureFt ▼

2019-01-13T17:05:04.730 [Information] Executing 'UpdateInventory' (Reason='New ServiceBus message detected on 'orders'.',
Id=11c82b11-e668-43fe-9b5f-f5301f58f609)

2019-01-13T17:05:04.763 [Information] C# ServiceBus queue trigger function processed message: {

    "ponumber": "10001",

    "name": "John Smith",

    "sku": "20223",

        "location": "New York"
```

Understanding the components of an Azure Function

In the previous section, we implemented the first part of our scenario by creating an Azure Function with a Service Bus queue trigger and running it locally. At this point, it is essential that we understand the various components of Azure Functions.

Application host file (host.json)

The host.json file is a configuration file containing the values that affect all the functions of a function app. This file is created as soon as we add an Azure Function project. This file will have at least one field to begin with, indicating the runtime version of Azure Functions.

The following is the content of the `host.json` file created in our sample project:

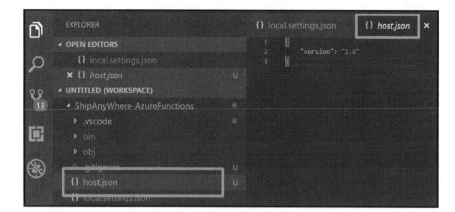

 To understand the various elements of a `host.json` file, please refer to the documentation: `https://docs.microsoft.com/en-us/azure/azure-functions/functions-host-json`.

Application settings (local.settings.json)

For the Azure Function to run, we need to add various application settings entries. In our sample project, the Service Bus connection string and `webjobsstorage` were the two application settings we used. When we run the functions locally, the configuration should be present in `local.settings.json`. The following is the `local.setting.json` file from our sample project:

```
"IsEncrypted": false,
"Values": {
    "AzureWebJobsStorage":
"DefaultEndpointsProtocol=https;AccountName=shipanywherestorage;AccountKey=
NX9E5gYe1vkSWEU0AFS0dgz2PKmrrOBf7Osk8XPpB0y+ZXLEPpxdQDjIN1oScg2393LuVemw4Ut
MRBEb/G9zJg==;EndpointSuffix=core.windows.net",
    "FUNCTIONS_WORKER_RUNTIME": "dotnet",
    "ShipAnyWhere_SERVICEBUS":
"Endpoint=sb://shipanywhere.servicebus.windows.net/;SharedAccessKeyName=Roo
tManageSharedAccessKey;SharedAccessKey=zG73Yvztm/XScB2BF98bOEZZZLjDhYXUT6bU
U6k/Di0="
    }
}
```

When you publish an Azure Function to Azure, application settings need to be added in the function app's **Application settings**:

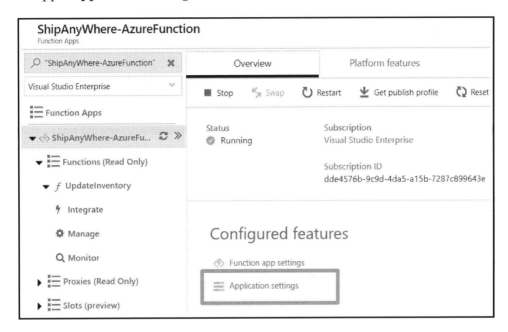

Ensure that all the entries from `local.settings.json` are available in the function app's application settings:

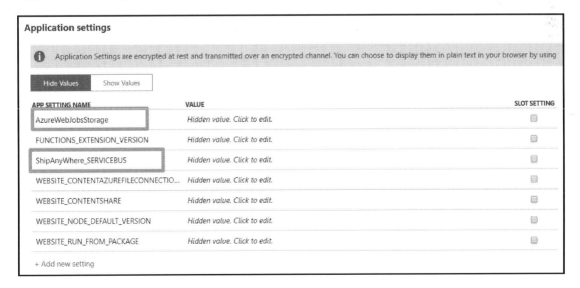

Function triggers

A trigger is a configurable way of defining how an Azure Function is invoked. In our sample scenario, we would like our Function to be invoked when there is a message is available in the orders Service Bus queue:

```
[FunctionName("UpdateInventory")]
        public async static void Run([ServiceBusTrigger("orders",
Connection = "ShipAnyWhere_SERVICEBUS")]PurchaseOrder order
```

The same configuration can also be done in the `function.json` file:

```
{
  "generatedBy": "Microsoft.NET.Sdk.Functions-1.0.24",
  "configurationSource": "attributes",
  "bindings": [
    {
      "type": "serviceBusTrigger",
      "connection": "ShipAnyWhere_SERVICEBUS",
      "queueName": "orders",
      "name": "order"
    }
  ],
  "disabled": false,
  "scriptFile": "../bin/ShipAnyWhere-AzureFunctions.dll",
  "entryPoint": "ShipAnyWhere.UpdateInventory.Run"
}
```

Function bindings

A binding is a declarative or a configurable way of connecting data to different types of sources or destinations, such as Azure SQL, Cosmos DB, Service Bus queues, and so on. When we create functions from the Azure portal, we always mention the bindings in the `function.json` file. Bindings come in two different types: input bindings and output bindings.

Input bindings are used to read data into Azure Functions from different sources. Input bindings are completely optional, and a function can have one or more input bindings. The following is an example of an input binding for Cosmos DB:

```
{
    "name": "Products",
    "type": "cosmosDB",
    "databaseName": "inventory",
    "collectionName": "products",
    "id" : "{Sku}",
    "partitionKey": "{Sku}",
    "connectionStringSetting": "ShipAnyWhere_SERVICEBUS",
    "direction": "in"
}
```

The preceding binding looks up a `cosmosDB` collection named `Products` using an `id` called `Sku`, which is a property in the trigger object.

Output bindings are used to create or update data in different sources. Output bindings are completely optional and a function can have one or more output bindings. The following is an example of an output binding for Cosmos DB:

```
{
    "type": "cosmosDB",
    "name": "Order",
    "databaseName": "Sales",
    "collectionName": "Orders",
    "connectionStringSetting": "ShipAnyWhere_SERVICEBUS",
    "direction": "out"
}
```

 Note: Since we are going to implement the Azure Function in Visual Studio Code, we will not be making using of the `function.json` file. We will be using a declarative way of defining input and output bindings.

Sample scenario continued

In the first part of the sample scenario, we created an Azure Function with a Service Bus trigger, ran the function locally, and deployed it to an Azure Function app. In this section, we will implement the logic for validating orders against **Inventory DB** and updating the order in **Sales DB**:

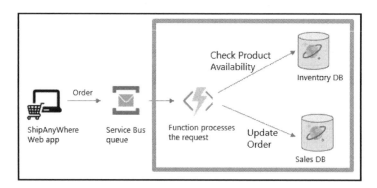

Installing the NuGet package for the Cosmos DB WebJobs extension

To install the NuGet package, you need to do the following:

1. Press *F1* in Visual Studio Code for the command pallet
2. Select the option for installing a NuGet package:

3. Select the package
   named Microsoft.Azure.WebJobs.Extensions.CosmosDB:

Adding input bindings to Inventory DB

Inventory DB contains a collection called **Products**. From the order message, we need to extract a field called Sku and look it up against productid of product documents. If the product with Sku is not available or the available quantity is less than the ordered quantity, we will mark an order status as Rejected:

1. Add a class file called PurchaseOrder.cs to our Function project:

```
namespace ShipAnyWhere
{
    using Newtonsoft.Json;
    using Newtonsoft.Json.Converters;
    public  class PurchaseOrder
    {
        [JsonProperty("ponumber")]
        public string Ponumber { get; set; }

        [JsonProperty("name")]
        public string Name { get; set; }

        [JsonProperty("sku")]
        public string Sku { get; set; }

        [JsonProperty("Location")]
        public string Location { get; set; }

        [JsonProperty("price")]
        public double Price { get; set; }

        [JsonProperty("quantity")]
```

```
            public long Quantity { get; set; }

            [JsonProperty("messagetype")]
            public string Messagetype { get; set; }

             [JsonProperty("status")]
             public string Status { get; set; }

              [JsonProperty("shipTo")]
            public To ShipTo { get; set; }

            [JsonProperty("billTo")]
            public To BillTo { get; set; }
        }
        public partial class To
        {
            [JsonProperty("name")]
            public string Name { get; set; }

            [JsonProperty("address")]
            public string Address { get; set; }

            [JsonProperty("city")]
            public string City { get; set; }

            [JsonProperty("state")]
            public string State { get; set; }

            [JsonProperty("zip")]
            public string Zip { get; set; }
        }
    }
```

2. Add a class file called `Product.cs` to our Function project:

```
        namespace ShipAnyWhere
    {
        using Newtonsoft.Json;
        using Newtonsoft.Json.Converters;
        public partial class Product
        {
            [JsonProperty("id")]
            public string Productid { get; set; }

            [JsonProperty("name")]
            public string Name { get; set; }

            [JsonProperty("location")]
```

```
public string Location { get; set; }

[JsonProperty("avialableQuantity")]
public long AvailableQuantity { get; set; }
    }
}
```

3. Change the Service Bus trigger with `PurchaseOrder class`. This ensures that the order message received from the Service Bus queue is deserialized into an object:

```
0 references
public async static void Run([ServiceBusTrigger("orders", Connection = "ShipAnyWhere_SERVICEBU")])PurchaseOrder order,
```

4. Add a `CosmosDb` input binding to run the method as shown:

```
public async static void Run([ServiceBusTrigger("orders",
Connection = "ShipAnyWhere_SERVICEBUS")]PurchaseOrder order,

                            [CosmosDB(databaseName: "inventory",
                             collectionName:"Products",
                             ConnectionStringSetting =
"dbConnectionString",

                             Id = "{Sku}",
                             PartitionKey="{Sku}"),]Product
product ,ILogger log )
```

This is all we need to do to get product details from the inventory database based on `Sku` which is one of the fields of the purchase order. The product object will be null if there is no document, else it will have the product details.

We will check this condition in the Function as follows:

```
if( product!=null && product.AvailableQuantity >= order.Quantity) {
order.Status = "Accepted"; }
```

Adding output bindings for the orders collection

Once the order status is updated, an order needs to be created in the orders collection in the Sales database. Add the following code to the Function parameters:

```
[CosmosDB(databaseName:"Sales", collectionName:"Orders",
ConnectionStringSetting ="dbConnectionString")]
IAsyncCollector<PurchaseOrder> writeResultsToCosmos
```

The binding is an output binding as we make use of IAsyncCollector. The wirteResultToCosmos object will be able to write the document to the orders collection. We will have to add the following line to update the orders collection:

```
await writeResultsToCosmos.AddAsync(order);
```

The complete Function code looks as follows:

```
using Microsoft.Azure.WebJobs;
using Microsoft.Azure.WebJobs.Host;
using Microsoft.Extensions.Logging;
using System.Collections.Generic;
using System.Collections;
using System.Linq;
namespace ShipAnyWhere
{
    public static class UpdateInventory
    {
        [FunctionName("UpdateInventory")]
        public async static void Run([ServiceBusTrigger("orders",
Connection = "ShipAnyWhere_SERVICEBUS")]PurchaseOrder order,

                                [CosmosDB(databaseName: "inventory",
                                 collectionName:"Products",
                                 ConnectionStringSetting =
"dbConnectionString",
                                 Id = "{Sku}", PartitionKey="{Sku}"),]Product
product ,

                                [CosmosDB(databaseName:"Sales",
                                 collectionName:"Orders",
                                 ConnectionStringSetting
="dbConnectionString")]
                                IAsyncCollector<PurchaseOrder>
writeResultsToCosmos,
                                ILogger log)
        {
            if( product!=null && product.AvailableQuantity >=
```

```
order.Quantity)
            {
                order.Status = "Accepted";
            }
            else
            order.Status ="Rejected";
        await writeResultsToCosmos.AddAsync(order);
            log.LogInformation($"C# ServiceBus queue trigger function
processed message: {order.Sku}");
        }
    }
}
```

Running the end-to-end sample scenario

Press *F5* in Visual Studio Code. From the Service Bus Explorer, post an order to the Service Bus queue.

Before posting the message, ensure that you are adding a brokered message header called **Content Type** with the value as `application/json` as follows:

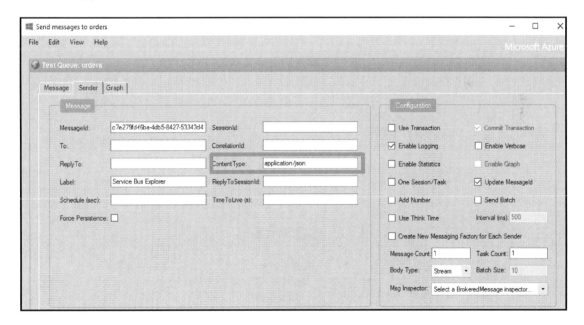

If the **Content Type** header is not set correctly, the Service Bus queue trigger fails with the following exception, stating that `There was an error deserializing the object`:

Once the run is successful, you can see a new order will be created with the appropriate status:

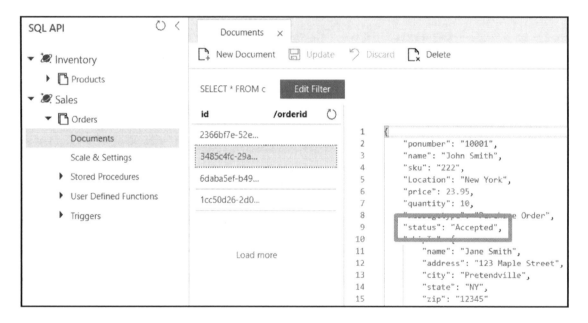

Azure Function use cases

Due to the ease of use and availability of a diverse set of triggers and bindings for Azure Functions, Azure Functions are being used more and more in various use cases. In this section, we will see some of the use cases in which Azure Functions can be used.

Again, we make use of our fictional company, ShipAnyWhere, to explain some use cases:

- **Extending Logic Apps functionality**: ShipAnyWhere has a logic app that processes orders. Though the transformation is done by executing maps, the order needs to be further enriched with master data lookups. The master data lookup is a functionality that will be shared across various integrations. ShipAnyWhere has decided to use Azure Functions to implement the lookup logic. Using Azure Function connectors, Logic Apps can make use of this lookup functionality:

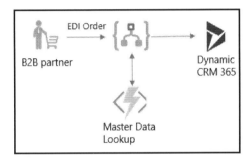

- **Extending SaaS applications**: At ShipAnyWhere, the invoices sent from the B2B partners need to be verified against contractual terms with the trading partner. The **customer relationship manager (CRM)** Microsoft Dynamics 365 handles the invoice processing. However, the custom validations require the extension of the built-in capabilities of Dynamics 365. So, ShipAnyWhere decided to use Azure Functions. When invoices arrive with Dynamics 365, it has built-in feature to place the invoice into a **Service Bus queue**. An Azure Function picks the invoice from the **Service Bus queue**, validates it against the contract, and based on results, takes action to either reject or process the invoice:

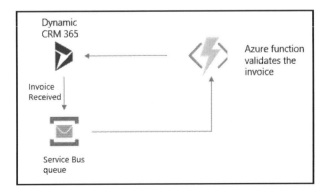

- **For application backend processing**: Regardless of whether it is a web application or mobile application, there will always be use cases where background processing takes place asynchronously. The following is an example of ShipAnyWhere's inventory management processing pipeline:

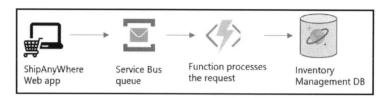

The **ShipAnyWhere Web app** places the order in a **Service Bus queue**. An Azure Function picks up the order from the queue, performs a transformation, and places it into **Inventory Management DB**.

- **Real-time file processing**: At ShipAnyWhere, everything is automated. However, when the goods are delivered, or inbound shipping is received, to improve the operational efficiency, they ask customers to fill in a paper survey form at the site. Keeping the survey form in a blob location is not going to bring ShipAnyWhere any benefits. They have to integrate this with their user experience system. They make use of Azure Functions to leverage Azure Cognitive Services for **optical character recognition (OCR)**:

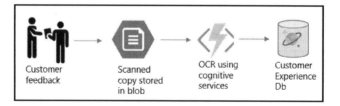

- **Automation of scheduled tasks**: ShipAnyWhere has a few blob locations that need to be cleaned up regularly. This includes deleting files older than few days in the **Blob location**. They decide to use Azure Functions to periodically execute a script to clean up the blob storage:

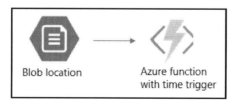

Important considerations when building Azure Functions

Azure Functions provide a rich set of functionalities to build enterprise-grade serverless functions. Though it is easy to create simple functions easily, when making enterprise-grade functions we need to follow some best practices. In this section, we are going to discuss a few best practices when implementing Azure Functions.

Securing application settings with Azure Key Vault

In our samples, we stored two connection strings: one for the Service Bus queue and another one for Cosmos DB. Both these application settings carry keys, which are sensitive and need to be secured in one place. Azure Key Vault is the best place to store any secrets. Storing connection strings, keys, and more in Azure Key Vault helps in two ways:

- It is a very secure service.
- When the keys are changed, you don't need to update all the services consuming them separately. Instead, the update can be done once, in the Azure Key Vault store.

 Here we assume that you are aware of how to create a Key Vault service and add secrets to it. Refer to the documentation for more information: `https://docs.microsoft.com/en-us/azure/key-vault/quick-create-cli`.

We can store our connection strings as follows:

Application setting	Value

ShipAnyWhere_SERVICEBUS	`@Microsoft.KeyVault`
	`(SecretUri=https://ShipAnyWhere.vault.azure.net/`
	`secrets/servicebusconnection/`
	`597EA7338A104F74BE25BF5B2CDF975E)`

dbConnectionString	`@Microsoft.KeyVault`
	`(SecretUri=https://ShipAnyWhere.vault.azure.net/`
	`secrets/CosmosDbConnection/`
	`597EA7338A104F74BE25BF5B2CDF975E)`

However, the following question arises: "how do we store the secret that connects the Azure Function to the Key Vault?" Azure Functions make use of service principles created by system-assigned managed identities. Please refer to `https://docs.microsoft.com/en-us/azure/app-service/overview-managed-identity` to find out how to create them.

Service plan versus consumption plan

When you are creating a Azure Function app, it is essential to choose between having a consumption plan and an App Service plan, based on the requirements. The following table explains the differences between these two plans:

Consumption plan	App Service plan
Scaling is automatically handled. Whenever there is a need for additional compute power, a consumption plan ensures that it is available.	The function app runs on dedicated **virtual machines** (**VMs**). As such, you can scale out can by adding more VMs or enabling auto scaling. Scaling up can be achieved by choosing a different service plan.
Billing is based on memory usage, the number of executions, and the amount of execution time.	Billing is based on the number of VM instances allocated.
A function cannot execute for more than 10 minutes.	A function can run for more than 10 minutes.
Not suitable for long-running Functions.	Suitable for long-running Functions.
Supports only one deployment slot.	Supports multiple deployment slots.

As a rule of thumb, use an App Service plan only for long-running Functions or for Functions that need more compute power than a consumption plan can provide.

Using deployment slots

If you have used app services to deploy web apps, you know how important deployment slots are. In the development life cycle, to establish the integrity of deployments, deployment slots are essential.

With a consumption plan, we can create a deployment slot, such as staging, and publish app services to appropriate slots:

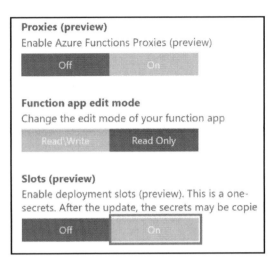

Leveraging Application Insights for monitoring

Azure Functions are tightly integrated with Application Insights. This means that all telemetry information will be logged to Application Insights. This is great for the debugging and monitoring of Azure Functions. The following are some examples of the kinds of information that can be logged from Azure Functions:

- All the requests coming into Azure Functions.
- All the exceptions thrown by the runtime.
- Application traces logged by Azure Functions. This can include information, errors, or warnings logged inside the Azure Function.
- Performance metrics to show the performance of servers that are running Azure Functions.
- Custom events and custom metrics logged within Azure Functions.

Application Insights can be enabled to a function app in the **Monitor** section as follows:

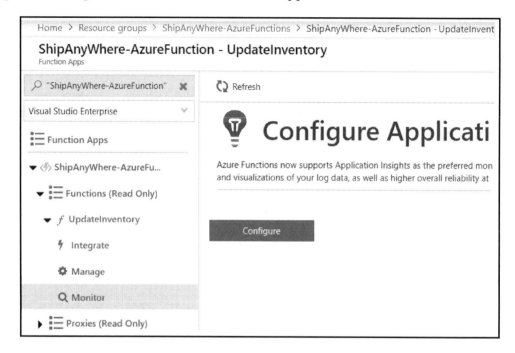

 Refer to `https://docs.microsoft.com/en-us/azure/azure-functions/` `functions-monitoring` to find out about how to use Application Insights in Azure Functions.

Function proxies

Function proxies provide a way to manage Azure Function endpoints within the scope of an application. There are many scenarios where a single API call will be handled by multiple Azure Functions. However, from an application point of view, it is a single API . In such scenarios, Function proxies become really useful.

The following things can be achieved using Function proxies:

- Creating facades for Azure Functions and logic apps
- Applying security to function calls

Refer to `https://docs.microsoft.com/en-us/azure/azure-functions/functions-proxies` to find out more about Function proxies.

Azure API Management provides superior features over Function proxies. For managing APIs across organizations, API Management is the right candidate.

Durable Functions

Durable Functions is an extension to Azure Functions that allows us to create code-based workflows by managing state, checkpoints, and restarts. Logic apps, on the other hand, provide all this functionality in a designer-based approach. The following are some of the patterns durable functions help us to achieve in code-based integrations.

Function chaining

A pattern formed by the execution of multiple microservices – in this case, Azure Functions – in a sequential order is referred to as function chaining:

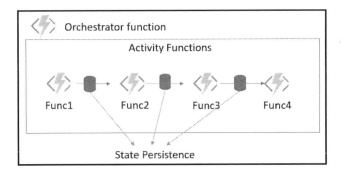

In the preceding example, there is a **Orchestrator function**, which executes the **Activity Functions** – **Func1**, **Func2**, **Func3**, and **Func4** – in a sequential manner. The state of every function execution is persisted to stage by the runtime. This way, if there is a failure, the flow can be resumed from the point of failure.

Fan-out or fan-in

In this pattern, the orchestrator function executes the parallel activity functions. Once all the parallel activities are complete, the results are aggregated:

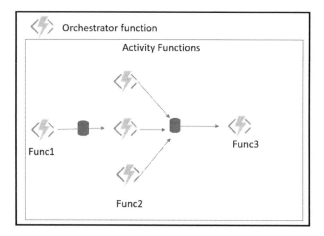

This pattern is similar to that for executing actions in a logic app parallel branch:

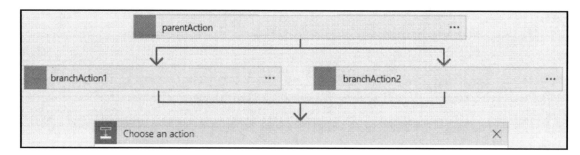

Async HTTP APIs

Consider a scenario when the user submits a registration form for a web application. The registration process takes a while as it has to verify details about the candidate from various crawling services.

Since it takes such a long time to process, it is better to provide a webhook that the web application can poll to find out the results rather than blocking the original request:

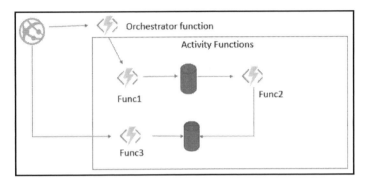

Generally, callbacks such as this will be handled by webhooks.

Monitoring

In many situations, we may want to execute a job until a specific condition is met. In the preceding scenario, we could have an Azure Function that executes until the response is returned. Similarly, this pattern can be used in many automation scenarios:

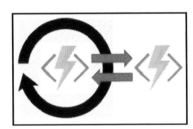

Human interaction

Consider an employee holiday request scenario. When an employee submits the request, it is not certain that the manager is available and able to approve or reject the request. They may be on leave. In such a scenario, where human interactions are required, workflows can take a while – from a few hours to a few days. However, there will always be escalations if the holiday request is not dealt with within a couple of days.

Durable functions have the ability to set a long-running timer and trigger actions when the timer elapses:

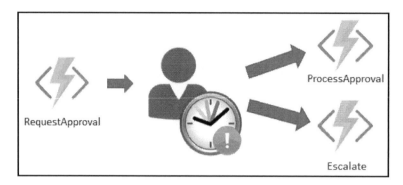

Creating a sample durable function

In this section, we will implement a function-chaining scenario. At ShipAnyWhere, when a new driver registers themselves, there are a few things that need to happen in a sequential manner. First, the driver's background needs to be verified. If the verification result is successful, they can be registered as a contract employee and assigned a driver ID. Once the driver ID is created, induction training will be scheduled. All these tasks are dependent on each other and are long running. Hence, we will implement the flow using durable functions.

Installing a durable task package

In Visual Studio Code, press *F1* to open the command pallet. Use the `NuGet` package install command and provide `Microsoft.Azure.Webjobs.Extensions.DurableTask` as the package name:

The following is the implementation of the durable function in Visual Studio Code:

```csharp
using System;
using System.IO;
using System.Threading.Tasks;
using Microsoft.AspNetCore.Mvc;
using Microsoft.Azure.WebJobs;
using Microsoft.Azure.WebJobs.Extensions.Http;
using Microsoft.AspNetCore.Http;
using Microsoft.Extensions.Logging;
using Newtonsoft.Json;
using System.Linq;
using System.Collections.Generic;

namespace ShipAnyWhere
{
    public static class DriverRegistration
    {
        [FunctionName("DriverRegistration")]
        public static async Task<List<string>> Run(
            [OrchestrationTrigger] DurableOrchestrationContextBase context)
        {
            var outputs = new List<string>();

            outputs.Add(await
context.CallActivityAsync<string>("BackgroundVerification", "success"));
            outputs.Add(await
context.CallActivityAsync<string>("RegisterDriver", "success"));
            outputs.Add(await
context.CallActivityAsync<string>("BookTraining", "success"));

            // returns ["Hello Tokyo!", "Hello Seattle!", "Hello London!"]
            return outputs;
        }

        [FunctionName("BackgroundVerification")]
        public static string BackgroundVerification([ActivityTrigger]
DurableActivityContextBase context)
        {
            string name = context.GetInput<string>();
            return $"success";
        }


        [FunctionName("RegisterDriver")]
        public static string RegisterDriver([ActivityTrigger]
DurableActivityContextBase context)
        {
```

```
        string name = context.GetInput<string>();
        return $"Id001";
    }

    [FunctionName("BookTraining")]
    public static string BookTraining([ActivityTrigger]
DurableActivityContextBase context)
    {
        string name = context.GetInput<string>();
        return $"trained";
    }


  }
}
```

Summary

Azure Functions are the linchpin in Azure's serverless offerings. With a range of triggers and bindings available, it is quick and easy for developers to spin up Azure Functions for given problems or APIs. Microsoft has made it possible for users to either use the Azure portal, Visual Studio, or Visual Studio Code for development.

In next chapter we will cover how to use Azure Event Grid and Event Grid Domain to publish and subscribe events from client application. We will also cover how you can utilize Azure Functions bindings to publish and subscribe events from Event Grid.

Introduction to Azure Event Grid

3

Azure Event Grid is a fully managed, intelligent event routing service available within the Microsoft Azure umbrella. With Azure Event Grid, enterprise applications can leverage event-driven programming models to build reactive interfaces that can be used to connect external or internal enterprise applications. Using Azure Event Grid as a middleware messaging layer for application and interface integration helps organizations to optimize the performance of their software resources with a notification-based design pattern rather than a data pull-based operation model.

On the architecture side, Azure Event Grid follows the publish-subscribe design pattern, where one or more client applications or software systems can publish events to an Azure Event Grid topic and there will be one or more systems reacting and listening to the broadcast events through an Azure Event Grid topic subscription.

Following a pattern similar to that of other serverless platforms and services available in the cloud, Azure Event Grid comes with many benefits for organizations, such as easy startup, on-demand scaling capabilities, multiple language support through a unified SDK, consumption-based pricing, and good monitoring capabilities through the Azure portal. Organizations can leverage these features to build next-generation integration frameworks based on microservices and the reactive programming model.

When it comes to supporting resource types for eventing, in addition to external applications and software resources to publish and route events, **Azure Event Grid** also has built-in support for multiple Azure components to publish and subscribe to platform-specific events. Some of the platforms that support eventing through Azure Event Grid are **Azure Subscription**, **Media Storage**, **Event Hub**, **Blob Storage**, **Data Factory**, **Azure Service Bus**, **Automation, IoT hub,** and **Resource Group**. The following diagram describes the current event publishing sources, along with multiple event subscribers for Azure Event Grid:

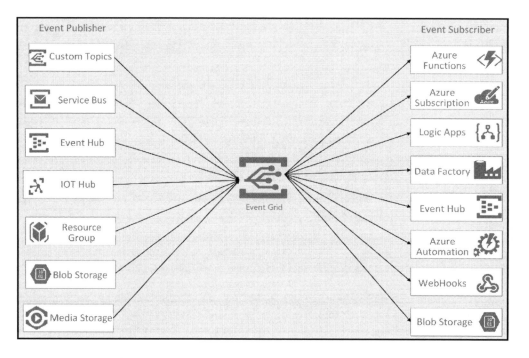

Eventing patterns and a reactive programming model help organizations to remain close to customer sentiments with near-real time communication. This also helps enterprises to remain competitive in the market, with frequent changes in product and service catalogs being based on customer and client requirements. To get started with Azure Event Grid and event-based design patterns, there are many great resources available in the Microsoft documentation and GitHub. In this chapter, we will follow the same steps to get our basic foundation covered before moving into many more granular and advanced integration patterns covering real-world implementations.

When we discuss Azure Event Grid's potential for offering modern integration and event-based architectures to organizations, one of the most important things to discuss is the difference between **events** and **messages**. What do we mean by **events** and **messages** in software development and enterprise system communications, and how can we differentiate between them? It's also important to choose the right communication pattern for system communication. For example, you can choose **eventing,** or **messaging,** or a combination of both, as per the requirements of your organization's solution.

In this chapter, we will learn about the basics of **events** and **messages**. This chapter will also help us to understand why we should care about emitting and consuming events when building applications on top of cloud resources or external resources.

The topics that we are going to cover are listed here:

- Eventing and messaging
- Event sources and event handlers
- Azure Event Grid topics
- Azure Event Grid security and authentication
- Azure Event Grid management access control
- Example 1 – storage events and Logic Apps single event listeners
- Example 2 – custom Azure Event Grid topics and event broadcasts
- Event domains and broadcast events

We will start our discussion with an introduction to **events** and **messages,** which are microcomponents of the messaging system. When discussing events, we will derive the **characteristics** of events and eventing. Moving on, we will cover important concepts such as **event sources**, **event subscribers,** and **event middleware**, and then we will move on to the **security** features of Azure Event Grid and the basic publish-subscribe design pattern. The concepts and exercises discussed in this chapter will give us some best practices for choosing patterns and implementing them in software integration. In the final section of this chapter, we will also cover **Event Grid Domains** and how we can get started with them to work with enterprise-wide eventing by using what we will learn about **Azure Event Grid topics**.

Eventing or messaging for enterprise solutions

With the rise of multiple cloud platforms and various **Software-as-a-Service (SaaS)** products, there has been a paradigm shift in the integration of architecture patterns. Concepts and patterns that might have been relevant a few years back do not make much impact now because of changes in the infrastructure and software market. This has been seen in the digital transformation paths of many enterprises. Organizations are taking advantage of machine learning, big data platforms, and serverless features (such as Azure Functions and Azure Logic Apps), and are moving to more granular microservice-based models of application design. Such application designs allow organizations to have real-time customer interactions and offer a better service model where further innovation is concerned.

As organizations move closer to the cloud with next-generation solutions in mind, integration is becoming more critical than ever. With current market trends, organizations are not dealing with serving a single customer base or working with a single set of software. Rather, most organizations have a global footprint and own a multitude of software and services to serve customers worldwide. As organizations' business dimensions grow& in different areas, such as marketing, service catalogs, and customer bases, we have seen a fast-paced shift toward better integrated solutions. These integrated solutions generally connect multiple applications over various protocols, such as HTTP, SFTP, AMQP, file-based transfers, and more.

Organizations are trying to take advantage of the data available to them and learn from existing systems by implementing hybrid communication models. In hybrid solutions, the structure of software and resources is scattered between on-premises environments and the cloud. With heavy investment on internal infrastructure already having been made in the past, most organizations are searching for ways to take advantage of the cloud while still keeping their own services on-premises, sitting behind a firewall.

In this section, we will discuss **events** and **event** utilization, along some definitions of basic concepts that we will deal with throughout this chapter. To get started, let's first define **events** and **eventing** in terms of software development.

We can define an **event** as a lightweight state change notification that is broadcast from the event source to participating event listeners through a subscription in an asynchronous pattern. On the other hand, **eventing** is defined as the process of notifying appropriate listeners about any specific events that have taken place within the event source system.

On Wikipedia, an event is defined as follows:

> "An action or occurrence recognized by software, often originating asynchronously from the external environment that may be handled by the software."

Let's get an understanding of the concept of event-based patterns with an e-commerce example. In e-commerce, when a customer places a new order through an e-commerce website, the website will send an order creation event to the warehouse and finance department for the basic inventory status and payment status checks. If both the inventory and payment status checks are successful, then a clearance event is fired to the shipment department, which will then send the order to the respective customer.

In cases where an ordered product does not exist in the warehouse or the payment status check has failed, the appropriate events will be sent from the warehouse and financial department to the respective system handling the order failure request. As you can see, all of this communication follows asynchronous patterns with real-time communications and connecting systems. With event-driven processes, an enterprise can limit the manual intervention required to process orders.

The following diagram describes a basic order-processing flow in an event-based architecture pattern. This diagram can be extended with other systems that might be interested in consuming or publishing events from one or more parties involved in overall communication:

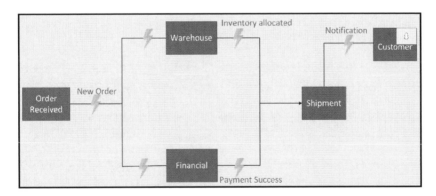

An event-based architecture has great benefits that can make it a next-generation solution utilizing the full power of cloud-hosted services. Another example of an eventing process could be found on a social media platform, when someone follows us on Twitter or when we get a friend request over Facebook or LinkedIn, for instance. All these interactions happen asynchronously, in real time, and through events raised by a specific entity involved.

As we have covered events and eventing, let's now discuss the basics of messages and messaging patterns.

Like events, messages are also micro components of a messaging platform. Usually, messages are pieces of conceptual data sent through the specified channel to a recipient in an asynchronous fashion. An example of this could be a postal order sent through the post office, or an email sent from an account to someone. Messaging can be defined as the overall process of sending data from the source to the desired recipient in an asynchronous way, while maintaining the contextual information of the communication.

So, what differentiates events from messages? The differentiating point here is the state. In event-based programming, events are tightly coupled to the object or entity state change without maintaining any other contextual information. When events are emitted, they only contain information about the state of an entity or object, such as when a blob is modified or when a message is published to a Service Bus.

On the other hand, messaging maintains contextual information while communicating with the end system or user. A great example of this would be an email thread between you and your friend, in which communication information and context are stored in the mail server and your inboxes.

If you have worked with integration before, you can easily correlate this with a pattern called the correlation properties pattern, in which context properties are used for message aggregation and routing. With message-based communication, pattern applications can transmit data along with its contextual information in an asynchronous manner without any human interaction.

To explain this definition with a visual representation, think of a use case in which an enterprise application creates jobs in the Microsoft Dynamics 365 **customer relationship management** (**CRM**) system, and part of the data needs to be replicated in Dynamics AX for financial invoicing. Here, there are multiple stages that need to be covered before the job can be invoiced to the customer.

Maintaining all these state changes—including creating an initial sales order number with job details, prepping the sales order line, assigning appropriate staff, performing servicing activities, and more—can be cumbersome with an event-based architecture. These are often long-running processes that can run over days. Communication channels, though, should be able to correlate all these actions and activities in a single transaction, like so:

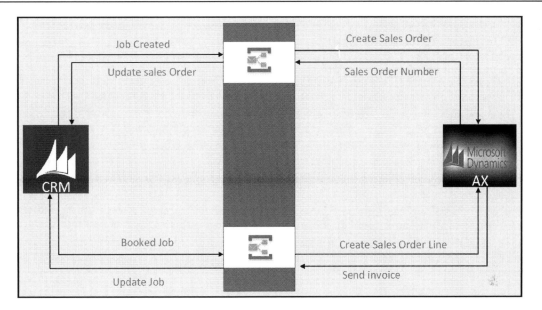

As we have completed our discussion of event and messaging patterns, we will move on to look at the various characteristics of events and event-based design patterns.

Characteristics of events and eventing

To work effectively with cloud resources, we need to choose the right set of patterns and services for our organization. Today, most cloud-native platforms and applications support **eventing**. In this section, we will cover the characteristics of events with some basic definitions:

- **Scatter communications**: The event source broadcasts the events to a wider audience. One or more interested event consumer applications or software instances can react and consume those emitted events.
- **Event timeliness**: The event source publishes events in real time, instead of storing them locally, for event consumers to consume the event.
- **Asynchronous communication**: Communication between the event source and the event handler is asynchronous. The event source does not wait for the consuming application to respond to events.
- **Single event**: The event source publishes an individual event, as opposed to a single aggregated event. This makes the event lightweight when traversing the communication channel, and means the event handler can run each event as a separate task.

- **Expression of interest**: This refers to receiving systems being able to express interest in the events of their choosing rather than having to react to all the events generated.
- **Dependency reversal**: This is another key characteristic of an event-driven architecture. As an enterprise moves to a distributed architecture, the enterprise does not want the application to be monolithic. An intermediate layer between applications and systems minimizes the dependency, and each application can be enhanced without breaking the communication pattern.

If all this is taken into account, an enterprise can make an informed decision about the messaging micro component to use, based on its business requirements. For the rest of the chapter, we will concentrate on the capabilities of Azure Event Grid, defining Azure Event Grid's building blocks and then moving on to Azure Event Grid's capabilities for building real-time, interactive solutions.

Event sources and event handlers

To understand the event-based architecture pattern, it is very important to go through the definition of event sources and event handlers. In the following section, we will describe the role of event sources, event middleware, and event listeners, and see how we can work effectively with these foundational blocks to build an enterprise-wide integration solution powered by events.

Event sources

State change is closely aligned with events. Let's start this discussion and understand what happens behind the scenes when there is a change to an object or entity within our enterprise application or software.

When we change an object or identity through a **create, retrieve, update, delete (CRUD)** operation, the properties of the associated entity are modified and a specific event will be aligned with the change. In the software world, entities where modification has occurred are called **event sources.** An example of this could be selecting a product from a list of products, clicking a submit button, mouse-hovering, and so on. Event sources are broadly classified into two categories: foreground events and background events.

Foreground events

Foreground events are state change events that occur when the user interacts with any graphical user interface, such as in a website or mobile app. These events require direct user interactions with applications. The following code is related to state changes when we add a new product to the product catalog list for an e-commerce website.

From the following code, we can verify that whenever there is a product catalog modification request that comes through the HTTP PUT operation in a website, there is a foreground event that is emitted through an entity state change modification. Capturing and routing those events will help an enterprise to synchronize multiple connecting systems that are interested in a product catalog entity:

```
[HttpPut("(id)")]
public async Task<IActionResult> PutProductCatalogueItem(long id,
ProductCatalogue Item)
{
if (id != Item.Id)
{
return BadRequest();
}
_context.Entry(Item).State = EntityState.Modified;
await _context.SaveChangesAsync();

return NoContent();
}
```

Background events

An application can register to listen and respond to any background system or software events. Background events run within infrastructure and application boundaries and do not interact with the user through a UI. Although background events do not interact directly, they provide contextual information through targeted notifications and updates. An example of a background event would be any event emitted when an application goes offline, or an SMS notification being received. Another example could be when a multiple failure occurs within a Logic Apps workflow.

Here, an auto-generated email is triggered from the Logic Apps framework:

Event handlers

Event handlers are programs or functions that are executed in response to a specific event. A good example of event handlers, also known as event listeners, would be webhooks reacting to an event raised from an application, or JavaScript responding to user input through a graphical UI:

```
<form action="#" method="post">
<input type="button" value="Display Message" onclick="window.alert('Hello
world!');">
</form>
```

In Microsoft Azure, multiple products and services support eventing, including Cosmos DB, Azure Resource Group, Azure Storage, and others. To understand events in Azure, let's look at the following example of an Azure Function reacting to a Cosmos DB change feed. This Function reacts to any object change in Cosmos DB and posts the change feed request to the external web URL:

```
[FunctionName("CosmosFeed")]
public static async System.Threading.Tasks.Task RunAsync([CosmosDBTrigger(
    databaseName: "socialwikigraph",
    collectionName: "sample01",
    ConnectionStringSetting = "CosmosDBConnection",
    CreateLeaseCollectionIfNotExists = true,
    LeaseCollectionName = "leases")]IReadOnlyList<Document> documents,
TraceWriter log)
{
    if (documents != null && documents.Count > 0)
    {
        log.Verbose("Documents modified " + documents.Count);
        log.Verbose("First document Id " + documents[0].Id);
```

```
        var jsonString = JsonConvert.SerializeObject(documents);
        var content = new StringContent(jsonString, Encoding UTF8,
"application/json");
        var response = await client
PostAsync("https://webhook.site/9d2ae6bf-cd79-4896-b44c-0e60a9e2061a",
content);
    }
}
```

Azure Event Grid topics

Azure Event Grid topics are micro components responsible for receiving and sending events from the event source to the event listener. To perform event routing, Event Grid topics follow the publish-subscribe pattern, where a source system publishes an event to an Event Grid endpoint and once the events are received, the Azure Event Grid topic uses subscription information to push the event details to multiple event listeners.

To create and manage an Azure Event Grid topic instance in Azure Resource Group, you can follow any of these processes:

- Use the Azure Portal
- Use **Azure Resource Manager (ARM)** templates
- Use the Azure CLI
- Use Azure PowerShell

To create an Event Grid topic manually through the Azure portal, you can follow the Microsoft documentation link shared here: `https://docs.microsoft.com/en-us/azure/event-grid/custom-event-quickstart-portal#create-a-custom-topic`.

If you want a simplified approach through the Azure CLI, then use the following code:

```
abhishek@Azure:~$ az eventgrid topic create -g myresourcegroupname --name
sampleintegration01 -l westus2
{
  "endpoint":
"https://sampleintegration01.westus2-1.eventgrid.azure.net/api/events",
  "id":
"/subscriptions/*************/resourceGroups/myresourcegroupname/providers
/Microsoft.EventGrid/topics/sampleintegration01",
  "inputSchema": "EventGridSchema",
  "inputSchemaMapping": null,
  "location": "westus2",
  "name": "sampleintegration01",
  "provisioningState": "Succeeded",
  "resourceGroup": "chapter7",
  "tags": null,
  "type": "Microsoft.EventGrid/topics"
}
```

In the preceding code, `myresourcegroupname` is the name of the resource group under which we are required to create an **Azure Event Grid topic**. `sampleintegration01` is the name of the custom Azure Event Grid topic and WestUs2 is the location of the resource.

When publishing events to the Azure Event Grid topic, the client application must follow the required data contract structure defined by the Azure Event Grid framework for pushing events to the Azure Event Grid. Once a message is sent to the consumer application's event grid topic, the consumer application can then read the event message and react as required by the system. The following example describes one of the request events fired through a custom event grid topic:

```
[{
    "id": "000023",
    "eventType": "NewOrderCreated",
    "subject": "New Order created with order number 0000123",
    "eventTime": "2019-01-10T21:03:07+00:00",
    "data": {
      "ordernumber": "0000123",
      "invoicenumber": "INV00012343",
      "CustomerId": "0000023"
    },
    "dataVersion": "1.0",
    "metadataVersion": "1",
    "topic": "/subscriptions/{subscription-id}/resourceGroups/{resource-
group}/providers/Microsoft.EventGrid/topics/{topic}"
  }
]
```

As we go though this chapter, we will understand more about the concept of event deserialization through the Azure Event Grid SDK. We will also become familiar with how you can post an event of your choice through Azure Event Grid.

Azure Event Grid security and authentication

Now that we have covered the basic components of the event-based architecture, let's focus on Azure Event Grid security and authentication features. By default, the Azure Event Grid supports three types of authentication:

- Webhook event delivery
- Event subscription
- Publishing events to a custom Event Grid topic

Webhook event delivery

Webhooks allow an application to listen for changing feed events with a push notification model. In the webhook model, an application is notified through an HTTP endpoint of any specific state change events. Unlike pull patterns, push event models save applications from using resources unnecessarily.

 To understand the importance of webhook event delivery in the real world, we would like you to read one of the blogs written by Jeff Hollan at the following link: https://medium.com/@jeffhollan/why-event-grid-is-a-game-changer-for-serverless-8979870a65d1.

As the software industry is growing with a shift toward event-based patterns, we are witnessing the large-scale use of platforms such as Azure Event Grid. To work with Azure Event Grid and listen for an event, every client application needs to validate the ownership of the HTTP endpoint before the Azure Event Grid can start publishing events to the registered HTTP subscriber listener. This process of validating HTTP ownership and handshakes prohibits malicious users from listening to events being emitted from the enterprise system or application.

In the following example, we have registered an Azure Functions HTTP endpoint as a webhook subscriber to perform initial validation handshakes with a validation token. This function performs two tasks, which are listed here:

- Performs the event grid validation process by sending a validation code in response to the initial request
- Reads the custom events from the event grid topic and posts the data to an external HTTP URL:

```
[FunctionName("EventGridhhtplistener")]
publc static async Task<HttpResponseMessage>
Run([HttpTrigger(AuthorizationLevel.Anonymous, "post", Route =
null)]HttpRequestMessage req, TraceWriter log))
{
    log Info("C# HTTP trigger function processed a request.");
    string requestContent = await req.Content.ReadAsStringAsync();

    EventGridSubscriber eventGridSubscriber = new EventGridSubscriber();
    EventGridEvent[] eventGridEvents =
eventGridSubscriber.DeserializeEventGridEvents(requestContent);
    foreach (EventGridEvent azevents in eventGridEvents)
    {
        if(azevents.Data is SubscriptionValidationEventData)
        {
            var EventData = (SubscriptionValidationEventData)azevents.Data;
            var responseData = new SubscriptionvalidationResponse()
            {
                ValidationResponse = EventData.ValidationCode
            };
            return req.CreateResponse(HttpStatusCode.OK, responseData);
        }
        else
        {
            var jsonString = JsonConvert.SerializeObject(azevents);
            var content = new StringContent(jsonString, Encoding UTF8,
"application/json");
            var response = await
client.PostAsync("https://webhook.site/9d2ae6bf-cd79-4896-0e60a9e2061a",
content);
        }
    }
}
```

In the case of Azure resources such as Logic Apps, Azure Automation, Azure Data Factory, and Azure Functions, the process of validation and handshake is automatically taken care of by the Azure infrastructure without having to write a single line of code.

In the following example, we have used an event grid input binding to listen in to Azure Functions to read events raised through blob storage and then write to an external HTTP endpoint. As you can see, in this process we are not performing any validation processes with Event Grid; it is all being taken care of by Azure:

```
[FunctionName("EventGridBinding")]
public static async
System.Threading.Tasks.Task.RunAsync([EventGridTrigger]JObject
eventGridEvent, TraceWriter log)
{
    log.Info(eventGridEvent.ToString(Formatting.Indented));
    if (eventGridEvent != null && eventGridEvent.Count > 0)
    {
        var jsonString = JsonConvert.SerializeObject(eventGridEvent);
        var content = new StringContent(jsonString, Encoding.UTF8,
"application/json");            var response = await
cllent.PostAsync(https://requestbin.fullcontact.com/lobunfk1", content);
    }
}
```

With version 2018-05-01, the Azure Event Grid has made another step forward with the manual validation of the ownership of HTTP webhook endpoints using the validation URI. This benefits software and applications that cannot participate in mutual validation communication processes through validation code.

To perform manual subscription validation and complete the trust between the client application and Azure Event Grid, the application needs to grab the validation URI property from the initial subscription request and use an HTTP client of our choice, such as Postman, an HTTP web client, or a web browser, to manually send a GET request, which will complete the subscription in Azure Event Grid.

It is important to note here that the URI provided in the initial subscription request is only valid for 10 minutes, and within this time period, the provisioning state for the event subscription is AwaitingManualAction. If an application failed to complete manual validation within 10 minutes, the provisioning state will change to *fail*.

We've covered various ways to perform a secure handshake with validation code and a validation URI in Azure Event Grid. There are other points that can be followed as a checklist when a client application is trying to register for event subscription:

- When an event subscription is created or updated, Azure Event Grid posts a subscription validation payload to the client application. An example of a subscription validation event is shown here:

```
[{
    "id": "d648bacd-9F5d-4e25-9aa0-ff0b37b1be3a"
    "topic": "/subscriptions/xxxxxxx-xxxx-xxxx-xxxx-
xxxxxxxxxxxx/resourceGroups/xxxxxxxxxxxxxxxx/providers/Microsof
t.Storage/storageAccounts/eventgridblobstroage",
    "subject": "",
    "data": {
        "validationCode": "4A73A2B0-C6D0-4C5D-
A13B-394A056330AA",
        "validationUrl": "https://rp-australiaeast.eventgrid.
azure.net:533/eventsubscriptions/webhook/validate?id=
xxxxxxxxxxxxx"
    }
    "eventType":
"Microsoft.EventGrid.SubscriptionValidationEvent",
    "eventTime": "2018-12-22T19:35:22.02665532",
    "metadataVersion": "1",
    "dataVersion": "2"
}]
```

- The subscription event contains the `aeg-event-type` header with the value as the subscription validation, the and body of the event follows the data contract of Event Grid events.
- The initial event subscription type is set to `subscriptionvalidationevent`, and the data property contains `validationcode` along with `validationUrl`.
- The subscription validation array contains only the validation event. Other events are sent as separate requests after the success of the initial handshake.
- During the validation handshake, the end system should return an HTTP status code of 200; the 202 status code is not recognized for event subscription.

Event delivery security

This is another way to secure webhook endpoints from an external user. To secure our webhook endpoint, we can add additional query parameters to the subscription webhook endpoint, such as the access token. Event Grid will include these query parameters in every event that is posted to the webhook endpoint. When modifying an Event Grid subscription, the query parameters are not displayed (unless specified with include-full-endpoint-url) to make the communication secure (`https://docs.microsoft.com/en-gb/cli/azure/ eventgrid/event-subscription?view=azure-cli-latest#az-eventgrid-event- subscription-show`).

Event subscriptions

As discussed in the previous section, to make a successful validation handshake with an Azure Event Grid topic, an event listener must return a valid validation code or validation URL when subscribing to the Event Grid topic.

In this section, we will extend the topic to include another event source, such as Event Hubs or a storage queue, that cannot perform the webhook-type validation process. To perform event subscription for such a system, Event Grid must have event writing permission for the specified resource or system. Azure Event Grid requires this privilege so that it can write a new subscription at the scope of the resource when required.

The requested resource will differ based on whether we are subscribing to a system topic defined within an Azure resource or Event Grid custom topic. An example of this would be an event raised from blob storage to listen for emitted events through Event Grid. Azure Event Grid requires having `eventsubscriptions` or write permission on the specified blob storage account:

```
/subscriptions/**********/resourceGroups/**********/providers/Microsoft.Sto
rage/storageAccounts/eventsubscription
```

In the Event Grid custom topic, the subscribing client should have `eventsubscriptions` or write permission on the specified topic to write the Event Grid subscription:

```
/subscriptions/**********/resourceGroups/**********/providers/Microsoft.Eve
ntGrid/stopics/wikieventsubscriptiontopic
```

Publishing events through custom topics

When working with an Azure Event Grid custom topic, we can either use a shared access signature or key authentication to publish the event to the Azure Event Grid custom topic. This option gives us the flexibility to choose the right option for new or existing applications. If we already have an application running and we are required to take advantage of the capabilities of Azure Event Grid, then the quickest way to integrate the application is via key authentication. When we have an enterprise-level application where security is vital, it is always recommended to work with a shared access signature for publishing events.

Key authentication with code

Azure Event Grid key authentication is the simplest way to publish an event to a custom Event Grid topic. In Event Grid key authentication, the client application has to pass `aeg-sas-key` as the header to event's POST operation. When using `aeg-sas-key`, it is always advisable to secure the keys within Azure Key Vault, or any secure storage of your choice, and retrieve the value at runtime.

The following function uses the Event Grid SDK, `aeg-sas-key`, and the topic endpoint for creating an Azure Event Grid topic connection before routing custom events. Once we have created a custom topic through the Azure portal or the Azure CLI, we can get the details of `aeg-sas-key` and the topic endpoint by navigating through the custom Event Grid topic resource:

```
[FunctionName("EventGridHttpPublisher")]
public static async Task<HttpResponseMessage>
Run([HttpTrigger(AuthorizationLevel.Function,"post", Route =
null)]HttpRequestMessage req,
{
    Productevent productname = await
req.Content.ReadAsAsync<Productevent>();
    string name = productname.Productname;
    List<EventGridEvent> eventlist = new List<EventGridEvent>();
    for (int i = 0; i < 1; i++)
    {
        eventlist.Add(new EventGridEvent()
        {
            Id = Guid.NewGuid().ToString(),
            EventType = "integration.event.eventpublished",
            EventTime = DateTime.Now,
            Subject = "IntegrationEvent",
            DataVersion = "1.0",
```

```
            Data = new Productevent()
            {
                    Productname = name
            }
        });
    }
    TopicCredentials topicCredentials = new TopicCredentials(eventgridkey);
    EventGridClient client = new EventGridClient(topicCredentials);
    client.PublishEventsAsync(topicHostname,
eventlist).GetAwaiter().GetResult();

    return req.CreateResponse(HttpStatusCode.OK);
}
```

The configuration settings for the Azure Event Grid are stored in the Azure Key Vault and retrieved from the app configuration file of the Function App. The configuration settings for interacting with Azure Key Vault and Azure Functions has already been discussed in the previous chapter:

```
private static string eventgridkey =
System.Environment.GetEnvironmentVariable("eventgridkey");
private static string eventgridendpoint =
System.Environment.GetEnvironmentVariable("eventgridendpoint");
private static string topicHostname = new Uri(eventgridendpoint).Host;
```

Using a shared access signature is the preferred approach when it is required to set a default expiry time for events emitted from the source system. This is also the preferred approach if you want to have granular permissions on the event write operation. To take advantage of shared access signatures with Azure Event Grid, we can use the following code snippet:

```
public static async Task<HttpResponseMessage>
Run(HttpTrigger(AuthorizationLevel.Function, "post", Route =
null)]HttpRequestMessage req, TraceWriter
{
    Productevent productname = await
req.content.ReadAsAsync<Productevent>();
    string name = productname.Productname;

    List<EventGrldEvent> eventlist = new List<EventGridEvent>();
    for (int i = 0; i < 1; i++)
    string sharedaccesstoken =
SharedAccessSignature.GeneratenSharedAccessSignature(eventgridendpoint,
DateTime.Now.AddHours(1), eventgridkey);
    using (var. reqclient = new HttpClient();
    {
        HttpRequestMesseqe requestMessape = new
```

```
HttpRequestMessage(HttpMethod.Post, eventgridendpoint);
        requestMessage.Headers.Add("aeg-sas-token", sharedaccesstoken);
        var jsonString = JsonConvert.SerializeObject(eventlist);
        var content = new StringContent(jsonString, Encoding UTF8,
"application/json");
        requestMessage.Content = content;
        HttpResponseMessage response = await
reqclient.SendAsync(requestMessage);
    }

    return req.CreateResponse(HttpStatusCode.OK);
}
```

In the preceding function definition, we are calling the GenerateSharedAccessSignature method, which will take three request parameters—EventGridTopicEndpoint, DateTime, and an Azure Event Grid key—and return the shared access token in response. The function definition for the GenerateSharedAccessSignature method is described here:

```
public static string GenerateSharedAccessSignature(string resource,
DateTime expirationtime, string key)
        {
            const char Resource = 'r';
            const char Expiration = 'e';
            const char Signature = 's';

            string encodedResource = HttpUtility.UrlEncode(resource);
            var culture = CultureInfo.CreateSpecificCulture("en-US");

            var encodedExpirationUtc =
HttpUtility.UrlEncode(expirationtime.ToString(culture));
            string unsignedSas =
$"{Resource}={encodedResource}&{Expiration}={encodedExpirationUtc}";
            using (var hmac = new
HMACSHA256(Convert.FromBase64String(key)))
                {
                string signature =
Convert.ToBase64String(hmac.ComputeHash(Encoding.UTF8.GetBytes(unsignedSas)
));
                string encodedSignature = HttpUtility.UrlEncode(signature);
                string signedSas =
$"{unsignedSas}&{Signature}={encodedSignature}";

                return signedSas;
            }
        }
```

Throughout this section, we have covered the authentication and security features available in the Azure Event Grid. We have gone through a code exercise to give us enough information to get started with Azure Event Grid.

In the next section, we will cover Azure Event Grid management access control, event filtering, Event Grid delivery, and event retries in the case of event delivery failure. Once we are done with these topics, we will go through some real use cases for utilizing Azure Event Grid and its features.

Azure Event Grid management access control

Like other Azure resources, the Azure Event Grid also supports granular role-based access control (RBAC). This is beneficial for organizations to set the right access and permissions rules to manage Event Grid within the enterprise's boundaries. An example of RBAC would be having a service principal application registered in the enterprise's Azure Active Directory, or using a Logic Apps workflow to read events from an Azure Event Grid topic.

The following table describes various operation types supported through RBAC in an Azure Event Grid topic:

Operation types	Action
Write rights to Event Grid topic	`Microsoft.EventGrid/*/write`
Read rights to Event Grid topic	`Microsoft.EventGrid/*/read`
Delete operation on Event Grid topic	`Microsoft.EventGrid/*/delete`
Get subscription details	`Microsoft.EventGrid/eventSubscriptions/getFullUrl/action`
Get Azure Event Grid keys	`Microsoft.EventGrid/topics/listKeys/action`
Regenerate Event Grid keys	`Microsoft.EventGrid/topics/regenerateKey/action`

The last three operations listed in the preceding table return potentially secret information about Azure Event Grid that gets filtered out of normal read operations. It's recommended that we should restrict access to these operations when giving access rights to any service principal user.

Azure Event Grid message delivery retry and event filtering

Azure Event Grid follows Durable Event delivery mechanisms. This means that Azure Event Grid delivers each event published through Event Grid at least once to the event listener registered through the validation subscription.

If a registered subscription listener does not acknowledge the event emitted through Event Grid, Event Grid will try to deliver the event again. This might be the case when a registered event subscribing endpoint is unavailable and throwing up a 404 (resource not found) exception. Azure Event Grid's event delivery exponential retry intervals are described here:

- 10 seconds
- 30 seconds
- 1 minute
- 5 minutes
- 10 minutes
- 30 minutes
- 1 hour

Events that are not delivered within 24 hours of event publication expire and become dead lettered. To make event retries more flexible, we can also customize event retry policies when creating the subscription; some of those customizations can also be done through the Azure portal:

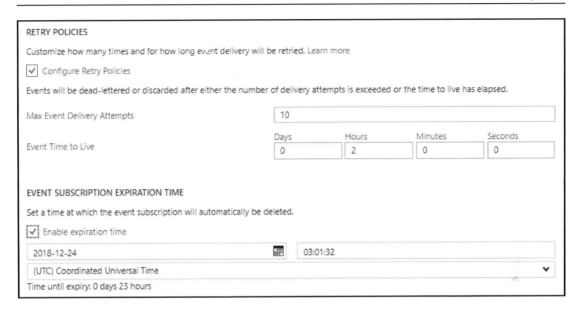

The maximum number of delivery attempts that we can set is 30, and the event time-to-live is 1,440 minutes. If the message is not delivered with these retries or within the time left before expiry, we can also configure the dead-lettering feature, which we will discuss in the next section.

Dead-letter events with Azure Event Grid

When events are not delivered to event listeners within the time **left before expiry**, we can route those delivery-failed events to our Storage account. The process of storing undelivered events in the Storage account is called **dead-lettering**. By default, the dead-lettering process is not enabled on Azure Event Grid, and the events are lost when not delivered within delivery time windows. To enable dead lettering for Azure Event Grid, we can use the Azure portal:

1. Log in to the Azure portal at `https://portal.azure.com`
2. Navigate to the resource group and click on the Event Grid instance
3. In the Event Grid blade, click on **Event Subscription**

4. On the Event Subscription page, click **Enable dead-lettering** and select the storage container:

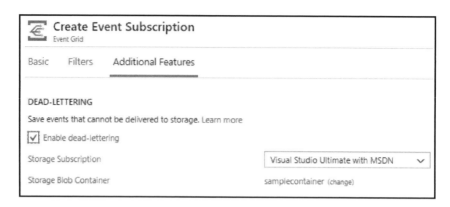

It is also worth noting that Azure Event Grid sends an event to the dead-letter location when it has tried all of its retry attempts or when Event Grid receives a 400 (bad request) or 413 (request entity too large) status response code from the subscription listener. To enable notifications for failed events, we can create an Event Grid subscription listener endpoint that can react to newly failed events stored in the dead-lettering blob storage.

Event delivery status codes

Let's familiarize ourselves with the use of various status codes when we do our event communication through Azure Event Grid:

Status description	HTTP status code
OK	200
Accepted	202
Bad request	400
Unauthorized	401
Not found	404
Request timeout	408
Too many requests	429
Internal server error	500
Service unavailable	503
Gateway timeout	504

Azure Event Grid has a simple monitoring dashboard. To look for events emitted and published to an Azure Event Grid topic or subscription, we can navigate to the instance of the Event Grid topic or subscription and verify the health of the overall integration flow.

Event filtering through Azure Event Grid subscription

In this section, we will describe the different ways to filter events when we create an Event Grid listener endpoint through subscription. An Azure Event Grid topic provides us with three options to filter out the event of our choosing:

- Event type filtering
- Subject filtering
- Advanced fields and operators

Event type filtering

By default, all the events broadcast via Event Grid should have the event type property in the actual event payload. We can use the event type within the filter condition to route events to the specified listener, which can then process those events. When filtering events on a subscription level, end client listeners can be saved from throttling conditions and can only listen for events of their choice. To enable filtering on the subscription, you can go to the specified Event Grid subscription, and in the advanced filtering tab, give the filter expression, as shown in the following screenshot:

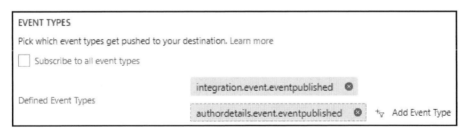

Subject filtering

Another method for filtering events is to use the event subject. This is a required property that is available with all events sent through the Event Grid topic. To filter data with the subject property, we need to specify the subject's string property, which can either be a start string for a subject, an end string, or a combination of both. When configuring an Event Grid subscription, we can also use a combination of both subject and event type filtering to have granular filtered data for our interface:

SUBJECT FILTERS

Apply filters to the subject of each event. Only events with matching subjects get delivered. Learn more

[✓] Enable subject filtering

Subject Begins With	IntegrationEvent
Subject Ends With	.jpg
Case-sensitive subject matching	[✓]

Advanced filtering

Advanced filtering options can use insights from the data field property to filter events along with the subject and event type. With the advanced filtering option, we can access multiple operator type comparisons, such as contains, does not contain, string in, Boolean equals, and more. To work with advanced filtering in Azure Event Grid, you can follow these steps:

1. Log in to the Azure portal at `https://portal.azure.com`
2. Navigate to the resource group and click on the Event Grid instance
3. In the Event Grid blade, click on **Event Subscription**
4. On the Event Subscription page, click **Advanced Filters**
5. Enter the required key value for event filtering for the specific subscription, and once done, click on **Save**:

In the next section of this chapter, we will do a hands-on exercise with Azure Event Grid. We will use Azure Event Grid as a middleware service for routing events from event source to event handler. We will also cover how we can easily connect Azure Event Grid with other cloud platforms and services, such as Logic Apps, Azure Functions, and Storage. Through this exercise, we will look at integration patterns such as event broadcasting.

Example 1 – storage events and Logic Apps single event listener

As we have learned in the preceding sections, Azure Event Grid has native support for multiple Azure resource components. In this example, we will connect to Azure Blob events via a Logic Apps workflow as follows:

- The Azure blob storage container will emit a blob event when a blob is added, modified, or deleted.
- Logic Apps will listen to the blob events through Event Grid or a webhook trigger.

- For each blob event, Logic Apps will route the event details to an Office 365 email account:

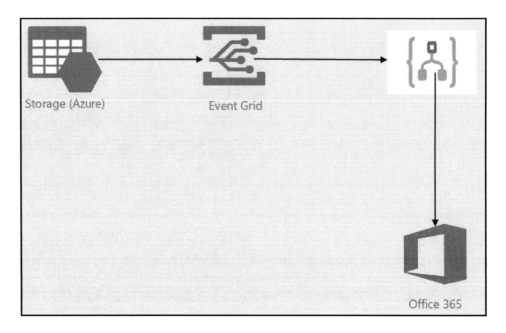

To get started with this example, you need to create a v2 version of a storage container in your resource group. To create a Storage account in your Azure subscription and resource group, follow the instructions described here: https://docs.microsoft.com/en-us/azure/storage/common/storage-quickstart-create-account?tabs=azure-portal.

In the next step, you need to create a Logic App workflow with an Event Grid trigger along with conditional statements, an email connector, and an HTTP connector to route the event details out of the Logic Apps workflow. If you are new to Logic Apps, do not worry; we have dedicated chapters that will cover Logic Apps:

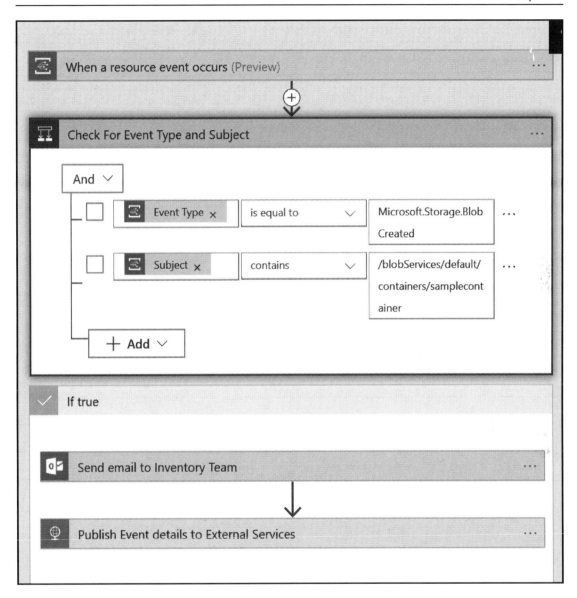

Once the Event Grid connection properties are validated in Logic Apps through the principal account, there will be one registered Event Grid listener endpoint in the blob storage event section. This Logic Apps event grid trigger endpoint will listen for a blob creation event and then route the event details to the Office 365 email account.

To test this communication and integration between Logic Apps and blob events through Azure Event Grid, upload content to the blob storage and verify the Logic Apps run history, along with the event monitoring section for the Storage account, as shown here:

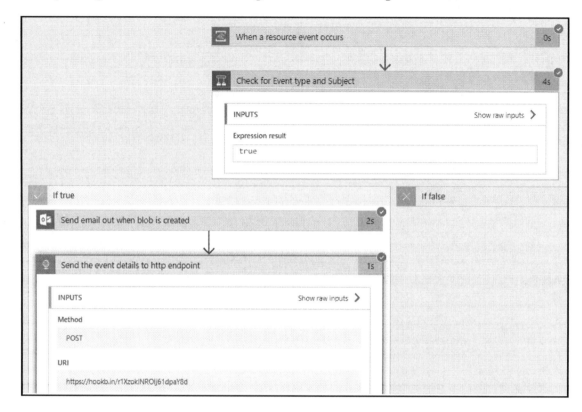

Example 2 – custom Azure Event Grid topic and event broadcast

This example will describe how we can work with a custom Event Grid topic to broadcast events from an event source to multiple event listener endpoints. In this example, we will use the Azure Functions code given in the previous section to publish custom events to an Event Grid topic endpoint.

The basic event flow architecture is described in the following diagram. The event flow details are listed here:

- The web app sends an event to Azure Event Grid.
- Azure Event Grid has three different subscriptions, Logic Apps, Azure Functions, and Webhooks, to read the event details.
- Logic Apps will write the incoming event to Service Bus, which will again be polled by the client application.
- Azure Functions will write the event details to a SQL database account.
- Webhooks will display the event details on the HTTP endpoint:

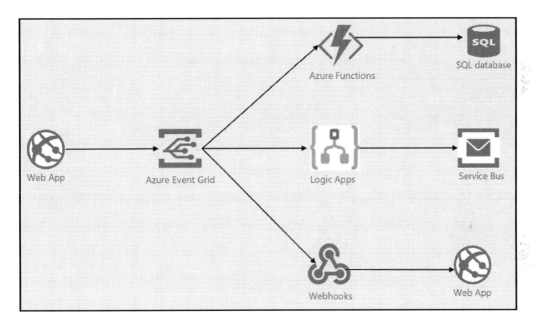

The first step here is to build a custom Event Grid topic in the Azure subscription. To do this, navigate to your resource group and search for `Event Grid topic`, populate the required fields, and click on **Create Blade**. This will create a new custom Event Grid topic in the specified resource group:

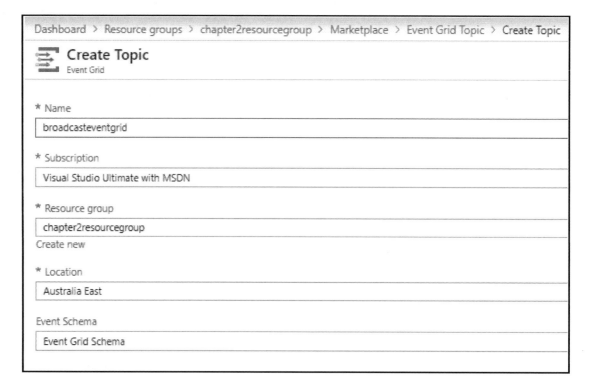

Next, we will create logic apps with a webhook trigger that will listen to events from an Azure Event Grid custom topic and route events to a Service Bus topic for further processing:

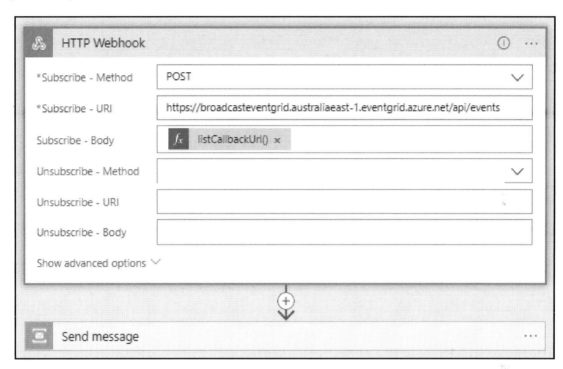

Once the Logic Apps workflow design is completed, the next step is to register the Logic Apps webhook endpoint as an Azure Event Grid subscription. To do this, navigate to the Event Grid resource, click on **Add subscription**, and register the Logic Apps webhook endpoint as one of the listeners for all events routed through the Event Grid topic.

In the next step, create a function in the Functions App with Event Grid input bindings. In Azure Functions, use the event entity details and entity framework to write event information into the Azure SQL database. The code for the described Function is listed here:

```
[FunctionName("EventGridEntityFramework")]
public static void Run([EventGridTrigger]JObject eventGridEvent,
TraceWriter log)
{
    log.Info(eventGridEvent.ToString(Formatting.Indented));
    if (eventGridEvent != null)
    {
```

```
            dynamic eventGridEvents =
eventGridEvent.ToString(Newtonsoft.Json.Formatting.None);

            foreach (var azevent in eventGridEvents)
            {
                using (var dbcontext = new
DbContext(System.Environment.GetEnvironmentVariable("DBconnection")))
                {
                    dbcontext.Database.Connection.Open();
                    dbcontext.Database.ExecuteSqlCommandAsync(string.Format
                        ("Insert into dbo.eventgridevents(eventid,eventsubject
,eventdata)values ({0},{1},{2})",
                        azevent.Id, azevent.Subject, azevent.Data));

                    dbcontent.Database.Connection.Close();
                }
            }
        }
        else
        {
            log.Info("Event payload is empty");
        }
    }
```

Lastly, we will add one more subscription to the external HTTP endpoint steps, such as `webhooksite` or `requestbin`, to list all the event details on the web page (we can use a static website along with a signal, R, to route events broadcast through Event Grid in a secure fashion). In this process, we will perform subscription validation through Postman using a validation URL, **Webhook successfully validated as a subscription endpoint**, as shown here:

As we are done with setting up all three different subscriptions of different types, let's submit some events through the Function application and validate the broadcast events from the Azure event monitoring blade.

As you can see in the monitoring blade in the following screenshot, there are 15 events that we have published to three different event listener endpoints, and each endpoint has performed the required business logic implementation as per the steps described previously:

To validate the event routing and Event Grid process, navigate to the external webhook site tab within the browser and verify the events posted to the external HTTP endpoint.

Azure Event Grid domain for enterprise integration

An Event Grid domain allows enterprises to work with a single event publisher endpoint within the enterprise domain. Each Event Grid domain is associated with multiple Event Grid domain topics and allows the enterprise to work with real broadcasting use cases across applications running on the cloud or on-premises.

To learn more about domain events, integration events, and their differences, look at the Microsoft documentation listed here: `https://docs.microsoft.com/en-us/dotnet/ standard/microservices-architecture/microservice-ddd-cqrs-patterns/domain-events-design-implementation`.

In this section, we will describe how you can work with Azure Event Grid domains and how you can publish/manage the flow of events emitted through your applications, either on the cloud or within your own network:

- When a new post or blog is uploaded, the Social Connect website sends events to Event Grid Domain.

- Event Grid Domain will then use two different Event Grid topics to route events to the event subscribers.
- The first Event Grid Topic will send events to Logic Apps and Azure Functions.
- The second Event Grid Topic will send events to Event Hubs and Webhooks:

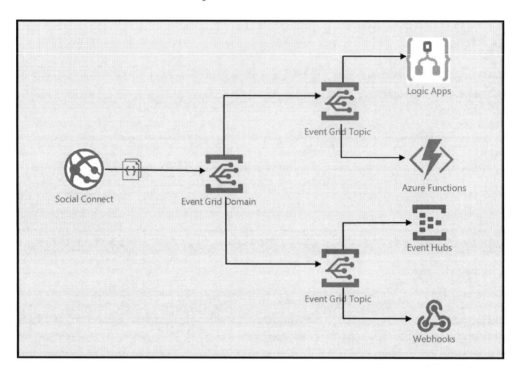

To get started with the Event Grid domain, create an Event Grid domain within your Azure subscription and resource group. To do this, you can either use the Azure portal, the Azure CLI, or Azure PowerShell. This is how you do so using the Azure portal:

1. Log in to your Azure portal and in the search blade, search for `Event Grid Domain` and click on **Create:**

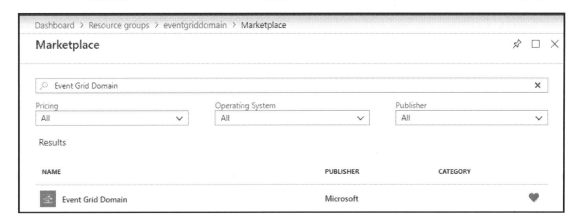

2. In the **Create Event Grid Domain** blade, enter the **Name** of your Event Grid domain; select your **Subscription**, **Resource group**, **Location**, and **Event Schema** (the default is `Event Grid schema`); and click on **Create** is will create a new instance of an Event Grid domain in your resource group:

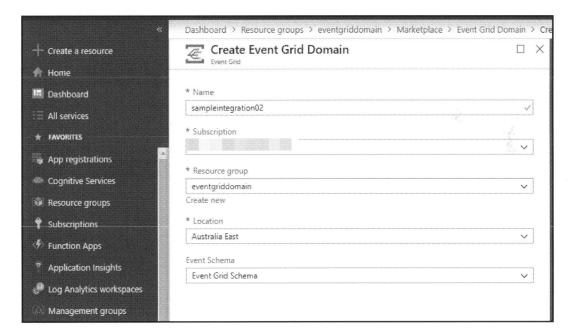

3. When working with the Azure CLI, you can create your Event Grid domain instance by using the following command:

```
abhishek@Azure:~$ az eventgrid domain create -g
myeventresourcegroup --name sampleintegration04 -l westus2

abhishek@Azure:~$ az eventgrid domain create -g
myeventresourcegroup --name sampleintegration04 -l westus2
{
  "endpoint":
"https://sampleintegration04.westus2-1.eventgrid.azure.net/api/
events",
  "id":
"/subscriptions/**********/resourceGroups/myeventresourcegroup
/providers/Microsoft.EventGrid/domains/sampleintegration04",
  "inputSchema": "EventGridSchema",
  "inputSchemaMapping": null,
  "location": "westus2",
  "name": "sampleintegration04",
  "provisioningState": "Succeeded",
  "resourceGroup": "chapter7",
  "tags": null,
  "type": "Microsoft.EventGrid/domains"
```

4. Once the command is successfully executed, you can verify the Event Grid domain resource instance in your specified resource group:

5. In the same Azure tenant, we will create event listeners, such as Events Hubs, Logic Apps, Functions, and webhook listeners. The following is a summarized view of the resources created as part of this exercise:

6. The next step is to define the Event Grid domain subscription for Logic Apps, Events Hub, and Azure Functions. As the event domain is built on top of the Event Grid domain topic, you can use the same subscription steps as covered in the Event Grid topic subscription. For example, to register a Logic Apps subscription to an Event Grid domain, within the Logic Apps designer and Event Grid trigger, select the resource type as **Microsoft.EventGrid.Domains**, and click on **Save**:

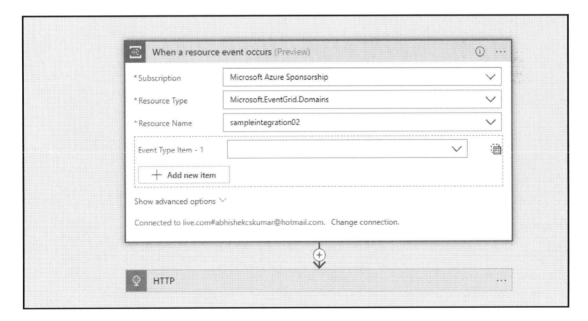

7. Once the event listener subscription is completed, we will add an Event Grid domain topic in the Azure Event Grid domain. To do this, navigate to the Event Grid domain, click on **Add subscription**, and populate the required data for the subscription:

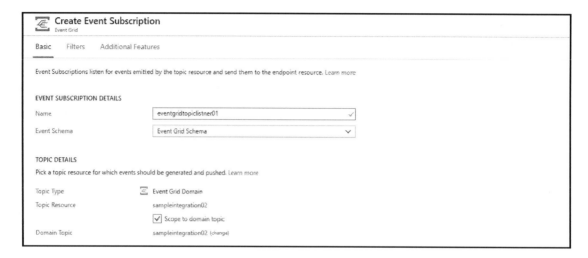

8. Repeat the same steps for the function listener, which uses the event grid input binding. The following screenshot shows how to add Function trigger bindings to an Event Grid domain:

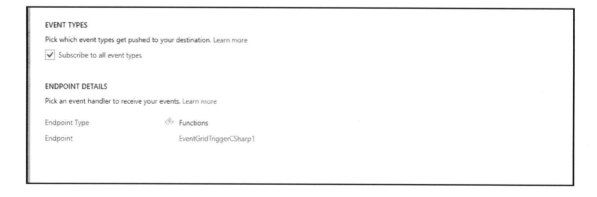

9. Add another Event Grid domain topic, and on the subscription listing for the new Event Grid domain topic, create an event subscription endpoint for the webhook along with the event hub. The complete event subscription setup for the Event Grid domain is shown here:

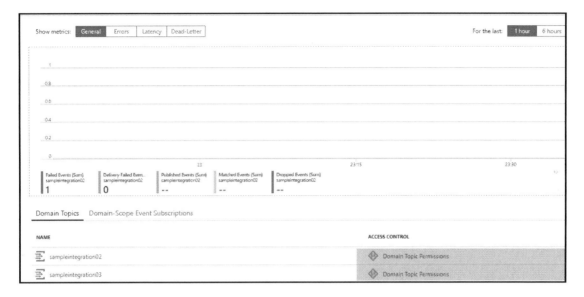

10. The last step is to publish events to the Event Grid domain topic and route them to a different topic and subscription. To do this, we have created an HTTP application with Azure Functions using the Event Grid Domain URI and access keys. This function will be used to publish events to the Event Grid domain endpoint. The sample code for the Event Grid domain publisher is shown here:

When you publish events to the Event Grid domain endpoint, you need to specify an Event Domain topic name in the event data so that the event can be routed to the correct event subscription handler.

```
public static async Task<HttpResponseMessage>
Run([HttpTrigger(AuthorizationLevel.Function,
        "post", Route = null)]HttpRequestMessage req,
TraceWriter log)
        {
            SocialPost post = await
req.Content.ReadAsAsync<SocialPost>();
            List<EventGridEvent> eventlist = new
List<EventGridEvent>();
            for (int i = 0; i < 1; i++)
```

```
        {
            eventlist.Add(new EventGridEvent()
            {
                Topic= "sampleintegration02",
                Id = Guid.NewGuid().ToString(),
                EventType = "integration.event.eventpublished",
                EventTime = DateTime.Now,
                Subject = "IntegrationEvent",
                DataVersion = "1.0",
                Data = new SocialPost()
                {
                    PostType = post.PostType,
                    PostedBy = post.PostedBy,
                    PostDescription = post.PostDescription,
                    id = Guid.NewGuid().ToString()

                }

            });
            eventlist.Add(new EventGridEvent()
            {
                Topic = "sampleintegration03",
                Id = Guid.NewGuid().ToString(),
                EventType = "integration.event.eventpublished",
                EventTime = DateTime.Now,
                Subject = "IntegrationEvent",
                DataVersion = "1.0",
                Data = new SocialPost()
                {
                    PostType = post.PostType,
                    PostedBy = post.PostedBy,
                    PostDescription = post.PostDescription,
                    id = Guid.NewGuid().ToString()

                }

            });
        }
        TopicCredentials topicCredentials = new
TopicCredentials(eventgridkey);
        EventGridClient client = new
EventGridClient(topicCredentials);
        client.PublishEventsAsync(topicHostname,
eventlist).GetAwaiter().GetResult();
        return req.CreateResponse(HttpStatusCode.OK);
```

11. You can monitor the event domain subscription through the Azure portal, which lists all the events that get published and emitted through the Event Grid domain:

12. The individual subscription resource can also track the events from the Azure portal and Event Subscription blade. When you navigate to individual resources, you can find details of the events subscribed to from the Event Grid domain. An example of an event published to an Events Hub resource is shown here:

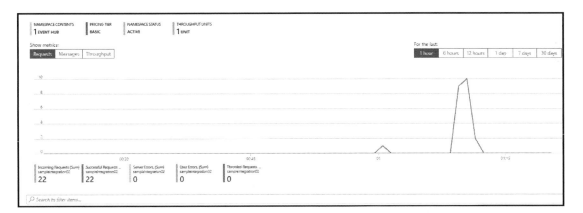

13. For the Function App, you can click on the **Event subscriber** function and then
    click either on the **Monitor** tab or on the Application Insights instance associated
    with the Function App:

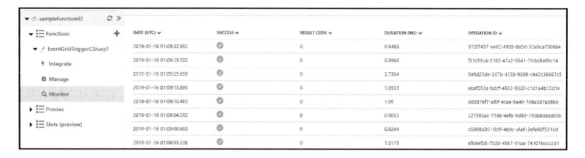

In this exercise, we have shown how you can work with scalable eventing solutions using
the Azure Event Grid domain. As this platform is currently in a preview state, there are
certain limitations on the throughput, information about which you can find in the
Microsoft documentation: `https://github.com/MicrosoftDocs/azure-docs/blob/master/`
`includes/event-grid-limits.md`.

Summary

In this chapter, we looked closely at the capabilities of Azure Event Grid and how we can
utilize Event Grid's features in a modern integration framework. We covered multiple
routing options with Azure Event Grid and looked at a few sample exercises with Azure
Event Grid topics and event domains. With this, you will be able to use Azure Event Grid
in integration solutions and publish events to Event Grid as well.

In the next chapter, we will continue our learning by looking at integration services such as
Service Bus, API Management, and Logic Apps. We will also look at how we can make the
most of Azure Event Grid in conjunction with these services.

4
Azure API Management

Today's enterprise technology landscape revolves around modern digital platforms that engage with internal and external customers more than ever before by exposing their assets, such as data and services, using **Application Programming Interfaces (APIs)**. APIs have become a tremendous opportunity for organizations to expand their business to new horizons.

According to Harvard Business Review (`https://hbr.org/2015/01/the-strategic-value-of-apis`), Salesforce.com (`https://searchsecurity.techtarget.com/news/2240222882/API-gateways-emerge-to-address-growing-security-demands`) generates 50% of its revenue through APIs, for Expedia.com (`https://www.slideshare.net/faberNovel/why-shouldicareaboutap-is4/45`) it's 90%, and for eBay (`https://www.programmableweb.com/news/ebay-opens-platform-to-3rd-party-developers/2008/06/16`) it's 60%. Salesforce.com has a marketplace (AppExchange) for apps created by hundreds of its partners. Expedia exposes its APIs to third-party applications for booking flights, hotels, and cars. eBay generates revenue by exposing APIs to list auctions, get customer information, retrieve information about the items listed, collect feedback, and more.

This data clearly shows that organizations have realized the significance of APIs in the modern era, and the trend is becoming so prominent that any organization without a proper API strategy is like an organization without an internet connection.

Huge growth in exposing services and information to internal and external customers brings various challenges and risks in terms of building, managing, maintaining, and securing APIs. The following are some important challenges in managing APIs:

- **Security**: Since enterprises expose their services and information through APIs, it is essential to be vigilant against potential threats and hacks. It is also vital to ensure that the usage of APIs is throttled and controlled in a way that supports the load on the backend and monitoring policies. APIs also need to be compliant with regulatory guidelines, with proper authentication, authorization, and auditing capabilities.

- **Exposing facades and versioning**: Developers publish APIs to internal and external applications in an organization. These APIs need to evolve and adapt to changes, which can be either breaking or non-breaking. It is vital that publishers ensure that changes they make do not violate the applications that consume those APIs. To ensure this, they need to expose facades to customers and make changes at their backend. However, if the publisher can't avoid breaking changes, they need to ensure they publish a different version of the same API. Handling these breaking and non-breaking changes is a challenge for any organization.

- **Faster onboarding and adoption**: Organizations need to ensure that developers can access APIs easily and without manual intervention. Application developers should be able to get up to speed quickly with the help of interactive documentation, sample code, and a developer console. If the process involves manual steps, then developer productivity decreases, the adaption rate goes down, and APIs will not be able to meet the reach expected of them.

- **API usage analytics**: APIs are becoming bread and butter for organizations. As such, organizations need to keep a check on the usage, performance, and reliability of services exposed through APIs. A straightforward approach to getting analytics from exposed APIs is essential for ensuring healthy and efficient operations.

The following topics will be covered in this chapter:

- Various building blocks for API Management
- Developer Portal and Administrator Portal
- Policies in API Management
- Handling large messages in hybrid integration scenarios

The API Management platform

To overcome the challenges in adopting APIs and to be innovative, organizations are making use of **API Management (APIM)** platforms:

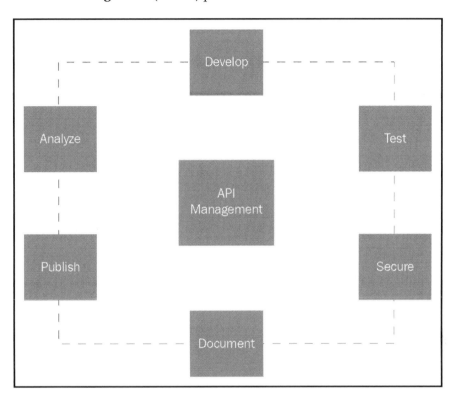

As shown in the preceding diagram, APIM platforms allow enterprises to **Develop**, **Test**, **Secure**, **Document**, **Publish**, and **Analyze** APIs in a holistic manner:

- **Design and develop**: APIM platforms help organizations to adopt an API-first approach, which, in turn, brings greater agility to development teams. APIs can be designed to help developers to consume them effortlessly by following best practices such as open API specifications, readable URLs, good error handling, data-centric modelling, non-hierarchical URLs, and more. It also helps teams to version control the APIs effectively.

- **Secure**: Badly designed and managed APIs are vulnerable to various cyber threats. APIM brings the ability to protect APIs against these cyber threats. The below screenshot shows the various cyber threats API Management deals with:

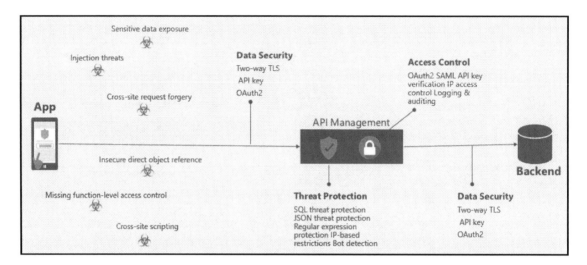

Azure APIM provides out-of-the-box traffic management capabilities, such as rate limiting, caching, spike arrest, and quotas, that are essential for handling volumetric attacks and business spikes.

- **Documentation**: The ability to provide documentation and a developer feedback mechanism is an important consideration when publishing APIs for developers. Developers need to know how to use those APIs and how to get the best results when integrating with the platform. Developers will be able to test the APIs interactively through developer portals.

- **Publish**: APIM brings the capability to create products out of APIs and provide differentiated access to various user groups. It helps organizations to be agile regarding pricing and business models. APIM also brings other things, such as rich documentation from the open API specification, a sandbox environment for testing APIs, and the understanding of request and response formats through interaction with APIs.

- **Analyze**: APIM platforms provide the ability to monitor performance and availability of APIs and also give appropriate metrics for measuring the success of an API program as. The below screenshot shows how the platforms will monitor the performance while providing an estimate metric value as well:

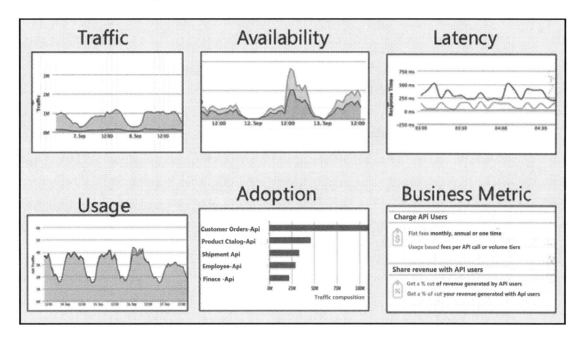

The Azure APIM platform

Azure APIM is Microsoft's service offering to address the challenges that organizations face when building an API strategy. With Azure APIM, organizations can expose their data and services to external partners, customers, and internal developers. As shown in the below screenshot, Azure API consists of three core components: an API gateway, the publisher portal, and the developer portal:

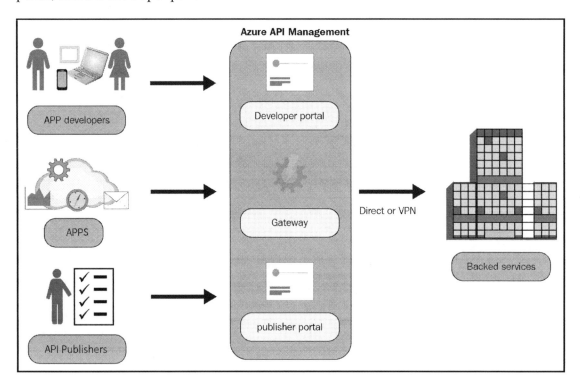

API gateway

The API gateway is the core engine and acts as an endpoint of Azure APIM. It is responsible for the following functionalities:

- **Policy-based routing**: It is responsible for accepting API calls from the client applications and routing them to backend systems based on routing policies.
- **CORS policies**: Applies cross-origin resource policies to inbound requests, if configured.

- **Security**: Verifies API keys, certificates, **Java Web Token (JWT)** security tokens, certificates, and other forms of credentials.
- **Throttling and rate limit**: Based on the load and policies, this applies rate limits and throttles requests.
- **Transformation**: Based on the policies, API requests are translated from one format to another format. For example, an XML message can be translated to JSON format.
- **Response Caching**: Whenever configured, the gateway caches the response for specific requests. This reduces the number of calls made to backend systems.

The publisher portal

The publisher portal is an administrative interface of Azure APIM that helps developers to manage their API program. The publisher portal has the following functionalities:

- **Creating proxies**: Provides the capability to create proxies to APIs by defining them or importing them from API schemas such as Swagger definitions, open APIs, and SOAP endpoints
- **Defining policies**: Provides the capability to define and apply various policies at various levels
- **Packaging APIs into products**: The publisher portal allows us to create products out of APIs to monetize them
- **User management**: Helps to add and remove users and assign appropriate permissions to them

The developer portal

The developer portal is where developers log in; understand the APIs, including their input, output, and terms of use; and subscribe to APIs that they are interested in. Naturally, developers expect APIs to be well documented in this portal. It also should allow them to leave their feedback and get in touch with communities using these APIs.

The Azure developer portal can be customized by making use of custom styling in order to add your own branding and custom content. A few main purposes served by the Azure developer portal are listed here:

- **Documentation**: This provides the proper documentation of the APIs
- **Testing APIs:** Helps developers to test or try out the API quickly through an interactive console

- **Subscription**: Helps developers to create an account and subscribe to API keys
- **Accessing analytics data**: Helps developers to access analytics data such as the number of requests on APIs they have subscribed to

API products

API products are used to package sets of APIs and attach usage constraints such as those to do with levels of access, functionality, and rate limits. Each API product will have its own identity, including a description, title, and usage terms. API products allow you to define **service-level agreements (SLAs)** with API consumer clients. They also help you monetize APIs by bringing them under organizational product lines.

Client application developers need to subscribe to these products in order to use APIs, or they have to be part of user groups that already have access to the products.

Technically, API products are used when you want to create API keys that enforce authorization policies and when you want to limit the number of requests to the APIs in the form of access quotas.

Authorization groups

Authorization groups provide a different level of access to APIs to developers. The following are the built-in authorization groups in Azure APIM:

- **Administrators**: The members of this group have access to manage APIM service instances, will be able to create APIs, manage operations, create products, and define SLAs for each product. They have the highest level of authority over the APIM service instance.
- **Developers**: Client application developers who have subscribed to the product and have got access to use the APIs in their application fall under the developers group. They will have full access to the developer portal, control the operations of the APIs, know the usage of the APIs, and call them in their client applications.
- **Guests**: These are the users who are not yet authenticated by the developer portal but are exploring and trying to understand the APIs for their client applications. Though these users have access to test the APIs in the developer portal, they will not be able to use them in their applications. These users could be potential clients for the organizations.

Azure APIM also provides an option to create custom user groups in order to provide access to a group of products or APIs to specific organizations or groups of users.

Policies

Policies help in modifying requests to APIs or responses from APIs in a configurable way. The Azure APIM portal allows users to apply these policies to requests or responses. One example could be the conversion of an XML payload in a request to JSON format. There is a wide variety of policies that give great control over changing the behavior of requests or responses. The following are a few capabilities and characteristics of the policies:

- Encapsulate common APIM functions
- Access control, protection, transformation, and caching
- Chained together into a pipeline
- Mutate request context or change API behavior
- Set inbound and outbound directions
- Can be triggered by an error
- Applied at a variety of scopes

Policy scopes

Policies can be applied at different scopes (such as API-level, operation-level, product-level, and global-level scopes). Some are allowed only on the inbound channel, while others are allowed only on the outbound channel:

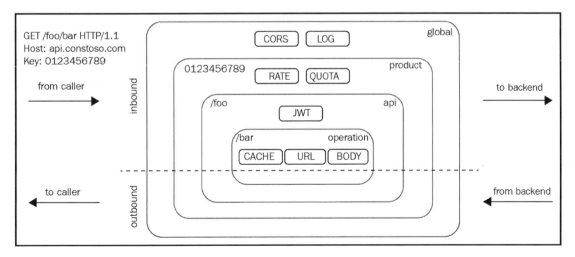

Policy scope in API Management has been divided into four categories global scope, product scope, API scope, and operation-level scope. The basic definition of each of the scope is listed as follows:

- **Global scope**: These are policies that are applied to all API requests. An example would be a cross-origin request policy or logging policy.
- **Product scope**: These policies are applied to all the APIs in a specific product. These policies are mainly used for monetizing purposes. Rate limit policies and quota policies are two examples.
- **API scope**: These are policies that are applied to only specific APIs. An example would be authorization policies that verify JWTs.
- **Operation-level scope**: These policies are applied at the operation level, such as caching and URL rewrite policies.

The following are example policies and the scopes at which they can be applied:

Category	Policy	Channel		Scope			
		Inbound	Outbound	Global	Product	API	Operation
Access Restriction	Check HTTP header	✓		✓	✓	✓	✓
	Limit call rate	✓			✓		
	Restrict caller IP	✓		✓	✓	✓	✓
	Set usage quota	✓			✓		
	Validate JWT	✓		✓	✓	✓	✓
Authetication	Autheticate with basic	✓				✓	
	Authenticate with Cert	✓				✓	
Caching	Get from cache	✓			✓	✓	✓
	Set to cache		✓		✓	✓	✓
Cross-Domain	Allow cross-domain	✓		✓			
	CQRS	✓			✓	✓	
	JSONP		✓	✓	✓	✓	✓
Transformation	JSON to XML	✓	✓	✓	✓	✓	✓
	XML to JSON	✓	✓	✓	✓	✓	✓
	Find and replace in body	✓	✓	✓	✓	✓	✓
	Mask URLs in content	✓	✓	✓	✓	✓	✓
	Set backend service	✓		✓	✓	✓	✓
	Set HTTP header	✓	✓	✓	✓	✓	✓
	Set querystring parm	✓		✓	✓	✓	✓
	Rewrite URL	✓					✓
Conditional	Control Flow	✓	✓	✓	✓	✓	✓
	Set Context variable	✓	✓	✓	✓	✓	✓

Logistical company ShipAnyWhere – case study

ShipAnyWhere is a fictional large logistical company that is specialized in commerce and fulfillment solutions for e-commerce businesses across the world. It has more than 100 distribution centers across more than 30 countries. It provides B2B, e-commerce, and multi-channel fulfillment solutions to its customers using cutting-edge technologies.

Traditionally, ShipAnyWhere has built numerous services for inbound processes across all fulfillment locations. All these services were built with different technologies and platforms and are living in silos. The following are the three main services that play key roles in their fulfillment solutions.

The product service

The product service is one of those old services implemented at ShipAnyWhere that makes use of a SOAP-based web service. When clients integrate with the product service, they will be shared with **Web Services Description Language (WSDL)** file.

The product service has operations for listing all products, creating a new product, modifying a product, and retiring a product.

The order fulfillment service

The order fulfillment service is being used by thousands of ShipAnyWhere's customers across the world. A strong integration platform was built with BizTalk Server. The order fulfillment service has operations for creating new orders, getting a list of orders, modifying orders, and canceling orders. This service is, again, SOAP-based, as shown in the following diagram.

The purchase order service

ShipAnyWhere sells its fixed-price or package service to their clients and receives purchase orders from them. However, this line of business is new to ShipAnyWhere and they need an integration layer with their **Software-as-a-Service (SaaS)**—based Salesforce system.

They have decided to use Azure Logic Apps and Azure Functions to implement their integration solution. All B2B purchase orders make use of EDI standard X12, and message transfer happens on a secure layer using AS2. They have created multiple Logic Apps and Functions, each acting as a service endpoint and creating a Service Bus, as shown:

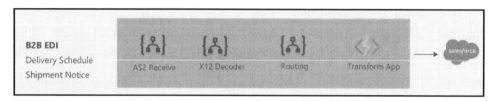

ShipAnyWhere digital transformation

ShipAnyWhere is implementing a digital transformation program with RESTful/JSON-based APIs as its backbone. They have taken an API-first approach. They already have lots of services up and running in silos. They do not want to replace these services in a 'Big Bang" approach. Rather, they start creating new services for their newer services using web APIs, Logic Apps, and Azure Functions, and they want to convert all the SOAP-based services to JSON-based services. They decided to make use of Azure's API gateways and expose their APIs to internal and external developers and manage all the APIs in one place. In all, ShipAnyWhere's aims here as are follows:

- They would like to build a strong security layer across all the APIs and services
- They would like to monetize these APIs wherever possible and generate revenue
- They want to create a very good developer portal that provides full-fledged documentation for the APIs

Creating an APIM service

You need an APIM service in order to expose APIs. This can also be done using ARM template deployment or the Azure portal. In our example, we will be using the Azure portal. Browse to `http://portal.azure.com`, and click **Create a resource | Enterprise Integration | API management**

In the **API Management service** window, enter the settings as shown here:

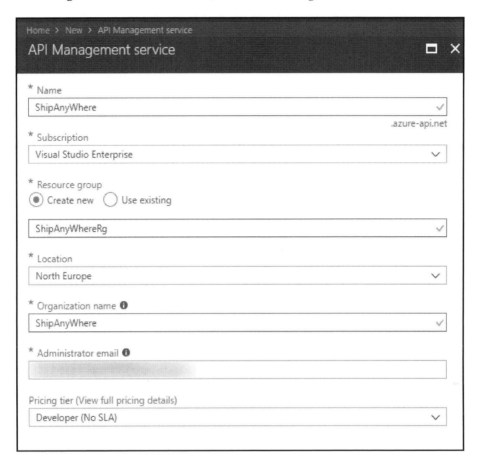

Following table contains list of required parameters to create API Management instance in Azure Resource Group:

Setting name	Setting value	Description
Name	ShipAnyWhere	The name is a unique identifier that becomes part of the domain name created for the APIM service. In our example, the domain name created will be `ShipAnyWhere.azure-api.net`.
Subscription	Your subscription	Name of the Azure subscription.
Resource group	ShipAnyWhereRg	Resource group under which the APIM service is created.

Location	North Europe	The name of the geographic location that is nearest to you.
Organization name	ShipAnyWhere	The organization name will be used for branding purposes, mainly in the developer portal.
Admin email	Email ID of admin	The APIM service sends notifications of various activities. Specify the email ID to which these notifications need to be sent.
Pricing tier	Developer	There are four pricing tiers—developer, basic, standard, and premium. We have selected the developer tier.

You can open the ShipAnyWhere APIM service by searching in the Azure portal:

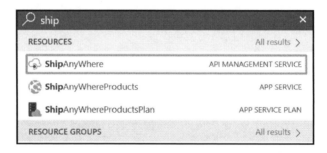

You will land on to a page similar to the one following. This page shows the name of the service and contains links for APIs, the publisher portal, the developer portal, and more:

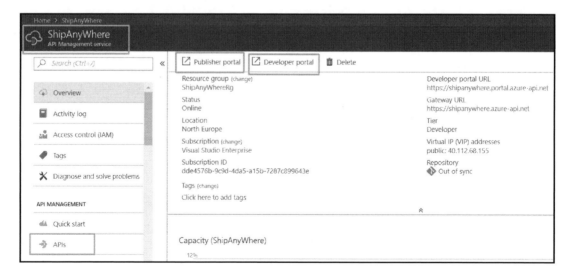

Creating REST endpoints for the ShipAnyWhere product service

ShipAnyWhere has decided to convert its product service SOAP operations into JSON-based REST APIs. This means the existing SOAP-based web service and its connectivity to the backend remain in operation and a proxy REST-based API will be created. The proxy API will be responsible for receiving REST-based requests, converting them to SOAP-based requests, and sending them to the backend, which is a SOAP-based web service in our scenario.

All this can be achieved in a matter of five minutes. This is the level of agility the Azure APIM platform brings to its customers. It saves a lot of cost to organizations. Here are the steps to follow to achieve this.

Existing ShipAnyWhere service

Open `http://shipanywhereproducts.azurewebsites.net/ProductService.svc` and click on the WSDL link: `http://shipanywhereproducts.azurewebsites.net/ProductService.svc?wsdl`:

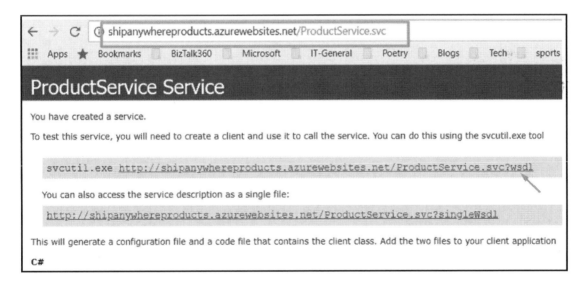

If you look into the WSDL file, you can clearly see that it has got four operations:

```
▼<wsdl:portType name="IProductService">
  ▶<wsdl:operation name="GetProducts">...</wsdl:operation>
  ▶<wsdl:operation name="CreateProduct">..</wsdl:operation>
  ▶<wsdl:operation name="ModifyProduct">..</wsdl:operation>
  ▶<wsdl:operation name="RetireProduct">..</wsdl:operation>
</wsdl:portType>
```

Importing WSDL

For importing WSDL, follow the steps:

1. Select APIs under the API MANAGEMENT section as shown below:

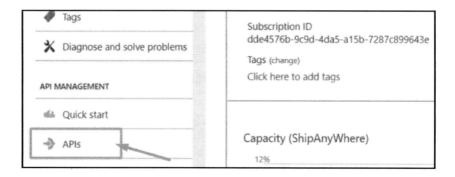

2. In the **Add a new API** section, select **WSDL**:

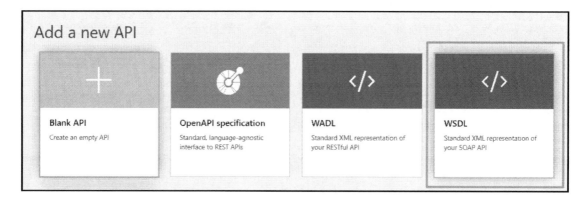

3. In the WSDL specification, enter the URL to where your SOAP API resides. Azure APIM automatically lists the service endpoints in the interface selection dropdown. We will have to select `http://shipanywhereproducts.` `azurewebsites.net/ProductService.svc?wsdl` for **WSDL specification** and `ProductService` as **Interface**:

4. In the import method, select the **SOAP to REST** radio button. When this is selected, Azure APIM attempts to transform the XML request-response specification to JSON so that the consumer application can use this as a RESTful API. All external requests will be converted back to SOAP requests by Azure APIM.

   Provide an appropriate display name, name, and description for the API.

   API URL suffix identifies the API hosted under the APIM instance. This name will become part of the base URL that application developers use to access the API. Type `Products` in the API URL suffix, which in turn creates a base URL: `https://shipanywhere.azure.api.net/Products`.

Tags provide you with an opportunity to categorize APIs. They help in searching for APIs in the Azure APIM portal. For example, if someone wants to search for all the APIs related to the catalog or products, then adding these words in tags would help to a great extent.

5. In the **Products** field, select the **Starter** product, which is one of the automatically created products when you create an APIM instance.

   We can create our own products and associate one or more APIs with them. The association can be done when creating an API or at later stages.

   By default, each APIM instance comes with two sample products:

   - Starter
   - Unlimited:

Azure APIM allows you to specify the version number for the APIs created. The version number can be part of the URL **Path**, or can be a request header, or can be part of a query string. In our example, we have selected **Path** as our versioning scheme. The version identifier indicates the exact version of the API. In our case, we are using v1 as our version identifier.

Since we have used a version number as part of the **Path,** the URL developers must use to access this API will be https://shipanywhere.azure-api.net/Products/v1.

6. When you click **Create**, a success message will be displayed, along with logs. Click **Done**:

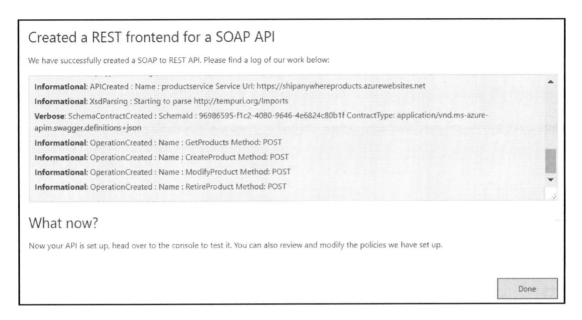

7. You will see all the operations from the WSL are converted to REST-based **POST** operations in v1 of the **ProductService** API:

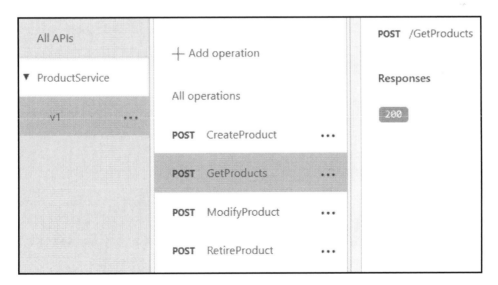

Testing the GetProducts service method

The Azure portal has a built-in console for testing API methods. It automatically prepopulates the HTTP headers required and the JSON file (in the case of the POST operations). This makes it easier for developers to quickly test the API methods that they have created or imported. By default, the following headers are pre-populated:

Header name	Value	Description
Content type	Application/JSON	This indicates that the request message is in JSON format.
Cache control	no-cache	This directive indicates the HTTP caching mechanism used for request and response messages. The following are the values this field can take: `max-age=10`, `max-stale=10`, `no-transform`, `only-if-cached`, `no-cache`, `no-store`, and `min-fresh=30`
`Ocp-APIM-Subscription-Key`	Subscription key from the developer portal	To access APIM service APIs, you will need a subscription key. By default, when you test an API in the testing console, the subscription key is automatically populated.
`Ocp-Apim-Trace`	True	This indicates whether the console should trace the logs or not.

Specify the body of the JSON message in the body section as a raw request body:

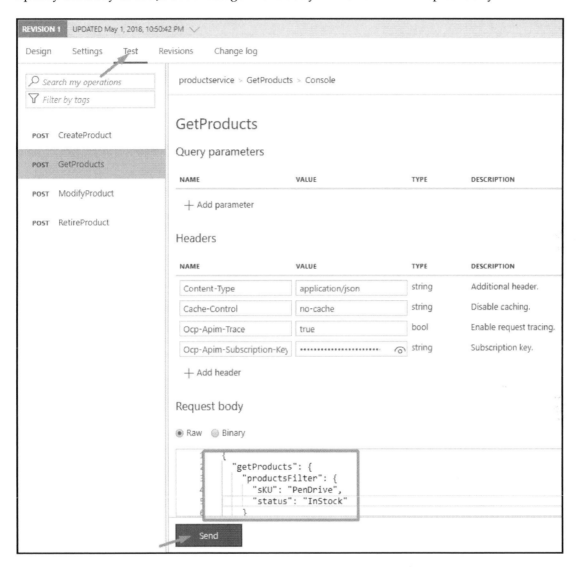

Once you click **Send**, you will get the response back as follows:

```
HTTP response

Message    Trace
_____

HTTP/1.1 200 OK

date: Tue, 01 May 2018 22:08:39 GMT
content-encoding: gzip
x-aspnet-version: 4.0.30319
x-powered-by: ASP.NET
vary: Accept-Encoding,Origin
ocp-apim-trace-location: https://apimgmtstsy0g19q6j0t768w.blob.core.
mqrtWTWI%2B5BKk3AfEh%2FCYNfw%3D&se=2018-05-02T22%3A08%3A39Z&sp=r&trac
content-type: application/json
cache-control: private
transfer-encoding: chunked

{
    "getProductsResponse": {
      "getProductsResult": {
        "Items": [{
            "availableCount": 200,
            "classification": "hardware",
            "sku": "Pen drive X13"
```

Since we have enabled tracing, the console contains detailed traces of inbound, backend, and outbound policy execution. Navigate to the **Trace** tab and select one of these options.

The **Inbound** section contains traces for all policy executions for the incoming request. The **Backend** section includes policies executed on the requests that are sent to the backend and responses are received back. The **Outbound** section contains traces for policy executions on the response sent back to the callers:

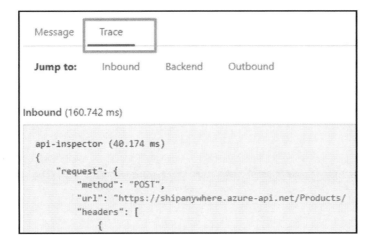

The developer portal

The developer portal is the place where the documentation of the API is published. It helps the customers to understand the APIs and get up to speed quickly. The developer portal not only contains documentation but also allows developers to sign in and get access to API products. The developer portal also provides the option try out the APIs.

The developer portal for the APIM service will be in the format `https://<ServiceName>.portal.azure-api.net`:

1. In our scenario, **ShipAnyWhere** is the service name and the portal URI will be `https://shipanywhere.portal.azure-api.net/`. You can navigate to the developer portal from the Azure portal itself as shown:

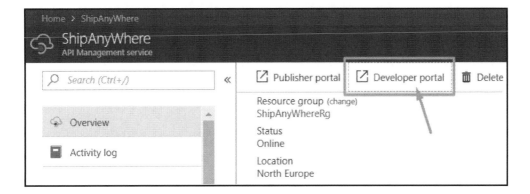

2. When you open the developer portal, you will land on a default landing page:

3. You can customize the portal to suit your organization's branding. Please follow
   `https://docs.microsoft.com/en-gb/azure/api-management/api-management-customize-styles` to understand how to configure the developer portal.

4. When you click on the API menu, you will have a page where all APIs to which you have access will be available:

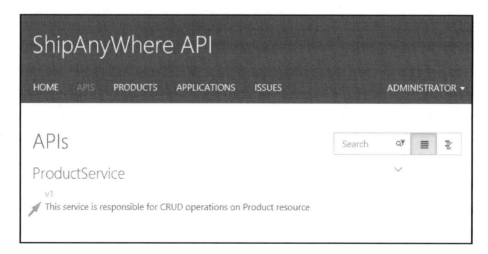

5. Click on the version of the API, which opens up a developer console listing all the APIs:

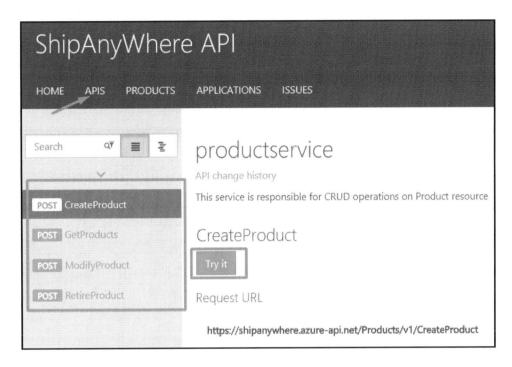

APIM policies

Policies are the set of configurable, execution statements that control the behavior of requests and responses in the APIM service. For example, a Validate-JWT policy reads a JWT and validates it for authorization. In this section, we will see various policies used in ShipAnyWhere's APIM service.

Inbound policies

Inbound policies are policies that are applied on the request message. **Frontend**, **Inbound processing**, and **Backend** are the stages in which inbound policies are being applied. Here is the designer view of the APIM policies applied at various stages:

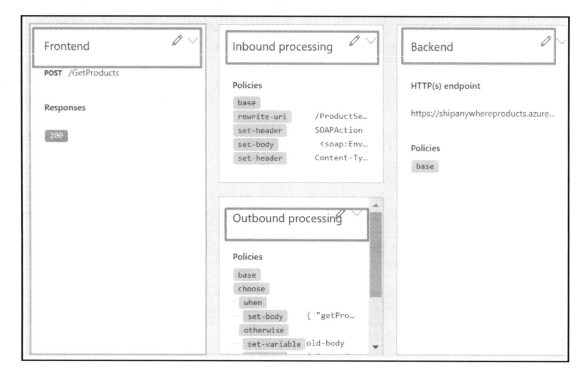

Apart from the designer view, Azure APIM also provides a code view as you can see below, which shows further details on each of the policies:

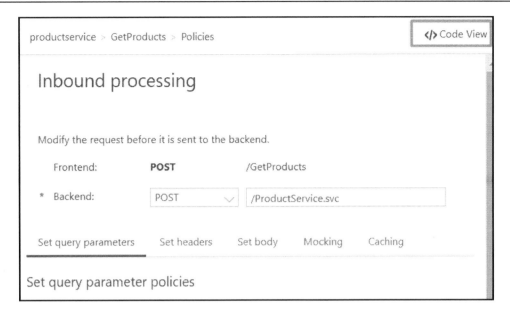

The rewrite-uri policy

The rewrite-uri policy helps in transforming the inbound URLs to the format expected by backend or client systems. In our scenario, we need to convert the public REST URL, `https://shipnywhere.azure-api/Products/v1/CreateProduct`, to a backend SOAP URL,

`https://shipanywhereproducts.azurewebsites.net/ProductService.svc`.

The policy can be written as follows. Note that the service URL is relative path to the backend service configured when creating the APIM service:

```
policies>
    <inbound>
        <base />
        <rewrite-uri template="/ProductService.svc" />
        <set-header name="SOAPAction" exists-action="override">
            <value>"http://tempuri.org/IProductService/GetProducts"</value>
        </set-header>
        <set-body template="liquid">
```

Rewrite-uri policies can be used to expose alternative, clean, user-friendly, RESTful, and SEO-friendly URLs.

When we run the APIs in the test console, we can see the rewrite policy execution in the trace:

```
rewrite-uri (0.051 ms)
{
    "message": "Updated request URL per specified rewrite template.",
    "request": {
        "url": "https://shipanywhereproducts.azurewebsites.net/ProductService.svc"
    }
}
```

The set-header policy

The `set-header` policy is useful for adding or removing HTTP headers to or from requests and responses. In our scenario, since we are invoking a SOAP-based endpoint in the backend, we will have to add two headers. One is the `SOAPAction` header, as shown:

```
<set-header name="SOAPAction" exists-action="override">
    <value>"http://tempuri.org/IProductService/GetProducts"</value>
</set-header>
```

The other is the `Content-Type` header:

```
<set-header name="Content-Type" exists-action="override">
    <value>text/xml</value>
</set-header>
```

The set-body policy

The `set-body` policy can be used to change the body of a request or response. To access the message body, you can use the `context.Request.Body` property or `context.Response.Body`.

In our scenario, `set-body` is used to create a SOAP XML message from the JSON content as shown:

```
<set-body template="liquid">
    <soap:Envelope xmlns:soap="http://schemas.xmlsoap.org/soap/envelope/" xmlns="http://tempuri.org/">
        <soap:Body>
            <GetProducts>
                <productsFilter>
                    <SKU xmlns="http://schemas.datacontract.org/2004/07/ShipAnyWhere"{{body.getProducts.productsFilter.sKU}}/SKU>
                    <Status xmlns="http://schemas.datacontract.org/2004/07/ShipAnyWhere">{{body.getProducts.productsFilter.status}}<,
                </productsFilter>
            </GetProducts>
        </soap:Body>
    </soap:Envelope>
</set-body>
```

Backend policies

Backend policies are the policies that are applied in the backend stage of the policy pipeline. In our scenario, we are not writing any policies explicitly:

```
24        <backend>
25            <base />
26        </backend>
```

Outbound policies

Outbound policies mainly act upon the response received from the backend service.

In our scenario, the outbound policy is responsible for converting the XML response from the backend SOAP service to its corresponding JSON format. It makes use of the `set-body` policy with a liquid template shown as following. We are making use of a liquid template to create a JSON response.

To find out more about liquid templates, refer to the documentation: `https://shopify.github.io/liquid/`:

```
27      <outbound>
28          <base />
29          <choose>
30              <when condition="@(context.Response.StatusCode < 400)">
31                  <set-body template="liquid">
32                                                  {
33      "getProductsResponse" :
34      {
35        "getProductsResult" :
36        {
37          "Items" :
38          [
39            {% JSONArrayFor item in body.envelope.body.GetProductsResponse.GetProduc
40              {
41                "availableCount" : {{item.AvailableCount}},
42                "classification" : "{{item.Classification}}",
43                "sku" : "{{item.Sku}}"
44              }
45            {% endJSONArrayFor -%}
46          ]
47      ,
48          "total" : {{body.envelope.body.GetProductsResponse.GetProductsResult.Total
49        }
```

The control flow policy

The control flow policy is applied to control the conditional execution of policies. This makes use of `choose`, `when`, and `otherwise` statements as shown:

```xml
XML

<choose>
    <when condition="Boolean expression | Boolean constant">
        <!- one or more policy statements to be applied if the above condition is true  -->
    </when>
    <when condition="Boolean expression | Boolean constant">
        <!- one or more policy statements to be applied if the above condition is true  -->
    </when>
    <otherwise>
        <!- one or more policy statements to be applied if none of the above conditions are true  -->
</otherwise>
</choose>
```

In our example, we mainly used the control flow policy to find out whether the backend service has returned status codes less than 400, and if so, to create a JSON response using the liquid template.

The XML-to-JSON policy

The XML-to-JSON policy converts a request or response body from XML to JSON. The syntax of the policy is as follows:

```
<xml-to-json kind="javascript-friendly | direct" apply="always | content-type-xml" consider-accept-header="true | false"/>
```

The `kind` attribute takes two values:

- `javascript-friendly`: The converted JSON has a form friendly to JavaScript developers
- `direct`: The converted JSON reflects the original XML document's structure

The `apply` attribute takes two values:

- `always`: This always converts the XML request to JSON
- `content-type-xml`: This converts the XML request only if the Content-Type header indicates the presence of XML

The `consider-accept-header` attribute takes two values:

- `true`: This applies conversion if XML is requested in the request accept header
- `false`: This always applies conversion

In our scenario, we did not use an XML-to-JSON policy as the web service returned a SOAP message and we should not be converting SOAP header XML elements into JSON. However, for demonstration purposes, I removed the logic and replaced the outbound policy with the following code:

```
<outbound>
    <base />
    <xml-to-json kind="direct" apply="always" consider-accept-header="false" />
</outbound>
```

When you test the `GetProducts` API method, we will get a response message as follows:

```json
{
  "s$Envelope": {
    "@xmlns$s": "http://schemas.xmlsoap.org/soap/envelope/",
    "s$Body": {
      "GetProductsResponse": {
        "@xmlns": "http://tempuri.org/",
        "GetProductsResult": {
          "@xmlns$a": "http://schemas.datacontract.org/2004/07/ShipAnyWhere",
          "@xmlns$i": "http://www.w3.org/2001/XMLSchema-instance",
          "a$Items": {
            "a$Product": [{
              "a$AvailableCount": "200",
              "a$Classification": "hardware",
              "a$Sku": "Pen drive X13"
            }, {
              "a$AvailableCount": "20",
              "a$Classification": "hardware",
              "a$Sku": "2 TB Hardrive X1"
            }]
          },
          "a$Total": "2"
        }
      }
    }
  }
}
```

The cross-original resource sharing (CORS) policy

CORS allows a browser and a server to interact and determine whether or not to allow specific cross-origin requests (such as `XMLHttpRequests` calls made from JavaScript on a web page to other domains).

In our scenario, we would like the product service to be accessed only by internal developers who are in the ShipAnyWhere domain. I add the following CORS policy to all the operations of the product service as shown:

```
ProductService                    14    <inbound>
                                  15      <base />
          All operations          16      <cors>
                                  17        <allowed-origins>
   v1              ...            18          <!-- allow any -->
                                  19          <!-- OR a list of one or more specific URIs
   POST   CreateProduct    ...    20          <origin>http://ShipAnyWhere.com</origin>   in>
                                  21          <!-- URI must include scheme, host, and pomd
   POST   GetProducts      ...    22        </allowed-origins>
                                  23        <allowed-methods>
   POST   ModifyProduct    ...    24          <!-- allow any -->
                                  25          <method>POST</method>
   POST   RetireProduct    ...    26        </allowed-methods>
                                  27        <allowed-headers>
                                  28          <!-- allow any -->
                                  29          <header>*</header>
                                  30        </allowed-headers>
                                  31      </cors>
```

When you test the API from POST, you will receive 200. But the response JSON will not be received as the inbound policy blocks the request:

Body   Cookies   **Headers (3)**   Test Results

content-length → 0

date → Thu, 03 May 2018 01:45:24 GMT

ocp-apim-trace-location → https://apimgmtstsy0g19q6j0t768w.blob.core.windows.net/apiinspectorcontainer/LsGwKdYD3QHOzIsO12B-vA2-16?sv=2015-07-08&sr=b&sig=hgkSc0MNeTVe9KEYi28%2Bphn%2FO4sm9CYj6bxGnpAYg90%3D&se=2018-05-04T01%3A45%3A24Z&sp=r&traceid=d6fdbd5e68894fa889a60a3224ec97b0

When you click on the trace location, you will see that the request is being terminated as the origin was different from the http://ShipAnyWhere.com domain:

Type","value":"application/json"},{"name":"Accept","value":"*/*"},{"name":"Accept-Encoding","value":"gzip,deflate,br"},{"name":"Accept-Language","value":"en-US,en;q=0.9"},{"name":"Host","value":"shipanywhere.azure-api.net"},{"name":"User-Agent","value":"Mozilla/5.0 (Windows N 10.0; Win64; x64) AppleWebKit/537.36 (KHTML, like Gecko) Chrome/66.0.3359.139 Safari/537.36"}]]}}},{"source":"api-inspector","timestamp":"2018-05-03T01:45:24.3298182Z","elapsed":"00:00:00.0003065","data":{"configuration":{"api":{"from":"/Products","to":{"scheme":"https","host":"shipanywhereproducts.azurewebsites.net","port":443,"path":"/","queryString":"","query":{},"isDefaultPort":true,"version":"v1","revision":"1"},"operation":{"method":"POST","uriTemplate":"/GetProducts"},"user":{"id":"1","groups":["Administrators","Developers"]},"product":{"id":"starter"}}}},{"source":"rate-limit","timestamp":"2018-05-03T01:45:24.3298182Z","elapsed":"00:00:00.0004072","data":{"message":"RateLimit counter 8150939447458989444 is incremented"}}],"outbound":[{"source":"cors","timestamp":"2018-05-03T01:45:24.3298182Z","elapsed":"00:00:00.0004640","data":"Origin header value `chrome-extension://fhbjgbiflinjbdggehcddcbncdddomop` was not on the list of allowed origins. Request was terminated."},{"source":"transfer-response","timestamp":"2018-05-03T01:45:24.3298182Z","elapsed":"00:00:00.0004970","data":{"message":"Response headers have been sent to the caller."}},{"source":"quota-by-key","timestamp":"2018-05-03T01:45:24.3298182Z","elapsed":"00:00:00.0005105","data":{"message":"Quota counter -8074385361110673278 is incremented by 1"}}]}}

Creating a SOAP pass through an API

Since the order fulfillment service is already being used by many customers, ShipAnyWhere has decided to keep the message format as XML over SOAP:

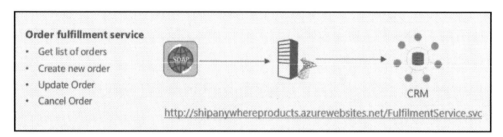

They recently upgraded their BizTalk 2016 environment with feature pack 2. Feature pack 2 provides an option to expose a WCF-BasicHTTP receive location as an endpoint with Azure APIM using the BizTalk Administration Console.

In the BizTalk Administration Console, right-click your WCF-BasicHTTP receive location, and select **Publish to API Management**:

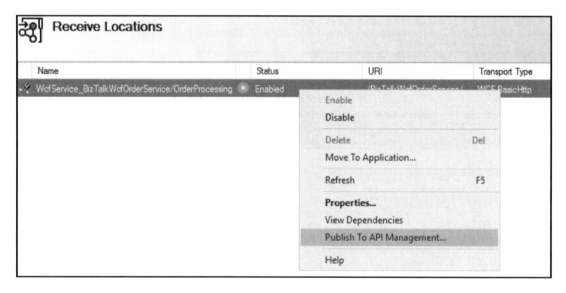

Press the **Sign-in...** button, which opens up an option to provide Azure credentials:

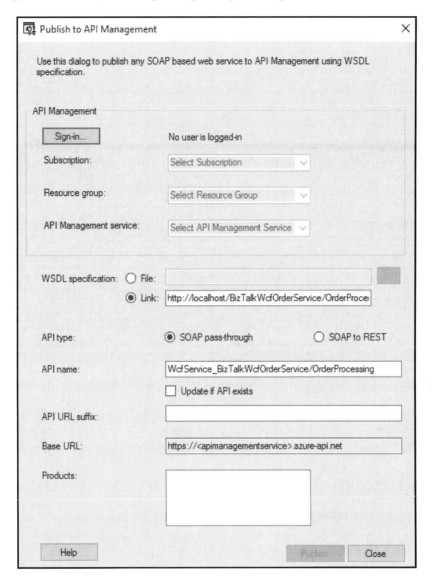

Once sign-in is successful, you can choose the resource group and the APIM service instance name. **WSDL specification** will be automatically populated from the wizard. If you want to provide a different **WSDL** file, you can explore a file location and select one.

You can either choose to select SOAP passthrough or SOAP to REST. If you choose the SOAP to REST option, a REST-based API will be created for the current SOAP-based web service. Since our intention is to expose the SOAP service as is, we select SOAP passthrough.

The API can be published both ways by changing the API URL suffix, and then publishing again using a different API type. The API name is automatically populated with the receive location name. Select an API URL suffix that is to be used by consumers of the API.

Creating purchase order APIs with Logic Apps and Azure Functions

ShipAnyWhere have built a number of Logic Apps and Azure Functions that together create a Service Bus layer:

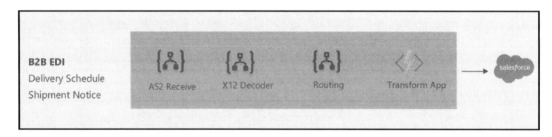

However, each Logic App or Azure Function is an API that internal and external developers can make use of. So, they decided to bring them also under the purview of APIM. Logic apps can be imported by following these steps:

1. Select **APIs** under **API MANAGEMENT**:
2. Select **Logic App** from the available types of APIs
3. In the **Create from Logic App** settings, select **Browse**:
4. This lists all the Logic Apps to which you have access. For example, I have got access to the following Logic Apps:

Selecting one of those is going to create an API.

5. Similarly, APIM provides an easy way to import Azure Functions. You have to follow the same steps we followed when importing the Logic Apps:

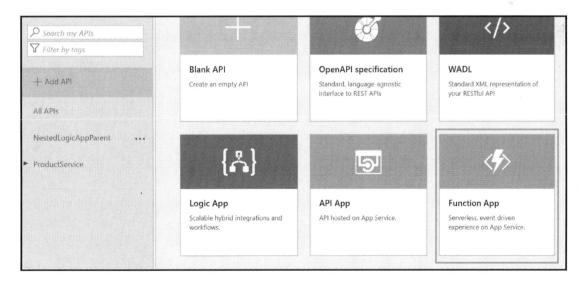

Handling large messages in hybrid integration scenarios

In hybrid integration scenarios, it is common that we need to send messages to BizTalk Server through Azure Service Bus queues or relays. However, the Service Bus has a restriction on the message size depending on the licensing tier. For example, if the Service Bus is of the standard tier, then the maximum size a message to the Service Bus can be is 256 kilobytes. If the Service Bus is on the premium plan, then the maximum size of the message is 1 MB. However, the premium plan costs a lot compared to the standard edition.

In order to resolve this issue, we can make use of Azure APIM to route messages depending on their size.

Azure APIM routes all messages that are larger than 256 kilobytes to a Logic App that stores the message in to a blob location, puts the blob location information into a message, and places it into a Service Bus queue from which BizTalk picks the messages. When the message arrives at BizTalk, it knows how to access the message from the blob location.

If the message size is less than 256 kilobytes, Azure APIM routes it to an Azure Function that puts the message into the Service Bus queue that BizTalk picks the messages from:

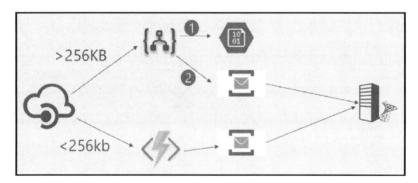

With an inbound policy, we can make use of control flow, `rewrite-uri`, and `set-backend-service` policies to achieve the scenario just described:

```
<inbound>
    <set-variable name="bodySize" value="@(context.Request.Headers["Content-Length"][0])" />
    <choose>
        <when condition="@(int.Parse(context.Variables.GetValueOrDefault<string>("bodySize"))
            <rewrite-uri template="?api-version=2016-06-01&amp;sp=/triggers/manual/run&amp;{{
            <set-backend-service base-url="https://prod-17.westeurope.logic.azure.com/workflc
        </when>
        <otherwise>
            <rewrite-uri template="?api-version=2016-10-01&amp;sp=/triggers/manual/run&amp;sv
            <set-backend-service base-url="https://TestFunctionApp.azurewebsites.net/
        </otherwise>
    </choose>
</choose>
```

Versioning and production testing Logic Apps

Let's consider a scenario in which ShipAnyWhere is building a new version of an already existing Logic App. However, they do not want to roll out the new version to all customers. They would like to test the latest version of the Logic App with a customer, Contoso, who sends a very small number of orders on a daily basis. Once there are no issues found with the new version, it will be rolled out to all trading partners.

In order to achieve this, ShipAnyWhere has decided to make use of Azure APIM's ability to route messages based on content. In this case, Azure APIM needs to check the trading partner. If the trading partner is Contoso, the inbound message must be routed to a new Logic App, and if not, it has to be routed to the old version of the Logic App as shown:

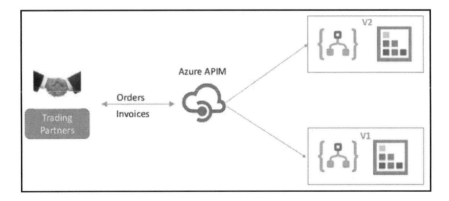

This can be achieved by adding a policy in Azure APIM as here:

```
<inbound>
    <set-variable name="parnterName" value="@(context.Request.Headers["PartnerName"][0])" />
    <choose>
        <when condition="@((context.Variables.GetValueOrDefault<string>("partnerName"))=="Contoso")">
            <rewrite-uri template="?api-version=2016-06-01&amp;sp=/triggers/manual/run&amp;{{orderProcessmanual
            <set-backend-service base-url="https://prod-17.westeurope.logic.azure.com/workflows/18267c7f0ec94d3
        </when>
        <otherwise>
            <rewrite-uri template="?api-version=2016-10-01&amp;sp=/triggers/manual/run&amp;sv=1.0&amp;sig=GXUr_
            <set-backend-service base-url="https://prod-16.westeurope.logic.azure.com:443/workflows/19b740311fb
        </otherwise>
    </choose>
    <base />
    <set-header name="Ocp-Apim-Subscription-Key" exists-action="delete" />
```

When ShipAnyWhere is happy with new version of the Logic App, all they have to do is remove the condition as follows. This ensures that end customers are not disrupted at all:

```
<inbound>
    <rewrite-uri template="?api-version=2016-06-01&amp;sp=/triggers/manual/
    <set-backend-service base-url="https://prod-17.westeurope.logic.azure.

    <base />
    <set-header name="Ocp-Apim-Subscription-Key" exists-action="delete" />
```

Summary

Companies are utilizing APIs innovatively to harness digital transformation. Supporting APIs at scale need a comprehensive APIM platform that helps in effective and efficient management of APIs.

Microsoft Azure APIM provides all the features required to manage all the organization's APIs which covers the legacy APIs as well. As it's a cloud offering, the companies can start using it instantly. It easy to on board with automatic generation along with easy maintenance of the developer portal reducing the tasks connected with API deployment. Microsoft has made an open turnkey solution for APIM which will have no dependencies on Microsoft technologies. Azure APIM is one of the best tools which will enable the companies to achieve their goal of digital transformation, while leveraging APIs that allow deployment due to its intrinsic advantages.

APIM is a prominent feature of Microsoft's integration landscape and is a linchpin in its **integration Platform-as-a-Service (iPaaS)** offering.

The next chapter will introduce azure serviced bus with latest updates from Microsoft for Azure Service Bus. This chapter will contain hand on lab which user can go through for working effectively with Azure Serviced Bus along with Azure Functions and Logic Apps.

5
Azure Service Bus with Integration Services

Azure Service Bus is a cloud-based messaging system that acts as a message broker to connect disparate systems that are on premises or on the cloud. This was one of the first **Platform-as-a-Service (PaaS)** offerings introduced by Microsoft, and has since become more trivial with greater cloud adoption among enterprises. With Azure Service Bus, you can decouple your applications using topics and queues and provide a secure platform for asynchronous data transfer across enterprise applications.

Service Bus messaging is based on a publish-subscribe messaging pattern and supports relayed, brokered, and byte message exchange patterns. We will cover all of these concepts in the coming sections. Throughout this chapter, you will gain hands-on experience of using Azure Service Bus and see how you can leverage the services of Azure Service Bus for system communication.

In this chapter, we will cover the following topics:

- Azure Service Bus use cases
- Building scalable solutions with Azure Service Bus and Azure Integration Services
- Service Bus in a hands-on lab with the .NET Core framework
- Publish and subscribe messages to/from Azure Service Bus
- Connecting your Azure Functions and Logic Apps to Azure Service Bus

Azure Service Bus use cases

There are a few common use cases for Azure Service Bus. Some of these are listed here:

- **Distributed applications**: Azure Service Bus is widely used to securely connect distributed applications. Azure Service Bus removes the dependency between the sender and consumer, and anyone can be taken offline without disturbing the overall communication.
- **Message-ordered delivery**: When ordered delivery is required during end-system communications, an enterprise can enable a session and implement workflows or code to maintain the order of the published data.
- **Broadcast messages with topics/subscription**: You can enable a 1 to *N* relationship between the sender and consumer using a Service Bus topic/subscription. This gives greater flexibility when there is more than one consumer for the same instance of a message.
- **Secure transfer:** Azure Service Bus communication with the publisher and subscriber is secured with **Shared Access Signature** (**SAS**). With SAS, the application is granted different access levels, such as listening to or sending a message to a Service Bus instance.

Before we explore the details of Azure Service Bus implementation and how it plays a vital role in the Microsoft Integration stack, there are some key parameters that we need to learn about. These will build our foundational knowledge to work effectively with Azure Service Bus.

Creating a Service Bus namespace

An Azure Service Bus namespace acts as a container for messaging components. In an Azure Service Bus namespace, you can create multiple topics/subscription and queues, and use them at runtime to publish and subscribe to a message through custom applications or software. To create a Service Bus namespace, you can either use the Azure portal, the Azure CLI, Azure PowerShell, or an **Azure Resource Manager** (**ARM**) template with a continuous integration and deployment pipeline in place. To get started on this exercise, we will use the Azure portal to create an Azure Service Bus resource in our resource group.

 To manage your cloud resources efficiently, we recommend using ARM or PowerShell for Azure Service Bus.

Creating a Service Bus namespace in the Azure portal

If you have not created a Service Bus namespace resource as part of an earlier exercise, then you can follow these steps to create a new instance of Service Bus through the Azure portal. To do this, you need an active Azure subscription. If you do not have one, then you can request the trial subscription at `https://azure.microsoft.com/free/`:

1. Log in to the Azure portal at `https://portal.azure.com`.
2. Click on the **Create a resource** blade on the left side of the Azure portal home page, and select **Integration** and then **Service Bus**.
3. Enter a meaningful name for the Service Bus namespace, and select the **Pricing tier** and your **Subscription.** In **Resource group,** select any existing resource group or create a new resource group and click **Create**. This will create a new Service Bus namespace resource within the specified resource group:

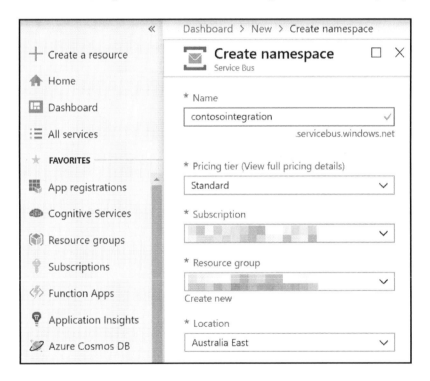

4. When using a Service Bus namespace as a messaging framework for your enterprise application, always follow the standard naming convention and use tags. This will help to locate the Service Bus resource in the Azure tenant. For the subscription owner, it can help them to derive billing patterns. With Azure DevOps, you can create an Azure Service Bus continuous integration and deployment pipeline by using either the ARM template or PowerShell. Here is the basic ARM definition for creating an Azure Service Bus namespace resource:

```
"resources": [
  {
    "apiVersion": "2017-04-01",
    "name": "[parameters('azureservicebusnamepaceName')]",
    "location": "[resourceGroup().location]",
    "type": "Microsoft.ServiceBus/namespaces",
    "sku": {
      "name": "Standard"
    },
    "properties": {},
    "tags": {
      "resourceType": "Azure Service Bus",
      "envionment": "[parameters('azureservicebusenv')]"
    },
    "scale": null,
    "dependsOn": []
  }
]
```

5. To create **an ARM** template from scratch, multiple open source solutions are available on GitHub. You can also use automation scripts from the Azure portal to work with a Service Bus ARM template. To look for an automation script, navigate to the appropriate resource group in the **Resource group** section and click on **Automation Script**. This will give you an example that you can use within your **Integrated Development Environment (IDE)**, such as Visual Studio Code.

6. Azure PowerShell also provides you with commands to manage your Service Bus namespace. To learn more about Service Bus management through Azure PowerShell, look at the Microsoft documentation: https://docs.microsoft.com/en-us/azure/service-bus-messaging/service-bus-manage-with-ps.

7. We can also use the Azure CLI to manage an Azure Service Bus namespace resource. To create an Azure Service Bus namespace, open the Azure CLI and follow the instructions. Open your Azure CLI Bash window through the Azure portal and run the following command:

```
abhishek@Azure:~$ az servicebus namespace create --resource-group
integrationpatterns05 --name dev-sb-integration --location westus2
--tags resourceType='Azure Service Bus' envionment='dev' --sku
Standard
```

Once the command has successfully executed, you can verify the result, which will describe the key parameters for the Service Bus namespace resource:

```
{
  "createdAt": "2019-01-25T01:19:12.680000+00:00",
  "id":
"/subscriptions/**************/resourceGroups/integrationpatterns06/provide
rs/Microsoft.ServiceBus/namespaces/dev-sb-integration",
  "location": "West US 2",
  "metricId": "***************:dev-sb-integration",
  "name": "dev-sb-integration",
  "provisioningState": "Succeeded",
  "resourceGroup": "integrationpatterns06",
  "serviceBusEndpoint":
"https://dev-sb-integration.servicebus.windows.net:443/",
  "sku": {
    "capacity": null,
    "name": "Standard",
    "tier": "Standard"
  },
  "tags": {
    "envionment": "dev",
    "resourceType": "Azure Service Bus"
  },
  "type": "Microsoft.ServiceBus/Namespaces",
  "updatedAt": "2019-01-25T01:19:35.313000+00:00"
}
```

In the preceding Bash script, `integrationpatterns05` is the name of the resource group, `dev-sb-integration` is the name of the Service Bus namespace instance, while `westus2` is the location of the Service Bus namespace resource. We have also added appropriate tags to identify resources based on tag values.

Service Bus tiers

Service Bus is available with multiple pricing models, and each model has a different set of features and capabilities. In this section, we will cover the basics of each model and how an enterprise can benefit from choosing the right option in different stages of the development and release pipeline.

Service Bus is available with three different pricing plans and service tiers. These are **Basic**, **Standard**, and **Premium**, and are described here:

- The **Basic** tier provides limited capacity with messaging through queues and scheduling, and has a limitation of 100 brokered connections at a single time.
- The **Standard** tier is more generic and provides capabilities such as messaging queues, topic/subscription, session, correlation, ForwardTo, and many more, which can be essential for building a highly scalable integration solution in the cloud.
- The **Premium** tier is built on top of the **Standard** tier and offers more features in terms of message size (1 MB), an increased number of brokered connections, resource isolation, and more, along with Azure Event Grid support for event routing on top of Azure Service Bus.

The **Premium** tier is priced daily at a flat rate based on the messaging units consumed. The **Premium** tier is suited for running production workloads as it is highly scalable and offers support for low-latency architecture solutions. For more information on features and pricing, you can visit the Microsoft documentation: `https://azure.microsoft.com/en-us/pricing/details/service-bus/`.

Azure Service Bus technology offerings

Azure Service Bus offers four distinct types of messaging communication patterns:

- **Service Bus queues**: Service Bus queues offer unidirectional asynchronous messaging for an enterprise. This messaging is durable and follows the **First-In-First-Out (FIFO)** pattern.
- **Topic/subscription**: Service Bus topics provide the publish-subscribe type of message exchange pattern. There can be many publishers along with a number of message listeners.
- **Event hubs**: This is used to store and route event type messages on a massive scale, such as telemetry data.

- **Relay**: Service Bus relays provide bidirectional communication and allow an enterprise to expose an endpoint in the cloud. With relay services, clients can securely expose services sitting behind a corporate firewall to the outside world.

As this chapter is all about messaging, we will concentrate on Azure Service Bus queues and topics, and provide you with the basic foundational knowledge to get started with the Azure Service Bus messaging platform.

Azure Service Bus architecture

Azure Service Bus is composed of scale units. A scale unit is defined as a deployment unit, consisting of different components that are required to run the service. Each Service Bus namespace (a container of different services provided by Service Bus) is mapped to the scale unit, and each scale unit consists of the following components:

- **Gateway nodes**: Gateway nodes are responsible for authenticating service requests.
- **Messaging broker nodes**: These forward messages to relevant entities after service authentication.
- **Gateway store**: The gateway store holds the data relevant to the entities, such as a topic subscription.
- **Messaging store**: There can be multiple messaging stores within a Service Bus namespace and scale unit. Each messaging store holds messages relevant to different queues, topics, and subscriptions. Except in the case of Service Bus **Premium** Messaging, messaging stores are implemented on top of SQL database instances.

The overall messaging process can be described with the following diagram taken from Microsoft's website:

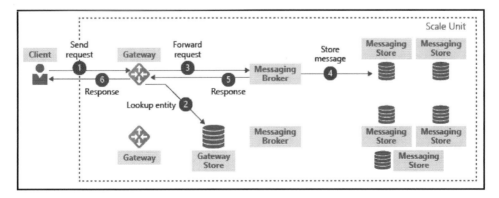

In the next section, we will discuss more concepts related to Azure Service Bus, such as brokered messaging, along with message headers and properties. These are key components of implementing messaging frameworks with Azure Service Bus.

Messaging with Service Bus

Azure Service Bus messaging with queues, topics, and subscriptions supports both byte message transfer with .NET Core and brokered messaging patterns with the standard .NET framework. With Service Bus messaging, the producer and the subscriber of the message should not remain online at all times. The messaging infrastructure stores the message reliably in a virtual queue (such as a Service Bus queue or topic) until the subscriber is ready to receive the message.

Message size

When designing enterprise-level distributed integration with Azure Service Bus queues/topics, we should also consider the size of each message published through the publishing system.

Currently, Service Bus queues support 256-kilobyte messages for the **Basic** and **Standard** tiers. When going with the **Premium** tier, the maximum message size you can publish through the Service Bus queue is 1 MB. In cases where incoming messages exceed those quotas, then those messages will be rejected and an exception will be thrown to the publishing application.

When working with a large message for integration, there are certain design patterns available, such as using session information and transactions, and breaking the large message into small parts. Each small message will then be placed with the same session information on the Service Bus topic. The Service Bus listener can then use the same session ID information and aggregate the chunked messages with an aggregator pattern, which we described in Chapter 6, *Introduction to Logic Apps*. You can find more details about this pattern in Michel Stephenson's write-up here: http://microsoftintegration.guru/2014/12/23/azure-service-bus-larger-messages/.

Another option would be to use Service Bus to hold only the metadata attribute of the message when placing the actual message into the blob container. While the message is processing the message, metadata is used to read the message from the blob container. This is the claim check pattern and has been described by Sean Feldman.

Message headers and properties

The brokered message class provides a set of properties that are used by the application for setting the content headers for messaging routing. The message properties in Service Bus are in key-value pairs derived from the IDictionary generic class and are used to define rules and actions for topics and subscriptions. Values assigned to the message properties are available on the message header as metadata properties.

The default brokered message properties are listed in the following table:

Property	Default value
ContentType	NULL
CorrelationId	NULL
EnqueuedTimeUtc	DateTime.MinValue
ExpiresAtUtc	DateTime.MaxValue
Label	NULL
MessageId	New GUID
Properties	IDictionary <string, object>
ReplyTo	NULL
ReplyToSessionId	NULL
ScheduledEnqueueTimeUtc	DateTime.MinValue
SessionId	NULL
Size	The size of the message body in bytes
TimeToLive	TimeSpan.MaxValue
To	NULL

In this section, we will discuss all these properties in detail. Many of these properties act as a basic framework for messaging in a Service Bus namespace:

- `MessageId`: This is a unique identifier of messages in a Service Bus namespace. When a message is created and published to a Service Bus queue/topic, a unique GUID is assigned as a `MessageId` property to the message, which will ensure message uniqueness across other published messages. The `MessageId` property is also used to implement duplicate detection. We will discuss the duplicate detection feature in a later part of this chapter.

- `ContentType`: This is a content type identifier utilized by the publisher and subscriber. The publisher can set the `ContentType` property of the message and the receiver reads the content type for proper serialization and deserialization of the message. `ContentType` is a string field that needs to be set in the key-value pair.

- `CorrelationId`: The `CorrelationId` property can be used for message routing across receivers. The user can set a `CorrelationId` property on the Service Bus message header and it can be used as a filter condition to subscribe to the message.

- `TimeToLive`: The `TimeToLive` property will determine the expiry time set on the message within the queue or topic subscription. Messages that are not processed within the `TimeToLive` timeframe will be routed to the dead-letter queue or removed from the queue or topic.

- `SessionId`: `SessionId` is a string property that is used to correlate messages at the receiving end. This is used for big message transmission through Service Bus when the sender sends the message in chunks. `SessionId` is also used for the request-response pattern over Service Bus' asynchronous channel.

- `ScheduledEnqueueTimeUtc`: `ScheduledEnqueueTimeUtc` allows the message to be sent to a queue where it will be stored until the specified time. It will then be batched at the receiving application.

- `Size`: The `Size` property can be used to determine the combined size of the message body in bytes. As discussed in the preceding section, it is worth noting that there are limitations on the published message size on the Service Bus message channel.

- `ReplyTo`: The `ReplyTo` message property is used to set the name of a specific queue to send a response to and from the recipient in a request-response operation. The publisher that sends the request message will set the `ReplyTo` property so that the subscriber knows the queue details in order to send the response message.

- `ReplyToSessionId`: In a request-response pattern message, the `ReplyToSessionId` property is used for correlating messages. The sender that is publishing the message will set the `ReplyToSessionId` property of the message with a value for correlation identification. Similarly, the receiving application will use the `SessionId` value when sending the response message to the caller application.

Service Bus queues and descriptions

An Azure Service Bus queue provides unidirectional message communications across distributed applications in a loosely coupled messaging pattern. This method of communication between a client and Service Bus instance can be done with either the Azure SDK, HTTPS, or by following the AMQP protocol.

The main advantage of using queues is that it provides load balancing across client-server applications by default. With a queue acting as a middleware client application, reading the message from the queue can be done at a leisurely pace rather than there being any throttling going on with a high number of concurrent requests. In cases where the rate of publishing messages in the queue is greater than the subscriber subscribing the message, an enterprise can always add additional subscriber applications to perform load balancing and to limit the queue depth.

If you are using multiple subscribers to subscribe to messages from the queue, then you should consider various lock types to suit the solution.

This type of distributed design has various advantages, some of which are listed here:

- **Offline/online message processing**: This is one of the greatest advantages of using Service Bus queues. The publishing and subscribing systems do not need to be online at the same time, as Service Bus queues will act as message brokers between distributed systems.
- **Hybrid integration**: With cloud adoption, most enterprises will move some or more of their workload to the cloud while keeping resources available on premises. Azure Service Bus queues will allow connecting on-premises resources to cloud-hosted services or applications in a secure manner.
- **Loosely coupled applications**: Using Service Bus queues as brokers, an enterprise can achieve a loosely coupled design where each system works independently without affecting the processing of other connecting systems.

Queue naming convention

A proper naming convention is one of the key requirements for building a robust integration framework in the cloud. With standardized naming, developers and architects can easily locate resources and services, thus decreasing duplicate resource creation. This also helps the enterprise to better manage the consumption of resources and limit billing patterns in the cloud.

Microsoft has come up with a standard naming convention, the details of which you can find at the Microsoft documentation site. As this section is dedicated to Service Bus and Service Bus-related artifacts such as queues and topics, let's take some time to learn about the naming conventions of the Service Bus namespace and Service Bus queue:

- The Service Bus namespace name must be between 6 and 50 characters long and can only contain letters, numbers, and hyphens.
- For queues, the standard naming convention dictates that the name should follow the enterprise pattern with between 3 and 63 characters, which will again be restricted to alphanumeric characters along with the hyphen character.

To keep building a foundation for understanding DevOps exercises through ARM, the following is the ARM definition for creating a Service Bus queue. The Service Bus namespace resource is a parent resource, and therefore the queue definition has a dependsOn section with the name of the Service Bus namespace, along with the queue name:

```
{
        "type": "Microsoft.ServiceBus/namespaces/queues",
        "name": "[concat(parameters('azureservicebusnamepaceName'),
'/',parameters('azureservicebusOrderProcessingqueue'))]",
        "apiVersion": "2017-04-01",
        "location": "[resourceGroup().location]",
        "scale": null,
        "properties": {
          "lockDuration": "PT30S",
          "maxSizeInMegabytes": 16384,
          "requiresDuplicateDetection": false,
          "requiresSession": false,
          "defaultMessageTimeToLive": "P14D",
          "deadLetteringOnMessageExpiration": false,
          "enableBatchedOperations": true,
          "duplicateDetectionHistoryTimeWindow": "PT10M",
          "maxDeliveryCount": 10,
          "status": "Active",
          "autoDeleteOnIdle": "P10675199DT2H48M5.4775807S",
          "enablePartitioning": true,
          "enableExpress": false
        },
        "dependsOn": [
          "[resourceId('Microsoft.ServiceBus/namespaces',
parameters('azureservicebusnamepaceName'))]"
        ]
    }
```

To create Service Bus queues programmatically, you can use the Service Bus SDK and create a management client, which can then perform read/write operations on Service Bus namespace resources such as queues or topics. The following code is the console code written in C# using the Microsoft Service Bus SDK to create Service Bus queues:

```
public async Task<object> CreateSbQueues(string queuename)
{
    var client = new ManagementClient(sbconnection);
    bool queueExists = await
client.QueueExistsAsync(queuename).ConfigureAwait(false);
    if (!queueExists)
    {
        QueueDescription queueName = new
QueueDescription(queuename);
        queueName.MaxSizeInMB = 1024;
        queueName.DefaultMessageTimeToLive = new TimeSpan(2, 0, 0,
0);
        var result = await
client.CreateQueueAsync(queueName).ConfigureAwait(false);
        return result;
    }
    else
    {
        return "Queue already exsits!!";
    }
}
```

Retrieving messages from a queue

Messages can be retrieved from a queue using one of the two locking mechanism available: PeekLock or AutoComplete. A lock mechanism indicates how messages retrieved for processing are handled by Service Bus.

In PeekLock, a client listener application keeps a lock on the messages available on the queue. This results in the queue message being invisible to other customers who may be listening to that message on the queue.

The message may reappear on the queue if the consumer does not issue a complete command within the specified visibility timeout period. If the customer doesn't issue a complete command within the stipulated visibility timeout span, the message may return on the queue. This can also happen if the customer calls the abandon method. When the guaranteed processing of a message is necessary, this is the ideal process.

AutoComplete mode is another option, and in this method, once the message is read, it will be erased instantly from the Service Bus queue, thereby ensuring that the message is processed. However, with AutoComplete mode, there is a risk that messages can get lost if the listener application fails to process the message.

To ensure messages are not lost in communication, there are certain patterns that can be adopted, such as setting the VisibilityTimeout parameter to a suitable period that will allow enough time for the message to be processed. Another method is to use DequeueCount to check how many times the message has been read from the queue. We can also use the message's unique transaction identifier, which can be persisted in a Storage account and matched against the unprocessed message.

In the coming section, we will also see how you can perform duplicate detection using a Service Bus MessageId (the unique identifier of a message). When setting up duplicate detection with the MessageId of our choice, we can prohibit any duplicate instances from being consumed by the listener application within a time window. Logic Apps and Azure Functions provide a robust framework to read and submit a message with either the PeekLock or AutoComplete feature.

The following code makes it possible to receive a message from a Service Bus queue through Azure Functions using the Microsoft Service Bus SDK:

```
using Microsoft.Azure.WebJobs;
using Microsoft.Azure.WebJobs.Host;
using Microsoft.ServiceBus.Messaging;
using System;

namespace azfunctonssb
{
    public static class ReadSBQueue
    {

        [FunctionName("ReadSBQueue")]
        public static void Run([ServiceBusTrigger("sample01",
AccessRights.Manage, Connection = "SbConnection")]
        string myQueueItem, Int32 deliveryCount,DateTime
enqueuedTimeUtc,string messageId, TraceWriter log)
        {
            log.Info($"C# ServiceBus queue trigger function processed
message: {myQueueItem}");
                log.Info($"C# deliveryCount: {deliveryCount}");
                log.Info($"C# enqueuedTimeUtc: {enqueuedTimeUtc}");
                log.Info($"C# messageId: {messageId}");
```

```
        }
      }
    }
```

When using logic apps, you have multiple sets of Service Bus connectors available that can work with both the `AutoComplete` and `PeekLock` features. This enables developers to build quick workflows to integrate distributed applications through Service Bus topics/subscriptions and queues:

Dead-lettering of Service Bus messages

Dead-lettering happens when a message cannot be processed before the `ExpiresAtUtc` time or when a filter condition exception has occurred when posting a message to a Service Bus topic. Other reasons could be that the message is not formatted correctly, or the subscriber is not available to pick up the message.

In Azure Service Bus, the message will be placed on the `$DeadLetterQueue` sub-queue for the following reasons:

- The read message fails to be processed and reappears on the queue more than 10 times by default. You can also change this default behavior through the Service Bus Explorer tool or by using the Serverless 360 third-party offering.
- When the message reaches the **Time-to-Live** (**TTL**) threshold and the dead-lettering flag has been set in the queue or subscription.
- When a subscription filter evaluation exception occurs and dead-lettering is enabled on the filter.

Automatic dead-lettering does not occur for `AutoComplete` mode. The reason for this is that the message is automatically removed from the queue once the listener sends a read command to the Service Bus queue. In the case of autocomplete, you should have a better exception handler in your workflow designer that can persist the exception state and the message for further processing.

Deferred message processing in Azure Service Bus

Deferring messages allows the processing of higher priority messages first and then servicing the lower priority messages once the higher priority messages are processed. To use this feature, we must use the `PeekLock` receive mode.

The client application reading the message from the Service Bus namespace then has the option of marking the message as deferred. When a message has been deferred, it will stay in the queue until it is retrieved and is then completed by the same or another application. The message will also be removed from the queue if a message's TTL timeout occurs. The message is read from the queue using the `QueueDescription` class and by passing the message sequence number that was persisted previously.

Security with an Azure Service Bus namespace

The client application gains access to the Azure Service Bus namespace resource through SAS authentication. In SAS authentication, the client application passes a security access token to the Service Bus namespace using a common symmetric key known to both the Service Bus resource and the client application.

The shared access token can either be generated using the Service Bus SDK or by using an intermediate token provider that the client interacts with to get the SAS token.

SAS authentication

SAS authentication grants the application access to the Service Bus namespace resource. In Azure Service Bus, you can configure multiple SAS authentication roles, which can either read, write, read/write, or manage a whole Service Bus resource environment.

To use SAS authorization, we can configure the `SharedAccess` authorization rule object on a namespace, queue, or topic. This rule consists of the following elements:

- `KeyName`: Identifies the rule
- `PrimaryKey`: A cryptographic key used to sign/validate SAS tokens
- `SecondaryKey`: A cryptographic key used to sign/validate SAS tokens
- `Rights`: Represents the collection of listen, send, and manage rights granted

You can configure up to 12 such authorization rules within a Service Bus namespace, including a queue and topic. By default, an SAS rule with all rights is configured for every namespace when it is first provisioned.

We've covered Service Bus namespace concepts and queues in detail, along with message properties. In the next section, we will cover Service Bus topics before diving into some of the basic patterns that can be implemented with Service Bus along with Logic Apps and API Management.

Azure Service Bus topics

Azure Service Bus topics are virtual queues that provide a one-to-many messaging system using subscription. Unlike queues, topics can have multiple listeners communicating with the same topic, as well as with different subscription properties associated with each listener.

Azure Service Bus topics have great support for broadcasting the same message to multiple subscribing clients using the subscription property associated with the client application. Like queues, Service Bus topics also support the `PeekLock` and `AutoComplete` features. The following code is the basic ARM template for a Service Bus topic:

```
{
    "type": "Microsoft.ServiceBus/namespaces/topics",
    "name": "[concat(parameters('azureservicebusnamepaceName'), '/',
```

```
parameters('azureservicebussocialgraphtopic'))]",
    "apiVersion": "2017-04-01",
    "location": "[resourceGroup().location]",
    "scale": null,
    "properties": {
      "defaultMessageTimeToLive": "P14D",
      "maxSizeInMegabytes": 1024,
      "requiresDuplicateDetection": false,
      "duplicateDetectionHistoryTimeWindow": "PT10M",
      "enableBatchedOperations": true,
      "status": "Active",
      "supportOrdering": false,
      "autoDeleteOnIdle": "P10675199DT2H48M5.4775807S",
      "enablePartitioning": true,
      "enableExpress": false
    },
    "dependsOn": [
      "[resourceId('Microsoft.ServiceBus/namespaces',
parameters('azureservicebusnamepaceName'))]"
    ]
  }
```

As with queues, we can also create a topic and associated subscription using code with the Service Bus namespace SDK, available through NuGet:

```
public async Task<object> CreateSbtopic(string topicname ,string
subscriptionName)
    {
        var client = new ManagementClient(sbconnection);
        bool topicExists = await
client.TopicExistsAsync(topicname).ConfigureAwait(false);
        if (!topicExists)
        {
            TopicDescription topicName = new
TopicDescription(topicname);
            topicName.MaxSizeInMB = 1024;
            topicName.DefaultMessageTimeToLive = new TimeSpan(2, 0, 0,
0);
            dynamic result = await
client.CreateTopicAsync(topicname).ConfigureAwait(false);
            if (result.Path != null)
            {
                SubscriptionDescription subName = new
SubscriptionDescription(result.Path, subscriptionName);
                subName.Status = 0;
                var result01 = await
client.CreateSubscriptionAsync(subName).ConfigureAwait(false);
                return result;
```

```
            }
            return result;
        }
        else
        {
            return "Topic already exsits!!";
        }
    }
```

To receive a message from Service Bus topic/subscription, we can either use Azure Functions, logic apps, or custom APIs. All these processes extend the Microsoft Service Bus SDK to perform SAS authentication and read the message from the topic with specified subscription properties, as described here:

```
using Microsoft.Azure.WebJobs;
using Microsoft.Azure.WebJobs.Host;
using Microsoft.ServiceBus.Messaging;
using System;

namespace azfunctonssb
{
    public static class ReadSBTopic
    {

        [FunctionName("ReadSBTopic")]

        public static void Run([ServiceBusTrigger("sample01", "sample01-
subscription", AccessRights.Manage,
        Connection = "SbConnection")]
        string mySbMsg, Int32 deliveryCount, DateTime enqueuedTimeUtc,
string messageId, TraceWriter log)

        {
            log.Info($"C# ServiceBus topic trigger function processed
message: {mySbMsg}");
            log.Info($"C# deliveryCount: {deliveryCount}");
            log.Info($"C# enqueuedTimeUtc: {enqueuedTimeUtc}");
            log.Info($"C# messageId: {messageId}");
        }

    }
}
```

Subscription rules

A subscription defines what type of message the subscriber is willing to receive from a Service Bus topic. Each Service Bus topic has one or more message listeners (subscribers) polling the Service Bus topic based on the subscription rule, and every subscription rule consists of a predefined conditional statement.

Subscription rule execution is done through the message properties set by the message publisher application or client when publishing a message to a Service Bus topic endpoint. Every newly created topic subscription has an initial default value, and if we do not explicitly define the filter condition, the default filter condition is always set to true.

Service Bus supports three filter conditions:

- **Boolean filters**: Boolean filters in a Service Bus topic are either `TrueFilter` or `FalseFilter`. With `TrueFilter`, all messages are consumed by the subscriber of the topic. In `FalseFilter`, the basic behavior is that none of the messages are pulled from the Service Bus topic by the client application:

```
public async Task<object> CreatetopicMatchAllSubscription(string
topicname)
  {
    var client = new ManagementClient(sbconnection);
    bool topicExists = await
client.TopicExistsAsync(topicname).ConfigureAwait(false);
    if (topicExists)
    {
      SubscriptionDescription subName = new
SubscriptionDescription(topicname, "AllMessages");
      subName.Status = 0;
      var result01 = await
client.CreateSubscriptionAsync(subName).ConfigureAwait(false);
      return result01;
    }
    else
    {
      return "Unable to create MatchAll Subscription!!";
    }
  }
```

- **SQL filters**: With `SqlFilter`, we can define SQL-like conditional expressions for a topic subscription. Each broker message arriving in the topic should be evaluated against the arriving message's user-defined properties and system properties. In the following example, we have created a subscription filter on the `messageType` user-defined property:

```
public async Task<object> CreatetopicsqlFilterSubscription(string
topicname)
   {
      var client = new ManagementClient(sbconnection);
      bool topicExists = await
client.TopicExistsAsync(topicname).ConfigureAwait(false);
      if (topicExists)
      {
         SubscriptionDescription subName = new
SubscriptionDescription(topicname, "SQLFilterSubscription");
         subName.Status = 0;
          RuleDescription subscriptionRule = new RuleDescription();
         var result01 = await client.CreateSubscriptionAsync(subName,
subscriptionRule).ConfigureAwait(false);
          return result01;
      }
      else
            {
                  return "Unable to create sqlfilter
Subscription!!";
            }
         }
```

- **Correlation filters**: A `CorrelationFilter` holds a set of conditions that are matched against one or more of an arriving message's properties. A common use case is to match against the `CorrelationId` property of the message or to have a match against user-defined properties, such as `ContentType`, `Label`, and `MessageId`.

`CorrelationFilter` provides an efficient filter that deals with equality. As such, the cost of evaluating filter expressions is minimal and almost immediate without extra computing resources being required for evaluating the expression filter:

```
public async Task<object>
CreatetopicCorrelationFilterSubscription(string topicname)
   {
            var client = new ManagementClient(sbconnection);
                bool topicExists = await
client.TopicExistsAsync(topicname).ConfigureAwait(false);
                if (topicExists)
```

```
            {
                    SubscriptionDescription subName = new
            SubscriptionDescription(topicname,
            "CorrelationFilterSubscription");
                    subName.Status = 0;
                    RuleDescription subscriptionRule = new
            RuleDescription();
                    subscriptionRule.Filter = new CorrelationFilter
                    {
                            Label= "Correlationfiltersample",
                            ReplyTo = "x",
                            ContentType="Finanical",
                    };
                    var result01 = await
            client.CreateSubscriptionAsync(subName,
            subscriptionRule).ConfigureAwait(false);
                    return result01;
            }
            else
            {
                    return "Unable to create CorrelationFilter
            Subscription!!";
            }
        }
```

Like other components of Service Bus, you can create ARM resources to define different subscriptions and filter conditions on the topic subscription:

```
{
    "type": "Microsoft.ServiceBus/namespaces/topics/subscriptions",
    "name": "[concat(parameters('azureservicebusnamepaceName'), '/',
parameters('azureservicebussocialgraphtopic'), '/',
parameters('azuresbtopicsubscription'))]",
    "apiVersion": "2017-04-01",
    "location": "[resourceGroup().location]",
    "scale": null,
    "properties": {
      "lockDuration": "PT30S",
      "requiresSession": false,
      "defaultMessageTimeToLive": "P14D",
      "deadLetteringOnMessageExpiration": false,
      "deadLetteringOnFilterEvaluationExceptions": true,
      "maxDeliveryCount": 10,
      "status": "Active",
      "enableBatchedOperations": false,
      "autoDeleteOnIdle": "P10675199DT2H48M5.4775807S"
```

```
        },
        "dependsOn": [
          "[resourceId('Microsoft.ServiceBus/namespaces',
parameters('azureservicebusnamepaceName'))]",
          "[resourceId('Microsoft.ServiceBus/namespaces/topics',
parameters('azureservicebusnamepaceName'),
parameters('azureservicebussocialgraphtopic'))]"
        ]
      },
      {
        "type": "Microsoft.ServiceBus/namespaces/topics/subscriptions/rules",
        "name": "[concat(parameters('azureservicebusnamepaceName'), '/',
parameters('azureservicebussocialgraphtopic'), '/',
parameters('azuresbtopicsubscription'), '/',
parameters('azuresbtopicsubscriptionrulename'))]",
        "apiVersion": "2017-04-01",
        "location": "[resourceGroup().location]",
        "scale": null,
        "properties": {
          "action": {},
          "filterType": "SqlFilter",
          "sqlFilter": {
            "sqlExpression": "MessageType='Socialconnect'"
          }
        },
        "dependsOn": [
          "[resourceId('Microsoft.ServiceBus/namespaces',
parameters('azureservicebusnamepaceName'))]",
          "[resourceId('Microsoft.ServiceBus/namespaces/topics',
parameters('azureservicebusnamepaceName'),
parameters('azureservicebussocialgraphtopic'))]",
        "[resourceId('Microsoft.ServiceBus/namespaces/topics/subscriptions',
parameters('azureservicebusnamepaceName'),
parameters('azureservicebussocialgraphtopic'),
parameters('azuresbtopicsubscription'))]"
        ]
      }
```

In the preceding sections, we have covered most of the theory of Azure Service Bus, along with sample code and the use of the ARM template. In the next section, we will cover how we can work with the Service Bus publish-subscribe model, using code along with the integration layer of Logic Apps and API Management.

Example 1 – Working with priority queues in Azure Service Bus

When you use Service Bus queues for an enterprise application, communication messages are picked up based the FIFO pattern. This means if a queue's length is 100, then a high-priority message will only be delivered after the subscribing application reads and commits all of the previous 100 messages.

To deal with this scenario, one option is to create separate queues for high-priority and low-priority messages, and the client application will be in control of setting up a queue endpoint when publishing a message to Service Bus queues:

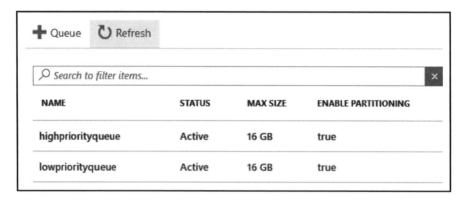

The code for routing the message to separate queues is listed here. In this method, the client application needs to make different a Service Bus connection object to send messages to high-priority and low-priority queues:

```
public async Task SendMessageToPriorityQueue()
        {

            QueueClient highpriorityqueueClient = new
QueueClient(sbconnection, "highpriorityqueue");
            QueueClient lowpriorityqueueClient = new
QueueClient(sbconnection, "lowpriorityqueue");

            for (int i = 0; i < 10; i++)
            {
                string messageBody = $"priorityqueue Message {i}";
                var message = new
Message(Encoding.UTF8.GetBytes(messageBody));
                await highpriorityqueueClient.SendAsync(message);
```

```
            }

            for (int i = 0; i < 10; i++)
            {
                string messageBody = $"lowpriorityqueue Message {i}";
                var message = new
Message(Encoding.UTF8.GetBytes(messageBody));
                await lowpriorityqueueClient.SendAsync(message);
            }
        }
```

Similarly to the preceding code, when working with Logic Apps and Service Bus, you can select different priority queues that can act either as publishers or subscribers to the message. In the following example, we have used Service Bus connectors for queues in logic apps to pull out the sent message and route the message to the HTTP endpoint:

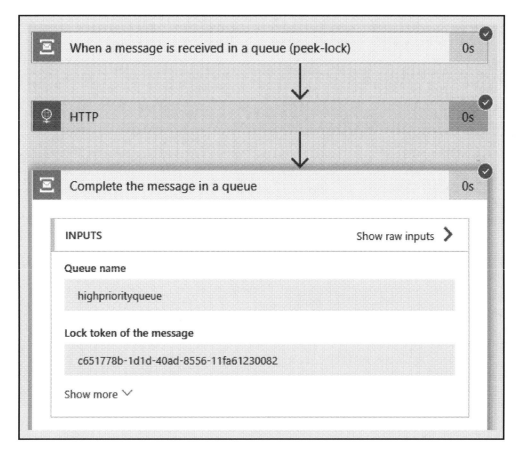

When working with logic apps and Service Bus connectors, you need to work with content type conversion from Base64 into a JSON string. This can be achieved through the Logic Apps expression language and the built-in `base64ToString` function:

```
"HTTP": {
  "inputs": {
    "body": "@{base64ToString(triggerBody()?['ContentData'])}",
    "method": "POST",
    "uri": "http://requestbin.fullcontact.com/15djfau1"
  },
  "runAfter": {},
  "type": "Http"
}
```

Another option is to use Service Bus topics, which can work as virtual priority queues with the Service Bus topic. There can be any number of applications subscribing to the same topic.

In the Service Bus topic approach, we need to pass additional user-defined properties along with a message body when publishing a message to the topic endpoint. Creating a priority topic with subscription uses the `SQLfilter` expression to differentiate between incoming messages.

To create a SQL filter rule for a priority, you can either use the Service Bus SDK, as shown in the preceding section, or you can use tools such as Service Bus Explorer or Serverless360. As this book focuses more on real implementations, we will use code to define the subscription filter condition for low-priority and high-priority messages:

```
public async Task CreatetopicprioritySubscription(string topicname)
{
    var client = new ManagementClient(sbconnection);
    bool topicExists = await
client.TopicExistsAsync(topicname).ConfigureAwait(false);
    string[] subscriptionarray = new string[] {
"highprioritysubscription", "lowprioritysubscription" };
    if (topicExists)
    {
        foreach (var item in subscriptionarray)
        {
            if (item == "highprioritysubscription")
            {
                SubscriptionDescription subName = new
SubscriptionDescription(topicname, item);
                subName.Status = 0;
```

```
                        RuleDescription subscriptionRule = new
RuleDescription();
                        subscriptionRule.Filter = new SqlFilter("Priority
>= 10");
                        var result01 = await
client.CreateSubscriptionAsync(subName,
subscriptionRule).ConfigureAwait(false);
                    }
                    else
                    {
                        SubscriptionDescription subName = new
SubscriptionDescription(topicname, item);
                        subName.Status = 0;
                        RuleDescription subscriptionRule = new
RuleDescription();
                        subscriptionRule.Filter = new SqlFilter("Priority <
10");
                        var result01 = await
client.CreateSubscriptionAsync(subName,
subscriptionRule).ConfigureAwait(false);
                    }
                }
            }
        }
```

When publishing messages to a Service Bus topic, the client application has to set the custom-priority property so that the Service Bus topic can publish messages to separate virtual queues, and each client subscribing to the topic can be associated with either priority subscription:

```
        public async Task SendMessageToTopicAsync()
        {
            TopicClient priorityClient = new TopicClient(sbconnection,
  "sample01");
            for (int i = 0; i < 15; i++)
            {
                string messageBody = $"priorityTopic Message {i}";
                var message = new
Message(Encoding.UTF8.GetBytes(messageBody));
                message.UserProperties.Add("Priority", i);
                await priorityClient.SendAsync(message);
            }
        }
```

Based on the custom-priority property of the Service Bus topic, any subscribing application can subscribe to a message from the topic subscription. In this example, we have logic apps that subscribe to messages from the high-priority `sample01` message topic. This technique of using the Service Bus topic and multiple subscription filters is advisable when you have a large set of Service Bus topic listeners.

In this section, we have covered how you can send and receive messages from virtual topic queues based on the custom property set for the message. In the next section, we will cover how you can leverage API Management as a message publisher to Azure Service Bus:

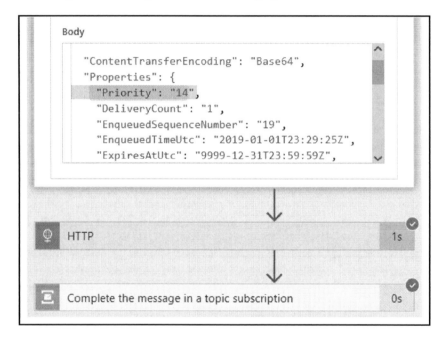

Example 2 – Working with API Management and Service Bus

When working with external customers, security is a major concern. With API Management's capabilities and Service Bus's robustness, you can create a secure channel for your external customers to interact with your backend system.

Leveraging API Management for Service Bus can help you to provide granular access to backend infrastructure without writing a single line of code, while still maintaining system security. This pattern of leveraging an API Management layer for Service Bus is important when you are dealing with public-facing applications or when your client is unable to implement an interface that can leverage the Microsoft .NET SDK.

In this example, we will be building an external-facing order-processing API powered by API Management, Service Bus, and Logic Apps. Azure Service Bus will act as the message broker platform and Logic Apps will take up the orders and write new orders into Cosmos DB:

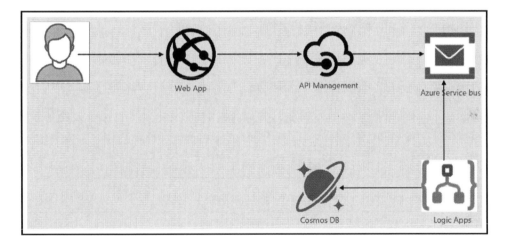

To work with this exercise, we will create an order queue in a Service Bus namespace instance and copy the Service Bus-required secret, along with a Service Bus queue URI property from the Azure portal into Service Bus queue resource:

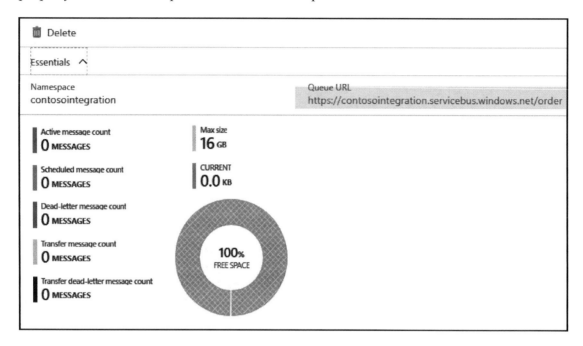

In the next step, we will add a Service Bus queue endpoint along with an SAS secondary key secret within the name-value pair of API Management. This will enable us to configure the order API policy with the required settings to post a message to the Service Bus queue:

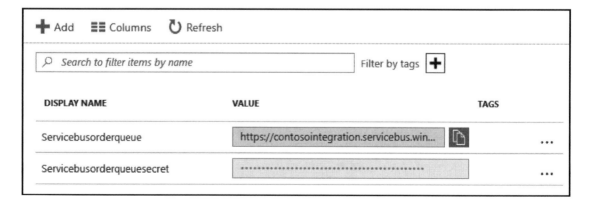

In the next step, we will create a blank API through API Management and add the required policies to it, including the content type, SAS token, broker properties, and backend service details:

```
<set-header name="Content-Type" exists-action="override">
    <value>vnd.microsoft.servicebus.yml</value>
</set-header>
<set-header name="Authorization" exists-action="override">
    <value>{{Servicebusorderqueuesecret}}</value>
</set-header>
<set-header name="BrokerProperties" exists-action="override">
    <value>@{

var requestBody= new JObject();
requestBody.Add("MessageId" ,context.RequestId);
requestBody.Add("Label" ,"Order");
// Format to a string and ready to go!
return requestBody.ToString(Newtonsoft.Json.Formatting.None);
}</value>
    </set-header>
    <set-backend-service base-url="                    ." />
    <rewrite-uri template="/order/messages" />
</inbound>
```

Once a new order request is posted, the Logic Apps listener will poll the order, update Cosmos DB, and complete the overall transaction:

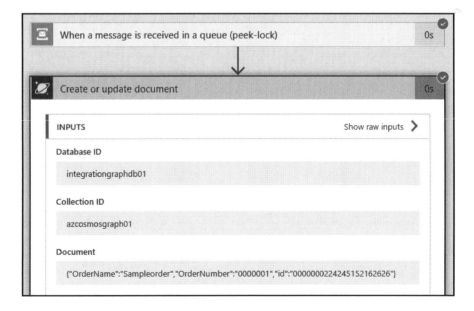

In the next example, we will cover how we can perform content-based routing using user-defined properties on a Service Bus message. We will also go through the process of enabling duplicate detection on a message through Service Bus and Logic Apps. This process comes in handy when you do not want to write duplicate records in your backend system.

Example 3 – Content-based routing based on message properties

Service Bus message properties come in very handy when working with multiple subscribing systems. In this example, we will show you how easy it is to route a message to different message listener subscribers using user-defined properties.

To work with this use case, we have created a logic app that will receive an HTTP request through a request trigger and post the message to the topic using content data and message properties. The logic app will set the message properties on each published message to the Service Bus topic using a defined key-value JSON string. This will enable the appropriate client application to subscribe to a message based on the filter condition.

To work with this, we have JSON inventory request data containing a set of properties for the message-subscription routing, along with the request body. The sample request data is shown in the following snippet and is used in the Logic Apps workflow to set the required message data and routing properties:

```json
{
  "properties": {
    "MessageType": "MessageType='Orders'",
    "department": "Inventory"
  },
  "RequestBody": {
    "OrderId": "000000000012",
    "OrderQuantitiy": 10
  }
}
```

The logic apps will use the JSON body and parse the content on the request trigger. This will enable the Logic Apps workflow to iterate through the incoming JSON and set the dynamic properties based on the request content. You can have *n* number of properties, which can enable an enterprise to have multiple subscription filters based on request content. For this specific payload to be subscribed to the end application, the filter condition is set as follows:

```
"properties": {
  "filterType": "SqlFilter",
  "sqlFilter": {
    "sqlExpression": "MessageType='orders AND department ='Inventory'",
    "requiredProcessing ": false
  }
}
```

Within the Logic Apps publishing workflow, we have set the required properties based on the dynamic requests coming through the request trigger:

```
"Send_message": {
    "runAfter": {},
    "type": "ApiConnection",
    "inputs": {
        "body": {
            "ContentData": "@{base64(triggerBody()?['RequestBody'])}",
            "Properties": {
                "Department": "@triggerBody()?['Properties']?['department']",
                "MessageType": "@triggerBody()?['Properties']?['MessageType']"
            }
        },
        "host": {
            "connection": {
                "name": "@parameters('$connections')['servicebus']['connectionId']"
            }
        },
```

Enabling duplicate detection on the specified topic or queue helps the enterprise to minimize the risk of having duplicate data in the backend system, and it also minimizes the overall processing cost of the integration framework when you work with the consumption-based model. To enable duplicate detection for messages coming through a Service Bus topic or queue, we need to enable the duplicate detection feature. This can be done either through code or by using the Azure portal, as described here:

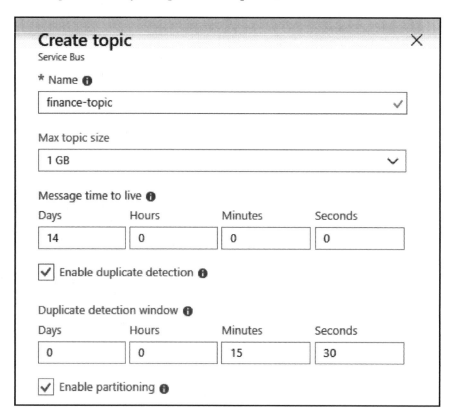

In the preceding topic, we have enabled duplicate detection. Any order that comes to this topic with the same MessageId within 15 minutes will be treated as a poisoned message and will not flow through the subscribing system. By changing only one MessageId property within the publishing framework, duplicate detection will be enabled:

```
"Send_message": {
    "runAfter": {},
    "type": "ApiConnection",
    "inputs": {
        "body": {
            "ContentData": "@{base64(triggerBody()?['RequestBody'])}",
            "Properties": {
                "Department": "@triggerBody()?['Properties']?['department']",
                "MessageType": "@triggerBody()?['Properties']?['MessageType']",
                "MessageId":"@triggerBody()?['RequestBody']?['OrderId']"
            }
        },
    },
```

The last thing to do now is to publish and test a sample message with some properties and verify that content-based routing is working well. As this is the HTTP request trigger, we have used Postman to invoke the publishing logic app workflow. We have submitted the same order twice, and can see only one order getting through to the subscribed logic apps:

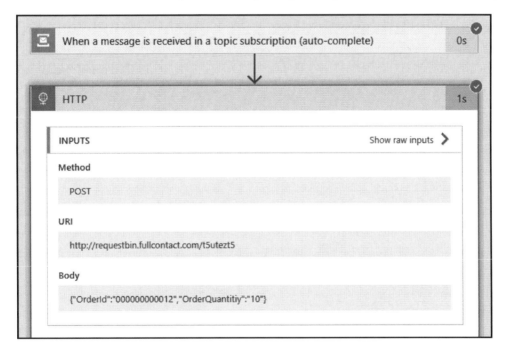

This exercise brings this chapter to a close. In the next chapter, we will cover more patterns that can help you to get a firm grasp of integration patterns and how you can work with multiple flow controls within Logic Apps.

Summary

In this chapter, we gave an introduction to Azure Service Bus and its related components such as Service Bus Namespace, Service Bus Queues, and Topics along with different message properties. In this chapter we have discussed how to work with .NET core Service Bus library and custom code to perform basic read/write message operation on Azure Service Bus resources. This chapter also demonstrated how you to leverage Azure functions and Logic Apps together with Service Bus to integrate with product and services.

In next chapter, we will learn about Logic Apps and demonstrate how you can work with the different types of triggers and actions that are available. We will also learn how to implement some complex design patterns with simple steps in Logic Apps.

Introduction to Logic Apps

6

Azure Logic Apps is Microsoft's premier cloud-based workflow engine. Azure Logic Apps allows enterprises to connect disparate systems using Microsoft's built-in connectors or the enterprise's own cloud-hosted APIs. Like some integration services in Azure, Logic Apps can run both in the cloud as a shared resource and within an enterprise's own Azure virtual network as a dedicated resource. Logic Apps supports both consumption-based and fixed pricing plans.

The following screenshot shows how, in a couple of minutes, you can build a traffic monitoring solution using a Bing connector with a Logic Apps webhook trigger and send an SMS whenever there is a large amount of traffic in your navigation path:

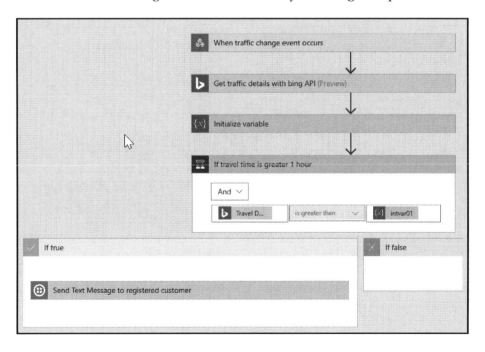

Azure Logic Apps is an event-based workflow engine. In order to build enterprise-grade and highly scalable integration solutions, Logic Apps has connectors for most common **Software-as-a-Service (SaaS)** products, such as Dynamics, Salesforce, and Office 365. It also supports and easily connects with other serverless platforms, such as Azure Functions, Azure Automation accounts, Azure Data Factory, Event Grid, Event Hub, and more.

Some common scenarios in which we might use Azure Logic Apps are listed here:

- An enterprise is moving to the cloud on a consumption-based pricing model. In this process, organizations make a shift toward a granular integration design, instead of having monolithic integration software that acts as a backbone for connection software.
- To take advantage of cloud innovation, organizations are moving to hybrid design patterns where services and software are scattered across multiple regions and data centers. Azure Logic Apps helps organizations to connect and use existing infrastructure and the data available behind an enterprise's own firewall.
- Azure Logic Apps provides an easy-to-learn platform with a simplified workflow engine. Most enterprises find using Logic Apps very easy compared to using more primitive integration software. This helps organizations make quick changes to their integration and their business processes according to market trends and requirements.
- With the shift toward microservices and the agile development methodology, Azure Logic Apps dominates the market with its robust workflow design and the ease with which we can create and update new and existing integration designs and patterns.
- Azure Logic Apps can run within an enterprise's own virtual network (integration service environment) or as a shared resource in the cloud. This is another great capability of Azure Logic Apps, which helps organizations choose the right option for its integration framework.
- For developers, Logic Apps can be built through the Azure portal or through an **integrated development environment (IDE)** of the developer's choice, such as Visual Studio Code or Microsoft Visual Studio. This makes it easy for any developer get started without having to think about setting up a new development environment only for integration resources.
- Azure Logic Apps has great support for DevOps through the workflow template. This helps organizations create continuous integration and deployment pipelines with ease, meaning they can smoothly switch over to multiple regions on the fly without making any code or workflow changes.

To find out more about how Azure Logic Apps fits your organization, check out the Microsoft Logic Apps learning site at `https://docs.microsoft.com/en-gb/azure/logic-apps/`.

With the introduction of the Logic Apps workflow, enterprise applications can now use cloud infrastructure to build their integration frameworks and automate business workflows using Logic Apps. With minimal coding skills required, it is very easy for a developer to start working with the Logic Apps workflow and the various connected services. In this chapter, we will describe various key components and best practices that can be followed when building an integration solution on top of Azure Logic Apps.

In this chapter, we will cover the following topics:

- Components of Azure Logic Apps
- An overview of Logic Apps triggers
- Actions in Logic Apps
- Parameters in the Logic Apps workflow template
- Outputs in the Logic Apps workflow template
- Debatching in Logic Apps with the `splitOn` property and the Azure Functions change feed with Cosmos DB
- Concurrency control and singleton patterns in Logic Apps with schema validation

The components of Azure Logic Apps

With great IDE support, development with Logic Apps is very easy. In this section, we will describe the various components of Logic Apps and their purposes.

Azure Logic Apps uses a workflow definition template to create Logic Apps workflows in JSON format. The workflow definition template schema consists of multiple sections, such as `parameters`, `triggers`, `actions`, and `outputs`. When we create a workflow within Azure Logic Apps, the Logic Apps workflow engine validates the workflow definition through this predefined schema structure.

The basic structure of a workflow definition schema is as follows:

```
{
    "$schema": "https://schema.management.azure.com/providers/Microsoft.Logic/schemas/2016-06-01/workflowdefinition.json#",
    "contentVersion": "1.0.0.0",
    "parameters": {},
    "triggers": {},
    "actions": {},
    "outputs": {}
}
```

Here, we will go through each of the sections described in the workflow definition schema. This will help us to understand how the Azure Logic Apps engine and the workflow schema validation work behind the integration framework:

- $schema: This section defines the location and the version of the workflow definition language. This is one of the required properties in the Logic Apps workflow definition schema. By default, Logic Apps uses the 2016-06-01 version of the workflow definition schema hosted in Microsoft Azure.

- contentVersion: This is an optional property that we use for versioning Logic Apps. This section is handy when we require multiple versions of the same logic within our enterprise integration solution.

- parameters: Parameters are key-value pairs in JSON format that are used during the deployment of Logic Apps resources. The parameters section enables us to customize the deployment of Logic Apps across multiple environments.

- trigger: The Logic Apps workflow definition schema can have one or more trigger instances. The purpose of trigger is to instantiate the Logic Apps workflow run when requested through the client application or according to the predefined schedule. Support for more than one trigger can be implemented through the code view of the Logic Apps workflow definition. A maximum of 10 triggers for Logic Apps are supported within the workflow definition schema.

- actions: These define executable steps within the Logic Apps workflow. These can consist of pre-built Microsoft connectors, along with an API endpoint hosted within the cloud or on premises. Each workflow definition can hold up to 250 actions.

- outputs: This defines the data that Logic Apps can return when it finishes running. By default, each Logic Apps workflow can return up to 10 outputs.

Let's now discuss some of these components in more detail.

An overview of triggers

The Logic Apps workflow is an event-driven integration platform and works with a combination of triggers and actions. In Azure Logic Apps, each workflow run starts with a trigger, which can be either external or scheduled. Every trigger is followed by one or more sets of actions, which are executed as part of the workflow.

It is always advisable to have a single trigger for each workflow instead of having multiple entry points for your logic apps. If you do require multiple triggers in Logic Apps for a single workflow, you need to update the code view of Logic Apps as shown:

```
"triggers": {
    "HTTP_Webhook": {
        "type": "HttpWebhook",
        "inputs": {
            "subscribe": {
                "body": "@listCallbackUrl()",
                "method": "POST",
                "uri": "
            },
            "unsubscribe": {}
        }
    },
    "Recurrence": {
        "recurrence": {
            "frequency": "Day",
            "interval": 3
        },
        "type": "Recurrence"
    }
},
```

Triggers in Logic Apps can be classified as **polling** triggers or **push** triggers. In the case of polling triggers, Logic Apps polls specified endpoints at scheduled intervals to look for any new messages or start the Logic Apps workflow instance at specified intervals. An example of this could be the Service Bus queue trigger connector or the scheduled trigger.

In the case of push triggers, a new instance of the workflow is started whenever there is a push event from an external source, such as an HTTP trigger, webhooks, or an Event Grid trigger.

Each of the triggers available in Logic Apps has a different set of interfaces and requires a different set of input parameters. Polling and push triggers can be divided into a further four categories, as listed here:

- HTTP webhook trigger
- Recurrence trigger
- Request trigger
- HTTP trigger

Any external API that is registered as a custom connector and has trigger actions for Logic Apps can also act as a trigger to the Logic Apps workflow. To learn more about custom connectors and triggers, look at the following Microsoft documentation: `https://docs.`
`microsoft.com/en-gb/connectors/custom-connectors/`.

Each trigger in Logic Apps has a different set of properties, such as the input type or the operation's runtime configuration. When you are required to control the behavior of a Logic Apps trigger, we can either use the Logic Apps designer or the code view to add or update the required trigger properties.

In the following section, we will go through each trigger type and list the important properties that can be used in the Logic Apps workflow to work with enterprise integration services.

Recurrence triggers

Recurrence triggers run on a schedule and have multiple properties associated that can change their behavior. Increasingly, Logic Apps' scheduler tasks are being replaced by recurrence triggers so that you can use the integration infrastructure available in Azure to your advantage.

In the following sample, we have set up a recurrence schedule trigger that runs only on Mondays at 2 A.M. and 4 A.M. This recurrence schedule also has a frequency of a week and an interval of three. The schedule parameters describe a Logic Apps schedule running with hours, minutes, and an array of weekdays:

```
"Recurrence": {
    "recurrence": {
        "frequency": "Week",
        "interval": 3,
        "startTime": "2018-11-26T18:41:00.9584103Z",
        "endTime": "2019-11-26T18:41:00.9584103Z",
        "timeZone": "New Zealand Standard Time",
        "schedule": {
            "hours": ["2","4"],
            "minutes": [15,30],
            "weekDays": [
                "Monday"
            ]
        }
    },
    "metadata": {},
    "type": "Recurrence",
    "description": "Recurrence trigger with scheduled"
}
```

The properties of the recurrence trigger are described here:

Name	Optional/mandatory	Description
recurrence	Mandatory	The name of the trigger
endTime	Optional	End time in the following format: *YYYY-MM-DDThh:mm:ss*
frequency	Mandatory	How often the scheduled trigger will run, such as daily or weekly
interval	String	The scheduled intervals, such as how often a schedule will run in a week
schedule	Optional	Provides specific information about the schedule of the trigger, such as the days of the week or the hours in the day in which it should run
startTme	Optional	The start time in the following format: *YYYY-MM-DDThh:mm:ss*
timeZone	Optional	The time zone (by default, this is UTC)
operationOptions	Optional	The default behavior of the trigger
type	Mandatory	The type of trigger

HTTP triggers

HTTP triggers are another type of scheduled trigger that can either poll or post to specific HTTP endpoints on a configured schedule. Apart from basic configuration settings, HTTP triggers support multiple authentication protocols such as basic, certificate, managed service identity, and OAuth authentication.

In the following code for the HTTP scheduled trigger, we can set the recurrence property with things such as frequency, interval, startTime, and endTime, along with its schedule. This HTTP trigger performs a GET operation against the external endpoint with the authentication type as Basic:

```
"HTTP": {
    "recurrence": {
        "frequency": "Week",
        "interval": 3,
        "startTime": "2018-12-25T15:00:00Z",
        "endTime": "2019-12-25T15:00:00Z",
        "timeZone": "Dateline Standard Time",
        "schedule": { …
        }
    },
    "splitOn": "@triggerBody()?.customer",
    "type": "Http",
    "inputs": {
        "authentication": {
            "password": "            ",
            "type": "Basic",
            "username": "sample_user"
        },
        "body": {},
        "method": "GET",
        "queries": {
            "operation": "publish"
        },
        "uri": "                              "
    }
}
},
```

As an HTTP trigger is a scheduled trigger, it has built-in support for all the properties available in the recurrence trigger. You can configure an HTTP scheduled task using properties such as schedule and runtime configuration. HTTP triggers also inherit some additional properties from the request trigger, such as `splitOn`, the retry policy, and support for headers.

HTTP trigger properties are listed in the following table:

Name	Optional/mandatory	Description
Recurrence	Mandatory	An object to define the `recurrence` property of the HTTP trigger
Headers	Optional	An object to define the HTTP header properties
Body	Optional	The body of the HTTP trigger
Authentication	Optional	Types of authentication include basic, OAuth, none, and managed service identity
`retryPolicy`	Optional	An object that customizes the retry behavior when failures occur with the HTTP status codes 408, 429, and 5XX
Queries	Optional	Query parameters to include with the HTTP request
`operationOptions`	Optional	The default behavior of the HTTP trigger
Type	Mandatory	HTTP trigger
`splitOn`	Optional	Splits incoming JSON arrays into objects
Method	Mandatory	The HTTP method to use for polling the specified endpoint: `GET`, `PUT`, `POST`, `PATCH`, `DELETE`
`runtimeconfiguration`	Optional	An object to change the runtime property of the HTTP trigger
URI	Mandatory	The endpoint URI

To work with HTTP triggers, the external endpoint should return a valid status code and understand the semantics of the HTTP protocol, such as the status code, retry-after header, and location header.

You can learn more about properties of HTTP triggers, such as HTTP status code and retry policies, in the Microsoft documentation: `https://docs.microsoft.com/en-us/azure/logic-apps/logic-apps-workflow-actions-triggers#http-trigger`.

Request triggers

A request trigger is a push trigger. You can use a request trigger to expose an HTTP endpoint externally to be consumed by client applications or services such as API Management or Azure Functions. The request trigger can accept various content types, such as application/JSON, application/XML, application/octet-stream, and application/JavaScript.

In the following code, we have a full definition of a request trigger with the `runtimeConfiguration` property. By default, `runtimeConfiguration` is not enabled in the request trigger. With the `runtimeConfiguration` property, Logic Apps controls the request trigger's run behavior, which we will discuss in a later part of this chapter:

```
"Request": {
    "metadata": { ···
    },
    "type": "Request",
    "kind": "Http",
    "inputs": {
        "method": "POST",
        "schema": { ···
        }
    },
    "description": "Logic apps request trigger",
    "runtimeConfiguration": {
        "concurrency": {
            "runs": 2,
            "maximumWaitingRuns": 12
        }
    }
}
```

With a request trigger, you have the option to validate the incoming JSON request with the schema validation property. To call the request trigger, the endpoint client should use `listCallbackRUrl`, which is generated once you save the Logic Apps workflow definition.

The request trigger properties are listed in the following table:

Name	Optional/mandatory	Description
Metadata	Optional	The metadata associated with the request trigger
Type	Mandatory	Request trigger
Inputs	Mandatory	The object to define the HTTP operation and the schema validation attribute
Description	Optional	The description of the request trigger
runtimeConfiguration	Optional	The object to change the runtime property of the HTTP trigger
Queries	Optional	Query parameters to include with the HTTP request

Webhook triggers

Webhooks are push triggers that work on the HTTP protocol and listen for events raised by the registered service. Webhook triggers give you the benefit of event-based design patterns within enterprise integration solutions.

In order to use a webhook trigger, you need to register the webhook endpoint to a service that supports eventing, such as Azure Event Grid.

In the following code, we have a definition of a webhook trigger with `runtimeConfiguration` and input properties. The input properties are used to hold the HTTP details of the external system.

This section is also used to perform validation with event subscribers during the initial subscription handshake. With the `runtimeConfigration` setting in webhook triggers, Logic Apps controls the run behavior of the webhook trigger:

```json
"HTTP_Webhook": {
    "metadata": {},
    "type": "HttpWebhook",
    "inputs": {
        "subscribe": {
            "authentication": {},
            "body": "@triggerOutputs()['queries']?['validationToken']",
            "cookie": "",
            "headers": {},
            "method": "POST",
            "queries": {},
            "uri": "https://graph.microsoft.com/v1.0/subscriptions"
        },
        "unsubscribe": {}
    },
    "description": "webhook trigger",
    "runtimeConfiguration": {
        "concurrency": {
            "runs": 1,
            "maximumWaitingRuns": 12
        }
    }
}
```

The webhook trigger properties are listed in the following table:

Name	Optional/mandatory	Description
Description	Optional	A description of the webhook trigger
Type	Mandatory	Webhook trigger
Inputs	Mandatory	An object to define the webhook trigger with subscribe and unsubscribe JSON objects
Metadata	Optional	The metadata about the webhook
runtimeConfiguration	Optional	An object to change the runtime property of the webhook trigger
Queries	Optional	The query parameters to include with the webhook request

In the preceding sections, we have covered all the available types of pre-built triggers in Logic Apps. In the next section, we will cover more about actions, which is another foundation block for creating a Logic Apps workflow on the cloud. We also encourage you to read the following Microsoft link on triggers and actions, along with the code available in this book, to gain a more in-depth understanding of the topic: `https://docs.microsoft.com/en-us/azure/logic-apps/logic-apps-workflow-actions-triggers`.

Actions in Logic Apps

The Logic Apps workflow is a combination of triggers and associated actions. In this section, we will give you an overview of actions and how they play an important role in creating the workflow in Azure.

In Logic Apps, each workflow can have one or more actions based on their workflow requirements. Actions are nothing but a set of Microsoft-managed APIs that allow you to develop your workflow design. At the time of writing this book, Logic Apps has built-in support for more than 200 connectors with different sets of action attributes associated with each connector:

Each action within Logic Apps takes a different set of inputs and provides a different set of outputs based on the request data. The

high-level schema definition of a generic action is listed here:

```
"<action-name>": {
    "type": "<Type of action>",
    "inputs": {
        "<input-name>": { "<input-value>" },
        "retryPolicy": "<retry policy behavior>"
    },
    "runAfter": { "<previous-trigger-or-action-status>" },
    "runtimeConfiguration": { "<runtime-config-options>" },
    "operationOptions": "<operation-option Type>"
},
```

In the following table, we will describe each property of the actions so that you can work easily within the designer and code views to update any of the properties if required:

Name	Optional/mandatory	Description
Action-name	Mandatory	The name of the action used in the Logic Apps workflow definition
Type	Mandatory	The action type, such as Service Bus, Events Hub, HTTP, or wait
Inputs	Mandatory	The input data for the listed action
retryPolicy	Optional	An object to describe the action's retry behavior
runAfter	Mandatory	The previous trigger or action associated with the logic app's workflow
runtimeConfiguration	Optional	An object to change the runtime property of a webhook trigger
operationOptions	Optional	The action behavior, such as DisableAsyncPattern or Sequential

Actions can be sub-divided into multiple categories:

- **Built-in actions**: Compose, Functions, HTTP, JOIN, PARSE JSON, Query, Response, Select, Table, Terminate, Wait, and Workflow.
- **Managed API actions**: Office 365, Salesforce, Azure blob storage, Azure Active Directory, OneDrive, and SharePoint.

- **Control flow actions**: Control flow actions help to include other actions and control the workflow design. Examples of control flow actions include `if...else`, `foreach`, `scope`, `do... until`, and `switch-case`.

Parameters in the Logic Apps workflow template

The `parameters` section is a placeholder for multiple parameters that are used by the Logic Apps engine during deployment. Parameters are key-value pairs and are required to automate your continuous integration and continuous deployment pipeline. The basic structure of the `parameters` section is shown here:

```
"parameters": {
    "<parameter-name>": {
        "type": "<Type of paramter>",
        "defaultValue": "<default value of the parameter>",
        "allowedValues": [ <multiple allowed values of parameter in array> ],
        "metadata": {
            "key": {
                "name": "<meta data value>"
            }
        }
    }
},
```

The `parameters` properties are described here:

Element	Required	Type	Description
Type	Yes	`int`, `float`, `string`, `SecureString`, `bool`, `array`, JSON object, `SecureObject`	The type of parameter
`defaultValue`	No	The same as for type	The default value of the parameter
`allowedValues`	No	The same as for type	The different allowed values
Metadata	No	JSON object	The additional parameter details

We will cover more details about parameters through various examples when we start building continuous integration and deployment pipelines for Azure Integration services.

In the following section, we will take a look at the output variables before we proceed with hands-on exercises with Logic Apps and connected systems such as Microsoft Graph, blob storage, Event Grid, and Service Bus.

Outputs in the Logic Apps workflow template

Outputs define the data that the Logic Apps workflow can return when finishing execution. This might include status or field tracking within a Logic Apps workflow with each run.

Output variables are key-value pairs and, once configured, you can track the values through a logic app's run history in the Azure portal, or you can pass the key-value pair to external systems such as Power BI to view on the dashboard:

```
"outputs": {
    "<key-name>": {
        "type": "<key-type>",
        "value": "<key-value>"
    }
}
```

The following table contains parameters for outputs in a Logic Apps workflow:

Element	Required	Type	Description
Key-name	Yes	`string`	The key name for the output return value
Type	Yes	`int`, `float`, `string`, `SecureString`, `bool`, `array`, JSON object	The default value of the parameter
Values	No	Same as type	The return value

We have now covered most of the theory, so it's time to work through some exercises to get a better understanding of how we can use these different components together to create a workflow in Logic Apps. In this book, we will use Visual Studio Code to build the logic apps. You can also use an IDE of your choice, such as Microsoft Visual Studio 2017 or the Azure portal, to create the same Logic Apps workflow.

Example 1 – Debatching in Logic Apps with the splitOn property and Azure Functions change feed with Cosmos DB

The `splitOn` property in Logic Apps debatches an item array and starts a new instance of Logic Apps for each item in the array list. In this example, we will be using the Cosmos graph change feed as an example of an item array and use logic apps and Azure Functions together to build an integration that will write the changed feed data into the Azure SQL database.

Whenever there is a change to one or more user documents in the Cosmos graph database, Azure Functions will trigger a Logic Apps endpoint, which will have the `splitOn` property set on the request trigger.

Logic Apps will send an email notification to a user to indicate that their profile has been updated. These change requests will also be synced with the Logic Apps unique identifier into an Azure SQL database for reporting purposes. The following diagram shows the pattern that we are going to develop as part of this exercise, and the steps for doing so are listed here:

1. Multiple users update their profiles in the Cosmos graph database.
2. Azure Functions listen to the change feed array list item.

3. Azure Functions call the Logic Apps HTTP endpoint, which has the `splitOn` feature enabled for the request trigger.
4. The request messages are debatched, and for each profile update, an automatic trigger email is sent.
5. Each item's data is also published to a Service Bus topic, where Logic Apps will poll the request message and update the Azure SQL database:

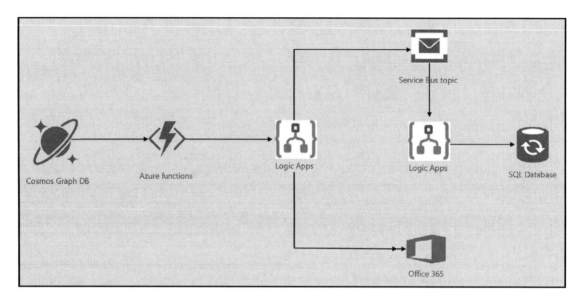

The first part of this exercise involves developing a Cosmos DB change feed function that will invoke the Logic Apps endpoint in real time. We will extend the Cosmos database change feed code developed in Chapter 3, *Introduction to Azure Event Grid*, to include the HTTP method. This HTTP method will POST the change feed document to the Logic Apps HTTP request trigger endpoint with the `splitOn` property set on `triggerBody()`:

```
[FunctionName("cosmosgraphchangefeed")]
public static void Run([CosmosDBTrigger(
    databaseName:"",
    collectionName: "",
    CreateLeaseCollectionIfNotExists = true,
    ConnectionStringSetting = "cosmosgraph",
    LeaseCollectionName = "leases")]IReadOnlyList<Document> documents,
TraceWriter log)
{
    if (documents != null && documents.Count > 0)
    {
        using (var client = new HttpClient())
```

```
    {
        var jsonString = JsonConvert.SerializeObject(documents);
        var content = new StringContent(jsonString, Encoding.UTF8,
"application/json");
        var response =
client.PostAsync(System.EnvironmentVariable("logicappsuri"),
content).Result;
    }
  }
}
```

After creating Functions to listen for the change feed, the next step is to develop logic apps with the HTTP trigger and use Office 365 to send emails along with the Service Bus send message action. The overall Logic Apps flow diagram is shown here:

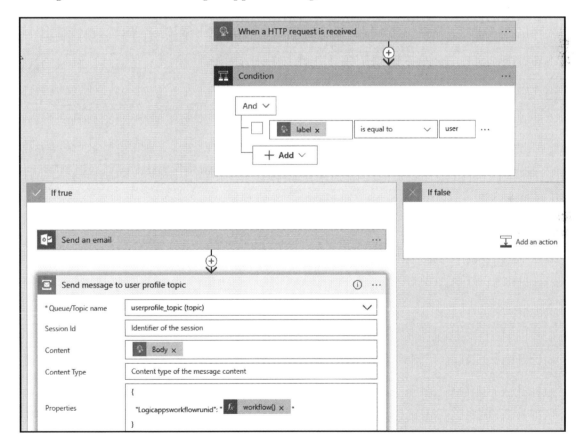

In the code of the Logic Apps workflow template, you need to set the `splitOn` property to split repetitive mode. In this case, as the Cosmos change feed is itself an array, we can split the array item at the `triggers` section:

```
"triggers": {
    "manual": {
        "splitOn": "@triggerBody()",
        "type": "Request",
        "kind": "Http",
        "inputs": {
            "schema": {}
        }
    }
},
```

The second Logic Apps workflow definition will poll the Service Bus topic for any new messages with a peek lock, so that the message is not lost if the change feed fails to be inserted into the SQL database:

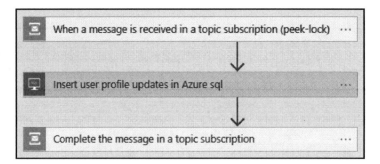

Now, to test the `splitOn` function in Logic Apps, we have performed a bulk update on the users' profiles in the Cosmos graph database with the Gremlin query, which updates Azure Functions with an array of change feed documents. The run details are shown here:

```
[FunctionName("cosmosgraphchangefeed")]
public static void Run([CosmosDBTrigger(
    databaseName: "integrationgraphdb01",
    collectionName: "azcosmosgraph01",
    CreateLeaseCollectionIfNotExists = true,
    ConnectionStringSetting = "cosmosgraph",
    LeaseCollectionName = "leases")]IReadOnlyList<Document> documents, TraceWriter log)
{
    if (documents != null && documents.Count > 0)
    {
        using (var client = new HttpClient())
        {
            var jsonString = JsonConvert.SerializeObject(documents);
            var content = new StringContent(jsonString, Encoding.UTF8, "application/json");
            var response = client.PostAsync(System.Environment.GetEnvironmentVariable("logicappsuri"), content).Result;
        }
    }
}
```

When navigating to the Logic Apps run history, we can verify that multiple runs with
`splitOn` on documents coming through Cosmos DB are being executed:

STATUS	START TIME	IDENTIFIER	DURATION
▶ Running	27/12/2018, 01:46	08586557317170104777485529043CU11	--
▶ Running	27/12/2018, 01:46	08586557317170104778485529043CU11	--
▶ Running	27/12/2018, 01:46	08586557317170104779485529043CU11	--
⊚ Succeeded	27/12/2018, 01:46	08586557317170104780485529043CU11	8.2 Seconds
▶ Running	27/12/2018, 01:46	08586557317170104781485529043CU11	--
⊚ Succeeded	27/12/2018, 01:46	08586557317170104782485529043CU11	1.65 Seconds
⊚ Succeeded	27/12/2018, 01:46	08586557317170104783485529043CU11	8.62 Seconds
⊚ Succeeded	27/12/2018, 01:46	08586557317170104784485529043CU11	9.48 Seconds
▶ Running	27/12/2018, 01:46	08586557317170104785485529043CU11	--

This can also be verified in SQL server. When you open up SQL server management studio and perform a select statement against the table, you can verify the run history along with the user profile information:

	logicappsrunid	userid	username	payload
1	08586557303984461236776750362CU31	U008	SampleUser8	{"id":"U008","_rid":"rlluAMgcR44IAAAAAAAAAA==","_...
2	08586557303984461232776750362CU31	U0012	SampleUser12	{"id":"U0012","_rid":"rlluAMgcR44MAAAAAAAAAA==",...
3	08586557303984461233776750362CU31	U0011	SampleUser11	{"id":"U0011","_rid":"rlluAMgcR44LAAAAAAAAAA==","...
4	08586557303984461230776750362CU31	U0014	SampleUser14	{"id":"U0014","_rid":"rlluAMgcR44OAAAAAAAAAA==",...
5	08586557303984461234776750362CU31	U0010	SampleUser10	{"id":"U0010","_rid":"rlluAMgcR44KAAAAAAAAAA==","_...
6	08586557303984461241776750362CU31	U003	SampleUser3	{"id":"U003","_rid":"rlluAMgcR44DAAAAAAAAAA==","_...
7	08586557303984461243776750362CU31	U001	SampleUser1	{"id":"U001","_rid":"rlluAMgcR44BAAAAAAAAAA==","_...
8	08586557303984461239776750362CU31	U005	SampleUser5	{"id":"U005","_rid":"rlluAMgcR44FAAAAAAAAAA==","_...
9	08586557303984461231776750362CU31	U0013	SampleUser13	{"id":"U0013","_rid":"rlluAMgcR44NAAAAAAAAAA==",...
10	08586557303984461229776750362CU31	U0015	SampleUser15	{"id":"U0015","_rid":"rlluAMgcR44PAAAAAAAAAA==","_...
11	08586557303984461237776750362CU31	U007	SampleUser7	{"id":"U007","_rid":"rlluAMgcR44HAAAAAAAAAA==","_...
12	08586557303984461238776750362CU31	U006	SampleUser6	{"id":"U006","_rid":"rlluAMgcR44GAAAAAAAAAA==","_...
13	08586557303984461235776750362CU31	U009	SampleUser9	{"id":"U009","_rid":"rlluAMgcR44JAAAAAAAAAA==","_...
14	08586557303984461242776750362CU31	U002	SampleUser2	{"id":"U002","_rid":"rlluAMgcR44CAAAAAAAAAA==","_...
15	08586557303984461240776750362CU31	U004	SampleUser4	{"id":"U004","_rid":"rlluAMgcR44EAAAAAAAAAA==","_...

As you can see, with the `splitOn` feature, you can use the simple Logic Apps workflow to split the incoming JSON array data and have Logic Apps run the ID as a unique identifier for the debatch operation. When you have a central depository, such as an Azure data lake, a Cosmos DB instance, or a SQL server, you can use gain insights from data using the Logic Apps unique run ID for the debatch operations.

In the next section, we will cover concurrency control and singleton patterns, along with request data validation.

Example 2 – Concurrency control and singleton patterns in Logic Apps with schema validation

When we are working in the cloud and connecting to multiple distributed systems across multiple regions, one of the basic requirements is to control the number of incoming and outgoing connections. A good example of this is a bank transaction, which defines a singleton pattern. Another example would be single-threaded communication with systems such as Salesforce, where you need to limit the read and write operations against the SaaS platform. Logic Apps has built-in support to cater to this critical enterprise requirement.

In this exercise, we will go through a few examples, demonstrating how you can work with concurrency control and singleton patterns within Logic Apps using operations and runtime configuration.

Let's take the example of registering to a social media site. Multiple users register at once and we need to limit the number of concurrent writes to our central graph database. Keeping Logic Apps in the overall solution makes it easy to implement patterns that are sustainable in the long term without any code or human intervention:

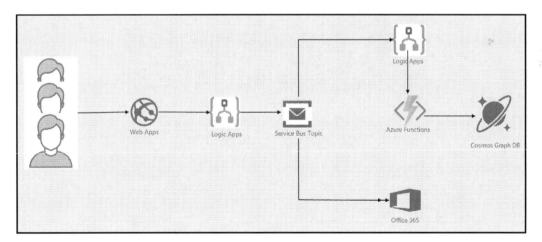

The first step here is to build logic apps with a request trigger and the runtime configuration set to sequential, with a maximum waiting run of 100 instances. Logic Apps will also include different actions, to send a welcome email to the user and to send the user profile information to the Service Bus for further processing.

The request trigger will also have schema validation on to reject any invalid requests posted to the Logic Apps request trigger. The basic configuration of the request trigger is as follows:

```json
"triggers": {
    "manual": {
        "type": "Request",
        "kind": "Http",
        "inputs": {
            "method": "POST",
            "schema": {
                "properties": {...
                },
                "type": "object"
            }
        },
        "runtimeConfiguration": {
            "concurrency": {
                "runs": 1,
                "maximumWaitingRuns": 100
            }
        }
    }
}
```

When testing logic apps with an HTTP client of your choice, such as Postman or Fiddler, you can verify the waiting property of your Logic Apps workflow, along with the sequential pattern. In the Logic Apps run history, we can see each message is processed sequentially and the rest of the Logic Apps run are in the wait state. Look at the following Logic Apps workflow, which describes the actual wait and run status of a Logic Apps instance.

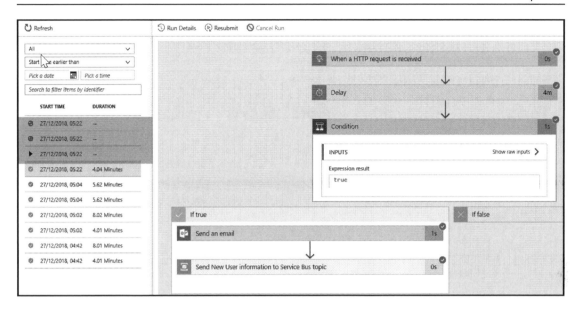

In the second Logic App, we will use the singleton pattern by setting the `operationOptions` property on the Service Bus queue trigger. This setting will limit our logic app's run to run on a sequence basis, rather than opening multiple threads and throttling the Cosmos graph DB:

```
"triggers": {
    "when_a_message_is_received_in_a_topic_subscription_(peek-lock)": {
        "recurrence": {
            "frequency": "Minute",
            "interval": 3
        },
        "type": "ApiConnection",
        "inputs": {
            "host": {
                "connection": {
                    "name": "@parameters('$connections')['servicebus']['connectionId']"
                }
            },
            "method": "get",
            "path": "/@{encodeURIComponent(encodeURIComponent('newuser_topic'))}/subscriptions/@{encodeURIComponent('newuser_subscription01')}/messages/head/peek",
            "queries": {
                "sessionId": "None",
                "subscriptionType": "Main"
            }
        },
        "operationOptions": "SingleInstance"
    }
},
```

When you look into the Logic Apps run history through the Azure portal, you can verify that the Service Bus trigger is running on a sequence basis rather than having multiple instances of the Logic Apps workflow. This way, we have limited our calls to Azure Functions, which creates a user profile node in the Cosmos graph database. We can also create a singleton pattern by using the runtime configuration settings instead of using the `SingleInstance` property operation option in the Logic Apps workflow definition.

An important consideration here is that the `runtimeConfiguration` property is immutable (at the time of writing this book). Once you set this property on a logic app, you will not be able to modify it unless you carry out a fresh release of the Logic Apps template:

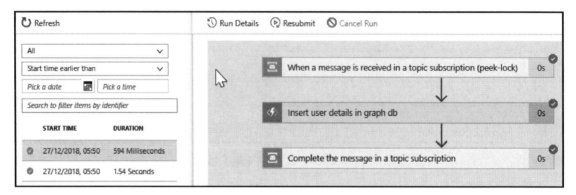

Now, with the two patterns discussed here, we will end this chapter. In the next chapter, we will continue our learning with the Microsoft integration stack and Logic Apps. We will also discuss control flow and custom connectors, along with other patterns that you can implement in your enterprise-grade solution.

Summary

Logic Apps is a great integration platform running on the cloud, as well as on-premises. In this chapter, we gave you an introduction to Logic Apps and demonstrated how you can work with the different types of triggers and actions that are available. We also learned how to implement some complex design patterns with simple steps in Logic Apps. This chapter also showed us a few highlights of the Cosmos graph database. We will continue our learning journey through more advanced integration use cases in the coming chapters. In the next chapter, we will build some really complex integration solutions with Logic Apps. Take a break and stay tuned.

7
Control Flow Actions and Custom Connectors

With digital transformation underway, enterprise applications are now running on a variety of platforms, resulting in a wide distribution of data. To benefit from existing data and distributed applications, integration is more important than ever. For an enterprise, the use of middleware can reduce business complexity and disruptions that can occur when new systems are connected through the enterprise environment.

Digital transformation is the key to successful business transformation, and integration plays an important role in this by connecting disparate systems and data sources:

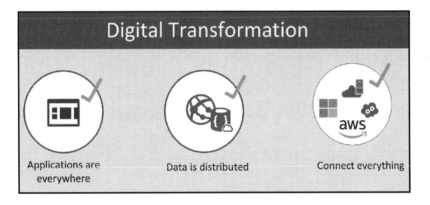

In the previous chapter, we introduced Logic Apps (Microsoft's cloud integration framework), and in this chapter, we will focus on the different features of Logic Apps, such as control flow actions and the workflow expression language. We will also discuss how you can leverage an existing build in APIs and custom connectors within Logic Apps.

To work effectively with integration, it is important to have a clear view of the business requirements and how you can utilize your knowledge and integration skills to create next-generation integration frameworks in the cloud.

In this chapter, we will cover the following topics:

- Logic Apps control flow actions
- The workflow expression language
- Working with content types – Logic Apps
- The custom connector in Logic Apps

Logic Apps control flow actions

To work effectively with a Logic Apps workflow, it is important to understand the utility of control flow actions. In this section, we will discuss the following pre-built control flow actions available in Azure Logic Apps and Microsoft Flow:

- Conditional actions
- Parallel actions
- Switch actions
- Foreach actions
- Scope actions
- Do…Until actions
- Terminate actions

We will describe how you can use these control flow actions against a set of triggers to build event-based cloud solutions in Azure. We will also discuss various data operation actions, such as Compose, Parse JSON, join, Filter array, and select.

Conditional actions

Conditional actions in Logic Apps provide if...else constructs. Each conditional action must have one or more conditional statements associated with it. When it is executed, it should return a Boolean true or false result. Conditional statements are executed using the Logic Apps workflow expression language:

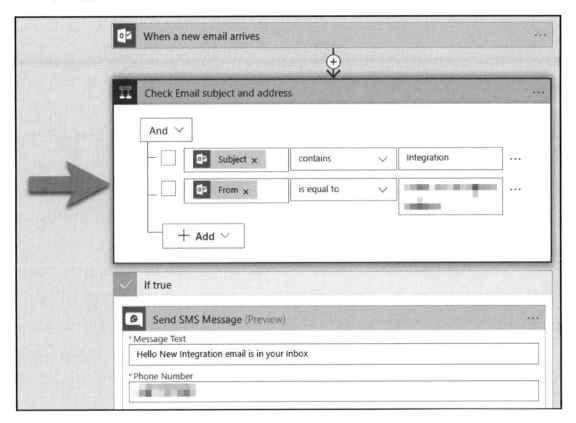

In the preceding workflow, Logic Apps polls for new emails in a user's inbox and performs a conditional check with the email subject and address parameters. In a Logic Apps conditional expression, the email subject and address parameters are used to derive the result of the conditional statement, as shown in the following screenshot:

```
"expression": {
    "and": [
        {
            "contains": [
                "@triggerBody()?['Subject']",
                "Integration"
            ]
        },
        {
            "equals": [
                "@triggerBody()?['From']",
                "sample01@hotmail.com"
            ]
        }
    ]
}
```

Parallel actions

With parallel control flow in Logic Apps, two or more actions are executed simultaneously without affecting the performance of any other actions. The advantage of parallel processing is you can route the same message across different branches of Logic Apps, thereby reducing the overall complexity of a workflow. To optimally utilize a parallel control flow, you can configure the runAfter property. This will ensure that the parallel branch can only be executed if the runAfter property is true or false in the Logic Apps run execution.

To add a parallel control flow in Logic Apps, you can either your either use Logic Apps designer or Logic Apps code view. Both will achieve the same result. In the following example, we have a Logic Apps instance with an HTTP request trigger. Based on the request trigger, we have a different set of actions, such as **Get document** from Cosmos DB, create or update the document in Cosmos DB, or use an HTTP action to post a message to the external API endpoint:

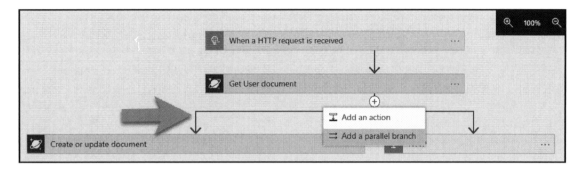

As you can see from the preceding example, creating or updating documents and triggering HTTP actions are in parallel, which means that once the **Get user document** action succeeds, other actions following the parent action will be executed in parallel.

Whenever possible, you should try to use parallel control flow actions with the asynchronous fire-and-forget pattern. This will help to remove tight coupling from the application and integration layers. Running parallel actions in an asynchronous manner will also improve overall application performance and remove any unnecessary and unwanted timeout exceptions

It's easy to implement a parallel control flow from Logic Apps code view. You just need to appropriately set the `runAfter` property with the parent action name. In the following code view example, we have an HTTP action with a parent action, `Get_User_document`. To add another action in the same level as the HTTP action, we only need to define the action definition and set the `runAfter` property to the `Get_User_document` action:

```
"HTTP": {
    "runAfter": {
        "Get_User_document": [
            "Succeeded"
        ]
    },
    "type": "Http",
    "inputs": {
        "body": "@triggerBody()",
        "method": "POST",
        "uri": "                                    "
    }
}
},
```

The `runAfter` property in a Logic Apps workflow is a string array with a value of either `Succeeded`, `Failed`, or `Skipped`. You can use a combination of `runAfter` properties or a single property to control the Logic Apps workflow. With the `runAfter` property, you can implement Logic Apps flows with greater control of exception conditions.

Switch control flow

Switch is a select statement in Logic Apps that chooses a single switch action based on the input. When you have lots of `if...else` logic in your workflow, switch can be more efficient in terms of performance and overall workflow design. In the following Logic Apps workflow example with switch, we have a Logic Apps instance that listens for user sentiment through an HTTP endpoint and, based on the result, sends an auto-response to the calling application over HTTP using the request-response pattern:

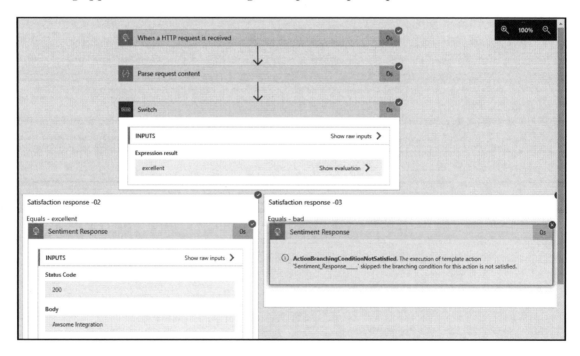

In the workflow displayed in the preceding screenshot, we've parsed the request JSON payload with the Parse JSON action and have used a sentiment property to send a response back to the caller. The switch uses the same pattern as a primitive language construct. The code for this Logic Apps definition is displayed here:

```
"Switch": {
    "runAfter": {
        "Parse_request_content": [
            "Succeeded"
        ]
    },
    "cases": {
        "Satisfaction_response_-01": {
            "case": "good",
            "actions": { …
            }
        },
        "Satisfaction_response_-02": {
            "case": "excellent",
            "actions": { …
            }
        },
        "Satisfaction_response_-03": {
            "case": "bad",
            "actions": { …
            }
        }
    },
```

Foreach action

The `Foreach` control flow action iterates over an array list. Within a `Foreach` control flow action, you can have one or more groups of actions, which can be executed in each item of the array.

By default, the `Foreach` control flow action can run 50 concurrent threads on array items. Logic Apps provides concurrency control for the processing of the `Foreach` action. You can also control the number of item lists within a `Foreach` loop using the filter condition on the array:

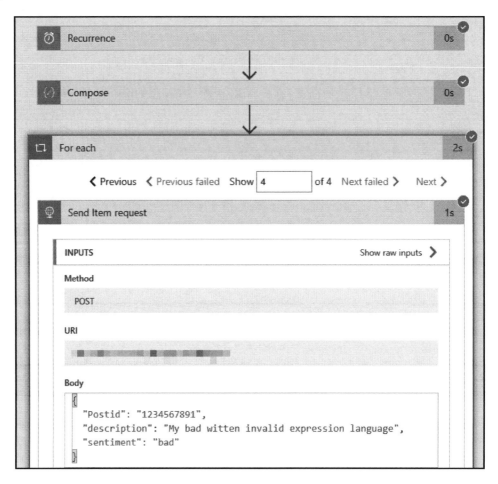

In this example, we have used a recurrence scheduled trigger along with `Compose` and a `Foreach` loop. In the Compose action, we have constructed a JSON array containing various hardcoded user sentiments. Compose actions are used to construct message shapes (such as transform and message assignment in BizTalk).

You can use the `Compose` action to build a dynamic or static message in a Logic Apps workflow and use them within subsequent sequential or parallel actions.

To control the degree of parallelism and concurrency in a `Foreach` loop, you can set the value within the Logic Apps designer through the `Foreach` action settings. You can also refer to the code view to manage concurrency control as shown here:

```
"For_each": {
    "foreach": "@outputs('Compose')",
    "actions": { ...
    },
    "runAfter": {
        "Compose": [
            "Succeeded"
        ]
    },
    "type": "Foreach",
    "runtimeConfiguration": {
        "concurrency": {
            "repetitions": 5
        }
    }
}
},
```

Scope action

The scope action provides grouping capabilities in the Logic Apps workflow designer. The scope control flow action is useful when we want to organize actions as a logical group within Logic Apps, evaluate that group's status, and perform any required actions that are based on the scope's status.

Using scope actions is a great way to handle logical group exceptions and take the necessary steps when scope execution is either failed or skipped. You can also use the runAfter property to control the flow of a logical set of grouped actions:

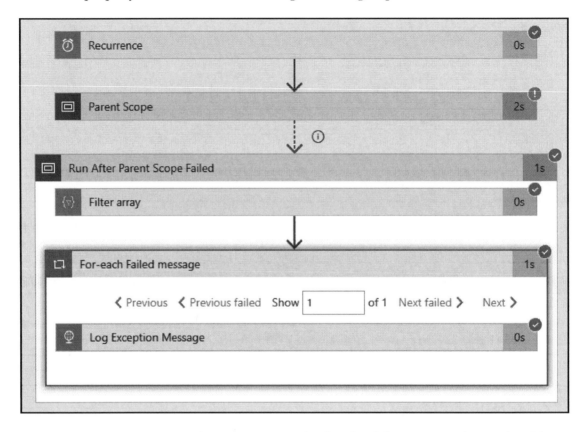

When an exception occurs in the parent scope, the details of the exception lies in the JSON array list. In the preceding screenshot, we've used a **Filter array** data operation action to filter the action, which has raised an exception in the parent Logic Apps instance. To learn more about Filter array data operation action capabilities, you can refer to https://docs. microsoft.com/en-us/azure/logic-apps/logic-apps-perform-data-operations#filter-array-action.

When looking into the Logic Apps code view, you can see how the logical grouping of actions is done through scope control flow actions. Here's the code for Logic Apps with the parent scope and two actions grouped within the parent scope:

```json
"Parent_Scope": {
    "actions": {
        "Compose": { ···
        },
        "For_each": {
            "foreach": "@outputs('Compose')",
            "actions": {
                "Send_Item_request": { ···
                }
            },
            "runAfter": {
                "Compose": [
                    "Succeeded"
                ]
            },
            "type": "Foreach",
            "runtimeConfiguration": { ···
            }
        }
    },
    "runAfter": {},
    "type": "Scope"
},
```

Do...until action

The Do...until control flow action is used when we have to repeat a set of actions until the required condition is satisfied. For example, in the asynchronous communication of a web API with an HTTP status of 202 (accepted), Logic Apps polls the API till it receives the final response body from the backend service.

In the following example, a Logic Apps workflow will perform the Do...until action till the variable count has reached 5. We have also used the select data operation action to select an item for the Compose JSON array. The Do...until loop helps to build long-running transactional workflows with Logic Apps, and like other actions within Logic Apps, you can also control the behavior of a Do...until loop.

In the example, we have also introduced the concept of variables. Like other language constructs, variables are placeholders for storing temporary data when executing logic apps. Logic Apps supports multiple variable types, such as `Boolean`, `String`, `Integer`, `Float`, `Object`, and `Array`. In Logic Apps, you need to declare the variable at a global level, and then you can perform multiple operations on variable sets, such as `increase`, `decrease`, and `append`, and you can set the variable value:

Using variables in the `Foreach` loop construct, it is advisable to run the `Foreach` loop with concurrency set to 1 to avoid unexpected results.

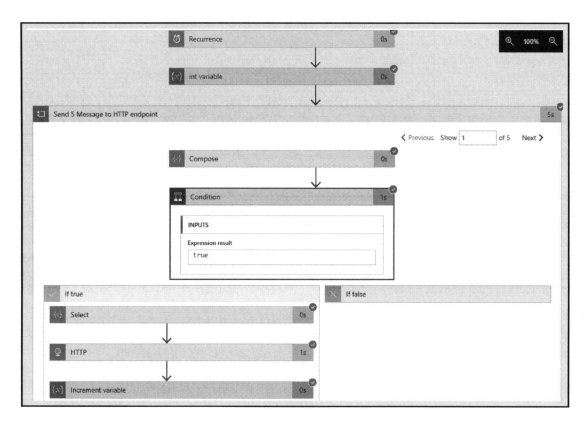

Through the following Logic Apps code view, you can verify the default limit and grouping of the actions within a Do...until loop. You can change the default limit configuration through either the Logic Apps designer or through the code view. It's important to remember that Do...until loops inherently run in sequence and that you don't need to change this default behavior:

```
"actions": {
    "Send_5_Message_to_HTTP_endpoint": {
        "actions": {···
        },
        "runAfter": {
            "int_variable": [
                "Succeeded"
            ]
        },
        "expression": "@equals(variables('intvarfordountil'), 5)",
        "limit": {
            "count": 60,
            "timeout": "PT1H"
        },
        "type": "Until"
    },
},
```

Terminate action

The Logic Apps designer allows us to add the Terminate control flow action simply by searching for terminate within the control flow action set. The Terminate action stops the run for a Logic App workflow instance and cancels any action runs that are in progress or skips remaining actions, and returns the status when requested.

Terminate, along with the scope action, can be used to build robust exception handlers within Logic Apps. In the following example, when there is an exception in the parent scope action, the terminate control flow is executed, and any secondary process depending on the **Parent scope** is skipped:

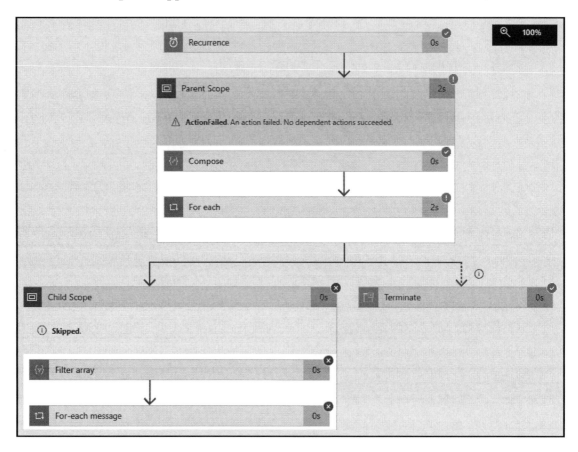

The `Terminate` action has enumerated status types of `Cancelled`, `Failed`, and `Succeeded`. You can select any of these types when you need to end an instance run of Logic Apps. The following code view represents the `Terminate` action:

```
"Terminate": {
    "runAfter": {
        "Parent_Scope": [
            "Failed"
        ]
    },
    "type": "Terminate",
    "inputs": {
        "runStatus": "Cancelled"
    }
}
},
```

So far in this chapter, we have covered all the pre-built control flow actions available in Logic Apps. We have also covered how you can use data operations actions in Logic Apps to perform message translation and select operations along with navigation through the Parse JSON action. We suggest that you practice these samples within your own Azure tool so that you get a firm understanding of the various patterns that can be implemented through Logic Apps' built-in control flows.

In the next section, we will discuss content type negotiation and the Logic Apps workflow expression language. Mastering both these elements can help you to build Logic Apps quicker.

The workflow expression language and content types

With Logic Apps, you can work with multiple content types, such as JSON, XML, Base64, and more. Logic Apps has built-in functions that are used within workflow expressions for conversion, transformation, and translation. For example, you can convert strings such as JSON and XML to @json() and @xml() workflow function expressions.

The following table displays the various content types along with casting types. You can also combine these content type functions to translate messages in your desired format:

Function	Cast operations
json()	Translates data to application/JSON
xml()	Translates data to application/XML
binary()	Translates data to application/octet-stream
string()	Translates data to text/plain
decodeDataUri()	Decodes a dataUri into a byte array
base64toString()	Converts a Base64-encoded string to text/plain
base64toBinary()	Converts a Base64-encoded string to application/octet-stream
base64()	Converts content to a Base64 string
encodeDataUri()	Encodes a string as a dataUri byte array

In the following example, we've used an HTTP request trigger to get the JSON request, and throughout the workflow, we've converted the request message into various content types before sending the same response back:

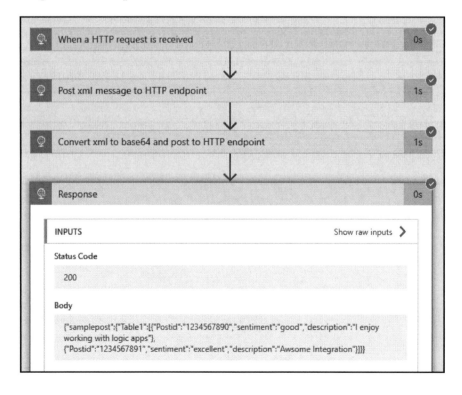

In the following code view, we can list various functions that are used together for content type modification:

```
"actions": {
    "Convert_xml_to_base64_and_post_to_HTTP_endpoint": {
        "runAfter": { ...
        },
        "type": "Http",
        "inputs": {
            "body": "@{base64(xml(triggerBody()))}",
            "method": "POST",
            "uri": "▚▚▚▚▚▚▚▚▚▚▚▚▚▚▚▚▚▚▚"
        }
    },
    "Post_xml_message_to_HTTP_endpoint": {
        "runAfter": {},
        "type": "Http",
        "inputs": {
            "body": "@xml(triggerBody())",
            "method": "POST",
            "uri": "▚▚▚▚▚▚▚▚▚▚▚▚▚▚▚▚▚"
        }
    },
    "Response": {
        "runAfter": { ...
        },
        "type": "Response",
        "kind": "Http",
        "inputs": {
            "body": "@{json(xml(base64toString(base64(xml(triggerBody())))))}",
            "statusCode": 200
        }
    }
}
```

When working with Logic Apps, it is also critical to understand how you can deal with NULL values in the request data. There are three different ways to gracefully handle NULL reference exceptions in Logic Apps:

1. **Stringify character**: The first option is to use a { } stringify character in the Logic Apps expression language; for example, changing your Logic Apps expression language expression from default to the { } stringify format is done as follows:

```
"Response": {
    "runAfter": {},
    "type": "Response",
    "kind": "Http",
    "inputs": {
        "body": "@{triggerBody()?['description']}",
        "statusCode": 200
    }
}
```

The execution of the Logic Apps expression will handle the NULL-to-string conversion, as displayed in the following screenshot:

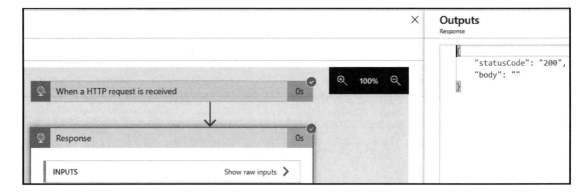

2. **Parse JSON**: The second option is to use the Parse JSON action with an array of the content type (for example, `string`, `null`) instead of the default. With this, any request data coming through action or trigger will have a valid content type:

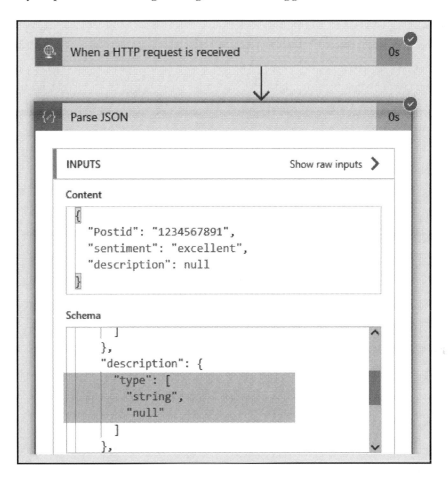

3. **Coalesce function**: When working with a Logic Apps conditional statement, you should use the `coalesce` function, which can help you to deal with NULL reference exceptions. The following example displays a conditional statement with the `coalesce` function:

```
"@equals(coalesce(triggerBody()?.description, 'nullcheck'),
'nullcheck')
```

Workflow and action tracking

Workflow and action tracking is enabled through the diagnostics settings of Logic Apps and uses Azure Log Analytics. To enable the custom tracking of action properties, you can use the Logic Apps designer and code view to set different actions' tracked properties, which can then be passed through Azure Log Analytics and the Logic Apps Management portal.

The following is the step-by-step guide to enabling tracking for Logic Apps using Log Analytics and the Logic Apps Management portal:

1. The first step is to create an Azure Log Analytics instance within your Azure subscription. To do this, log into the Azure portal and in the search blade, search for `Azure Log Analytics`.

2. In Azure Log Analytics, create the blade, enter a proper workspace name for the Azure Log Analytics resource, select a **Resource group**, appropriate **Subscription**, **Location**, and **Pricing tier**, and click on **OK** to create a Log Analytics workspace in the resource group:

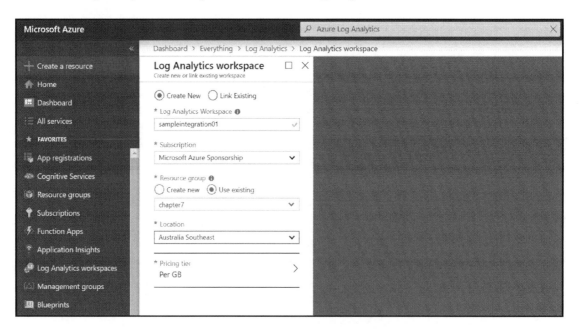

3. In the next step, add **Logic Apps Management Solution** to the Azure Log Analytics workspace resource. To do this, you need to navigate to the Log Analytics instance in your resource group. In the **Configure monitoring solutions** section, click on **View solution**.

4. Click on **Add** and this will open up the list of different management solutions under the Azure Log Analytics workspace. Select **Logic Apps Management (preview)** for Logic Apps monitoring and then click on **Create**:

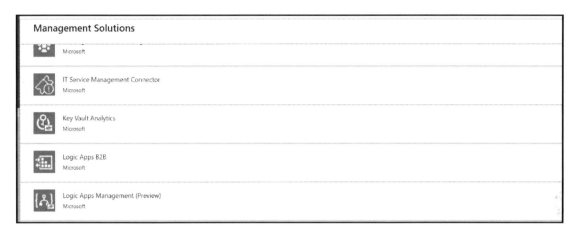

5. In the steps discussed previously, we have completed the initial setup for **Logic Apps Management solution** with the Azure Log Analytics workspace solution. The next step is to publish tracked properties from **Logic Apps workflow** using the tracked properties' built-in features. To do this, we have created a Logic Apps instance with a request trigger and a set of actions, including **Parse JSON** and **HTTP**, to send the request message to an external HTTP endpoint:

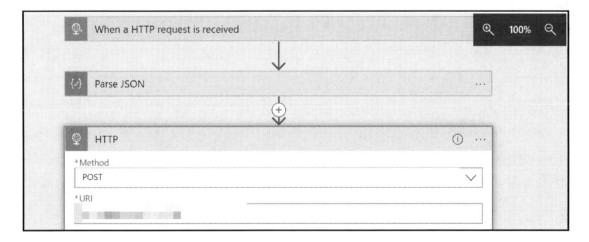

6. The next step is to configure action-level tracking with a Logic Apps workflow definition. To work with tracking properties, open the Logic Apps code view and add the tracked properties in an HTTP action definition.

7. Once the action-tracking configuration is completed, click on the **Save** button to save the Logic Apps workflow definition.

8. The last thing to do is to enable the diagnostic feature with Logic Apps. To do this, navigate to the Logic Apps resource in the **Monitoring** section and click on **Diagnostics settings**.

9. On the **Diagnostics settings** page, click on **Turn on diagnostics**. Fill in the **Name** field and click on **Send to Log Analytics**. We also need to enable the tracking of **WorkflowRuntime** and **AllMetrics**. Once completed, you can save the **Diagnostics settings** page by clicking on the **Save** button:

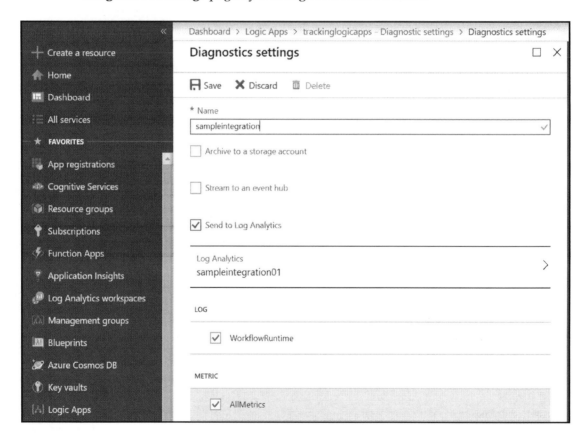

10. This completes the tracking of actions and Logic Apps instances with Azure Log Analytics. To test the tracking, we will post data to a Logic Apps endpoint and validate the Logic Apps Management Solution through Log Analytics. After sending test data to the request-triggered logic app, we can see the tracked properties are being captured in the Log Analytics workspace and displayed through Logic Apps Management Solution:

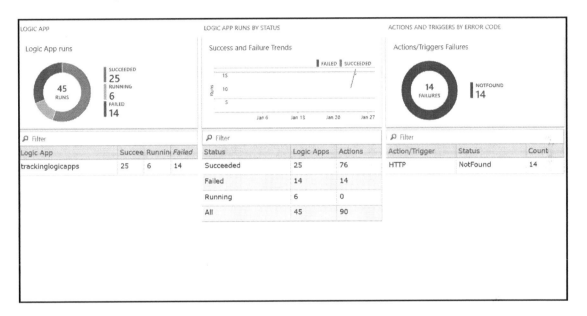

In this section, we have covered Logic Apps tracking with an Azure Log Analytics workspace along with content types in Logic Apps. We have also discussed how to work with the Logic Apps expression language using Logic Apps' built-in functions.

In the next section, we'll discuss how to create custom connectors for Azure Logic Apps. We will discuss the process of creating custom connectors for an enterprise-owned API and using them in Logic Apps definitions, just like any other standard connector.

Custom connectors and Cosmos graph databases

As we have seen throughout this book, we can build integration workflows powered by Logic Apps, Microsoft Flow, or Power Apps without having any hand in the code. In this section, we will discuss how we can leverage existing APIs and make standard custom connectors to connect integration platforms and services, whether they are cloud resources or on-premises applications.

To get started with the custom connector, we have created a Gremlin API to connect with a Cosmos graph database using the `Gremlin.Net` library. To find out more about graph databases and the Gremlin query language, you can read through the Cosmos DB documentation available at `https://docs.microsoft.com/en-us/azure/cosmos-db/graph-introduction`.

The Gremlin custom API performs create, retrieve, update, and delete (**CRUD**) operations on graph nodes (documents) with the Gremlin query language. The following code blocks show the operation definitions for `create`, `get`, and `delete` graph database vertexes (nodes):

- **Method to create graph database vertexes (nodes)**:
  The `PostComosGraphVertex` operation creates a node document in a Cosmos graph database using the `Gremlin.net` driver. In this method, the client application (for example, Logic Apps) sends vertex content, which includes the type of vertex and a JSON string. Once the request is received through the `post` operation, Logic Apps iterates through the JSON string and creates a Gremlin query using the request data:

```
// POST api/GraphVertex Create Vertex with JSON string
        [HttpPost]
        public async Task<ActionResult>
PostCosmosGraphVertex(GraphVertex graphcontent)
        {
            try
            {
            var result = (dynamic)null;
            dynamic content =
JsonConvert.DeserializeObject<dynamic>(graphcontent.Content);
            string type = graphcontent.VertexType;

            StringBuilder builder = new StringBuilder();
                foreach (var item in content)
                {
```

```
                     string query =
$".property('{item.Name}','{item.Value}')";
                builder.Append(query);
            }
        var queryString =
string.Concat($"g.addV('{type}')",builder);
            result = await
_client.SubmitAsync<dynamic>(queryString);


            var responsemessage =
JsonConvert.SerializeObject(result);
            return this.Content(responsemessage,
"application/json");
        }


        catch (Exception ex)
        {
            return Content(ex.Message);
        }


    }
```

- The operation then calls the Gremlin client with the SubmiteAsync method and sends the Gremlin query to the Gremlin driver to create a record in the graph database. If there are any exceptions while processing the request message, the controller method will return the exception details to the calling application.

- **Method to get graph database vertexes with properties (nodes)**: The GetVertexByProperty operation queries the graph database to find the node (documents) with a specific set of properties and values using the Gremlin.net driver. In this method, the client application sends vertex details in the form of a key and a value. The operation will send the key-value details of the node to the Cosmos graph database using the Gremlin query language and get the required node information from the graph database:

```
// Get Graph Node with key value Property

[HttpGet]
public async Task<ActionResult> GetVertexByProperty(string
Property, string Value )
{
  try
  {
    var queryString = $"g.V().has('{Property}', '{Value}')";
    dynamic result = await
_client.SubmitAsync<dynamic>(queryString);
    var responsemessage = JsonConvert.SerializeObject(result);
```

```
        return this.Content(responsemessage,"application/json");
    }
    catch (Exception ex)
    {
        return Content(ex.Message);
    }
}
```

- Similar to the preceding method, to create a node in the graph database, the GetVertexByProperty operation uses the Gremlin client with the SubmiteAsync method and sends the Gremlin query to get the record document from the graph database. If there are any exceptions while processing the request message, the controller method will return the exception details to the calling application.

- **Method to delete graph database vertexes with properties (nodes)**: DeleteGraphVertex performs the delete graph node operation on the graph database. This operation requires a property set in the key-value pair to identify the record in the graph database. Again, this method uses the Gremlin.net driver to post a Gremlin query to the Cosmos graph database:

```
[HttpDelete]
public async Task<object> DeleteGraphVertex(string Property,
string Value)
{
    try
    {
        var queryString = $"g.V().has('{Property}',
'{Value}').Drop()";
        dynamic result = await
_client.SubmitAsync<dynamic>(queryString);
        var responsemessage = JsonConvert.SerializeObject(result);
        return this.Content(responsemessage, "application/json");
    }
    catch (Exception ex)
    {
        return Content(ex.Message);
    }
}
```

- Like other methods in this graph web API, DeleteGraphVertex also uses the Gremlin client to send a Gremlin query to the SubmiteAsync method. If any exceptions occur when deleting the node from the graph database, the controller method will return the exception details to the caller.

The PATCH operation is the same as the POST operation. It will overwrite the graph vertex property or create a new if none of the vertices are found with request data.

In the web API, we have defined the dependency injection to pass the Gremlin connection properties that are defined in the `startup.cs` file of the web API. The definition for `Startup.cs` contains properties and a method to retrieve the Cosmos graph database connection from Key Vault using `application.configuration` of the web API:

1. The code to retrieve a Cosmos database secret from Azure Key Vault through the web API `application.configuration` file is shown in the following code snippet:

```
public class Startup
    {
        private static string hostname =
System.Environment.GetEnvironmentVariable("cosmosDbHostaddreess
");
        private static string port = "443";
        private static string collection =
System.Environment.GetEnvironmentVariable("cosmosDbdatabasecoll
ectionName");
        private static string authKey =
System.Environment.GetEnvironmentVariable("cosmosDbdatabaseAuth
Key");
        private static string database =
System.Environment.GetEnvironmentVariable("cosmosDbdatabase");

        private GremlinClient client;
}
```

2. Once the Cosmos graph database secret has been retrieved from the application settings, the next step is to create a connection to the Cosmos graph database through the `gremlin.net` driver. To do this in the `Startup.cs` file, update the startup method to create a Cosmos DB connection using Cosmos graph database properties:

```
public Startup(IConfiguration configuration)
{
  Configuration = configuration;
  var server = new GremlinServer(hostname, 443, enableSsl:
true, username: "/dbs/" + database + "/colls/" + collection,
password: authKey);

  client = new GremlinClient(server, new GraphSON2Reader(), new
GraphSON2Writer(), GremlinClient.GraphSON2MimeType);
}
```

3. Finally, we need to enable the OpenAPI definition for the custom connector through a swagger definition. To do this, open the `Startup.cs` file and update `ConfigureServices` and the `Configure` method as shown:

```
void ConfigureServices(IServiceCollection services)
        {
            services.AddMvc();
            services.AddSingleton(client);
            services.AddSwaggerGen(c =>
            {
                c.SwaggerDoc("v1", new Info { Title = "Cosmos
Graph Database", Version = "v1" });
            });
        }

        // This method gets called by the runtime. Use this
method to configure the HTTP request pipeline.
        public void Configure(IApplicationBuilder app)
        {
            app.UseSwagger();

            app.UseSwaggerUI(c =>
            {
                c.SwaggerEndpoint("/swagger/v1/swagger.json",
"My API V1");
            });

            app.UseMvc();
        }
    }
}
```

The build setup for the Gremlin web API is complete now. You can host your web API in multiple environments, including on-premise, on virtual machines, in a container, or an App Service in an Azure resource group.

4. In this example, we have deployed our web API in an Azure resource group through the DevOps pipeline. When you browse to the OpenAPI definition of the Gremlin API, you can see the list of operations in the swagger definition file:

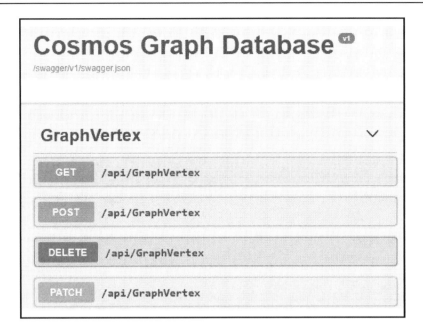

We will now create a custom connector for this web API:

1. Search for `logic apps custom connector` and click on **Logic Apps Custom Connector**:

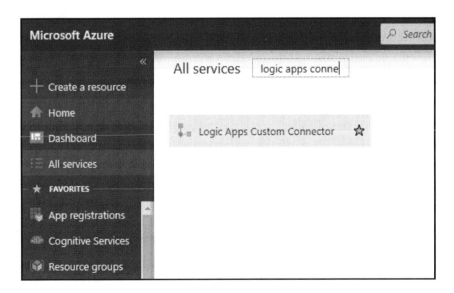

2. Populate the custom connector's **Name** field, choose your **Subscription**, **Resource group**, and **Location** (choose a location near to your Logic Apps instance), and click on **Create**. This will open up the definition section for the Logic Apps custom connector:

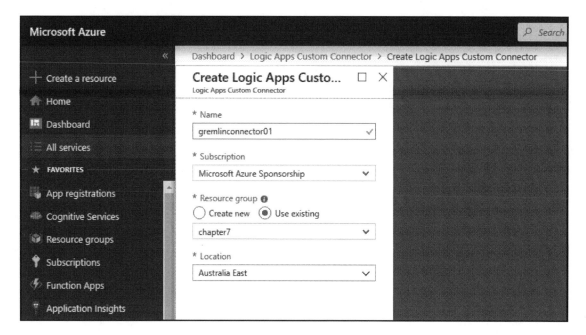

3. Choose your **API endpoint**. As we have our web API running over the REST protocol, we have chosen **REST** and imported the swagger definition. You can also use the OpenAPI URL or collection details from Postman. Based on the method of import definition, you will be prompted to use a collection, URI, or swagger definition:

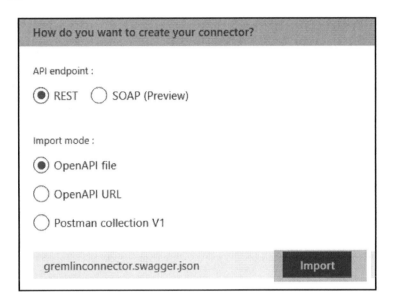

4. In the next section, you can list the Gremlin API image along with the description. As we've hosted our API in Azure, we have not ticked **Connect via on-premises data gateway**. If you are hosting within your own infrastructure, then you can connect your API through the API gateway. We have also chosen **HTTPS** as the **Scheme** for our web API invocation. It's important to list the web API host to appropriately identify the HTTP endpoint:

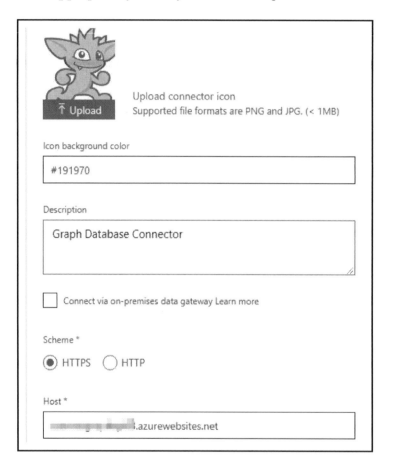

5. In the security section, you can choose a security model. In this custom connector, we have chosen **OAuth 2.0** with Azure Active Directory as **Identity Provider**. To do this, you need to register an application with Azure Active Directory and provide management access to the Azure resource:

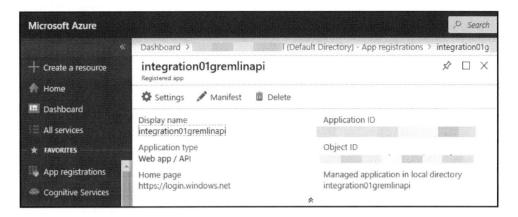

6. You need to update the **Security** section with the client ID, also known as the **Application ID**, and the security key that is generated during app registration. Once saved, the custom connector will generate a redirect URI, which needs to be updated:

In this case, the custom connector definition section will use information from the OpenAPI definition of the swagger file, or you can also manually enter the properties of the custom connector:

- As we have already used swagger, we can see the list of available operations in the custom connector. We will only update the basic information, such as the summary and description.
- Now you need to close the custom connector configuration. Within a couple of seconds, you'll see your custom connector listed within Logic Apps for CRUD operations, along with other Microsoft built-in connectors:

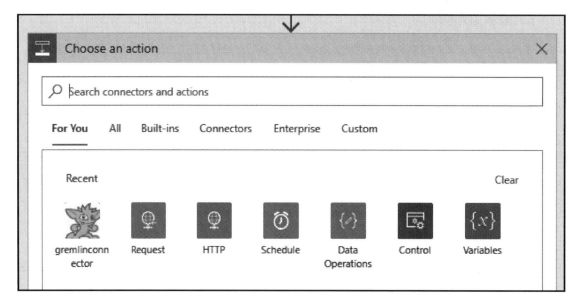

- To test the connector's behavior, create a recurrent Logic Apps instance to find the vertex details with a property name and value:

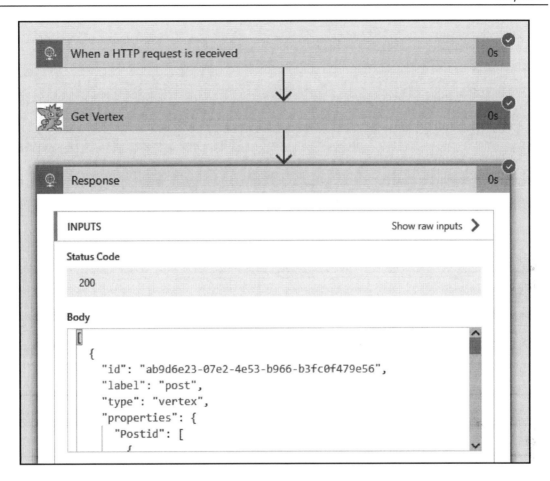

When working with real use cases, it is advisable to lock your web API with a Logic Apps IP range, or you can implement mutual OAuth authentication both on the web API and the custom connector to provide an extra layer of protection.

In this section, we have discussed how to build and leverage custom connectors for Azure Logic Apps and how to leverage the custom connector definition with a Logic Apps workflow. As we discussed in the previous chapter, logic apps and Azure Functions communicate through HTTP endpoints and webhooks. You can also enable the OpenAPI definition in Azure Functions to work efficiently within a function app. To find out more about how you can enable an OpenAPI definition in a function app, you can read through the following resource: `https://docs.microsoft.com/en-us/azure/azure-functions/functions-openapi-definition`.

Summary

In this chapter, we discussed the different control flow actions available in Logic Apps. We also learned to write in the Logic Apps expression language both through the designer and code views. Finally, we discussed how you can leverage your existing API as a custom connector in Logic Apps and how to build your own custom connector for Logic Apps.

In the next chapter, we will continue to learn about integration patterns with advanced workflows implemented through Logic Apps and connecting services.

8

Patterns with Azure Integration Services

This is a continuation of the previous chapter on Azure Logic Apps. In this chapter, we will continue our learning by looking at advanced integration patterns using Azure integration services, a robust serverless platform that includes Logic Apps, Azure Functions, Event Grid, Service Bus, and API Management.

In this chapter, we will cover integration patterns such as batching, session management with Service Bus, message broadcasting, layered service design, and so on. These can be directly implemented in our enterprise-grade solutions. As an example, the following diagram shows the broadcasting pattern using Event Grid and connected services such as Azure Functions, Logic Apps, and API Management:

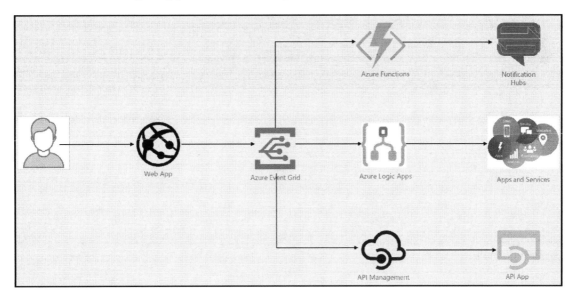

Azure Functions and Logic Apps

Before we dive into various integration patterns, let's discuss the difference between Logic Apps and Azure Functions. As we know, Logic Apps and Azure Functions are both part of the serverless family and both have a robust platform engine running behind the scenes. It's very important for us to know the difference between the two, as this will enable us to pick the right option for our compute operations.

Development experience: Azure Functions follow an event-based programming model and works with a code-first approach, whereas Logic Apps are workflows triggered through events and messages.

From a development point of view, the developer can choose a language of their choice, such as C#, F#, JavaScript, Node.js, or PowerShell, to develop event-based executable code with support for multiple integrated development environments, including Visual Studio Code, Visual Studio, and the Azure portal.

When it comes to Logic Apps, developers can develop event-based workflows that connect disparate systems through connectors, triggers, and visual designer. Like Azure Functions, Logic Apps supports multiple integrated development environments, such as Visual Studio Code, Visual Studio 2015 or later, and the Azure portal.

Pricing model: With the introduction of the Azure integration services environment, Logic Apps work on both consumption and fixed pricing plans. On the consumption-based plan, you pay for the number of actions and triggers executed as part of your Logic Apps workflow and your resources are shared in the Azure environment. With a fixed pricing plan, on the other hand, Logic Apps runs in private and in an isolated integration runtime within your virtual network, and you pay a fixed price to run your integration solution in the cloud.

Azure Functions also has a flexible pricing plan and supports consumption, fixed, and premium pricing structures. On the Azure Functions consumption plan, you are billed for server memory utilization per second, while on the fixed and premium plans, you have dedicated compute resources allocated to your Functions app. To learn more about the Azure Functions premium offering, we suggest that you go through the Microsoft documentation at the following link: `https://azure.microsoft.com/en-au/pricing/details/functions/`.

Monitoring: Both Logic Apps and Azure Functions have a robust monitoring feature powered by Log Analytics and Application Insights. Logic Apps provides monitoring through the Azure portal and with the Logic Apps management solution hosted on Azure Log Analytics. In Logic Apps, you can also send Logic Apps run logs either to storage or event hubs for better data analysis through machine learning. In the following screenshot, we have used Azure portal monitoring for Logic Apps to give a visual representation of the Logic Apps workflow run history:

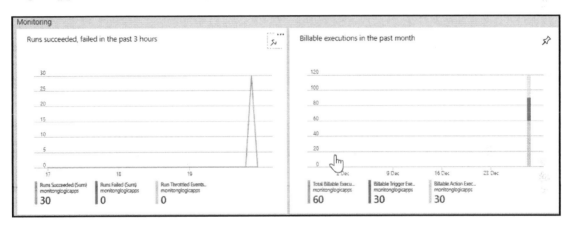

Azure Functions, on the other hand, has built-in support for Azure Application Insights to monitor the runtime behavior of all of the functions running in an Azure Functions App. Azure Application Insights are used to monitor custom telemetry data for functions and any exceptions raised during the execution of code.

The following screenshot shows an example of Application Insights monitoring for Azure Functions:

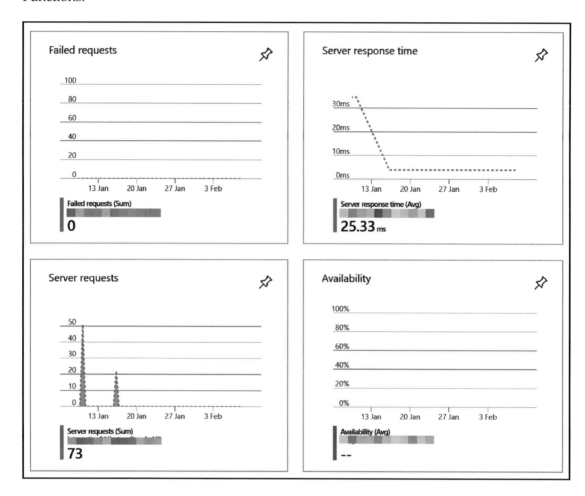

Deployment: Azure Functions and Logic Apps have great support for continuous integration and deployment through DevOps. With Logic Apps, you can deploy your workflow template through a DevOps pipeline in real time without affecting your environment. Better usage of DevOps with integration services such as Logic Apps, API Management, Service Bus, and Event Grid can help you to build disaster recovery points in Azure within a couple of minutes.

Azure Functions also has a flexible deployment method. You can deploy functions directly from Visual Studio, or use an ARM template in the DevOps pipeline. With DevOps, you can also deploy functions in different slots for a Functions app and enable the autoswitch feature through a DevOps task.

Exception Handling: Cloud solutions must have robust exception-handling capabilities. As the Logic Apps workflow runs on a managed API connector, exception handling capabilities are included by default, with multiple connectors through retry policies and `runAfter` policies. You can configure retry policies, which can either be fixed or exponential, with a specific connector through the code view or the Logic Apps Designer.

In the following example, we have an HTTP action and will describe exception handling with `retryPolicy`. The retry policy action on Logic Apps contains `type`, which is exponential, along with a retry `interval` and `count`:

```
"HTTP": "{
    "runAfter": {},
    "type": "Http",
    "inputs": {
        "body": "@triggerBody()",
        "method": "POST",
        "retryPolicy": {
            "type": "exponential",
            "interval": "PT7S",
            "count": 4,
            "minimumInterval": "PTSS",
            "maximumInterval": "PT1H"
        },
        "uri": "place_ur_url_here"
    }
}
```

Another way to manage exceptions is to implement exception patterns such as the `runAfter` property, scope, or with the switch case control flow, as shown in the following Logic Apps workflow:

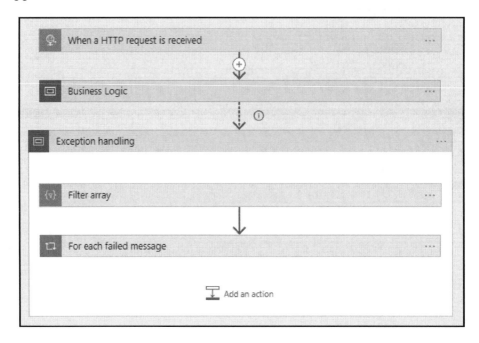

In Azure Functions, exception handling is done with code control, using try-catch blocks and retry polices that are available with some input and output bindings, such as Blob Storage, Cosmos DB, and Service Bus. You can read more about exception handling in Azure Functions at the following link: `https://docs.microsoft.com/en-us/azure/azure-functions/durable/durable-functions-error-handling`.

Azure Functions, on the other hand, supports development and testing in a local environment. You can simulate the testing of Azure Functions with frameworks such as Xunit, NUnit, or the Visual Studio unit testing project.

Execution context: Logic Apps follow a cloud-first approach. We can use the support for Visual Studio Code to develop Logic Apps in a local environment or Azure portal. You can also use the Logic Apps template to integrate the runtime environment. At the time of writing this book, it is currently very difficult to simulate unit testing in a local environment using Logic Apps unless we push the workflow template to the Azure resource group with a proper API connection and connector configuration.

In Azure Functions, however, you can use a testing framework such as xUnit or NUnit to write unit test cases. With Azure Functions unit testing, you can take advantage of the various input and output bindings available and simulate a production run in your local environment:

```
[Fact]
public void GetHttprequestResultAsync()
{
    var query = new Dictionary<String, StringValues>();
    query Add("name", "Abhishek");
    var body = "";

    var result = Httpfunctions01.Run(req: GenerateRequestBody(query, body),
traceWriter);
    var resultset = result;
}
```

Security: A secure integration environment is one of the critical requirements of any enterprise-grade solution. Azure Logic Apps uses managed API connections to secure endpoint configuration details. With support for managed service identity in Logic Apps, any key secret can be stored in the Azure Key Vault and the secret value can be retrieved at runtime.

In Azure Functions, security is managed by various types of input and output bindings that are available for cloud resources, along with support for Azure Key Vault and managed service identity. In Azure Functions, you can also store secrets in the application settings and use the values at runtime (although this is not advisable for production workloads).

Connectors and connectivity: Azure Logic Apps has more than 200 connectors that can help you to connect to external systems such as Salesforce, Zapier, SurveyMonkey, and the Xero accounting platform. In Azure Functions, you have connections to a broad range of Azure resources, such as CosmosDB, Blob Storage, and Event Grid. With recent advancements in Azure Functions, you can also create custom bindings to work using a code-first approach.

In this section, we have tried to cover some of the main differences between Logic Apps and Azure Functions. Both services work on serverless platforms and are vital for the overall success of any enterprise integration solution.

In the next section, we will start our discussion of batch patterns and look at how you can utilize Logic Apps' built-in connectors to build batching patterns.

Example 1 – The batching or aggregator pattern in Logic Apps

Batch processing is a critical requirement for most organizations. With event-based patterns and cloud consumption models, working with batch files is cost-effective and provides the end user with better insights into the business data. Logic Apps has built-in connectors for batch-processing use cases, in which the batch connector groups related messages and events in a collection until a specific criteria is met.

To understand this more clearly, let's take the example of a social media website. When we post an update on a social media site, we may get some comments. To analyze those comments, it is important to batch them up and pass them to a central repository such as a data lake for analytical purposes, or Cognitive Services for sentiment analysis.

In this example, we have used a Cosmos graph database to trigger Azure Functions whenever a comment is added to a specific post:

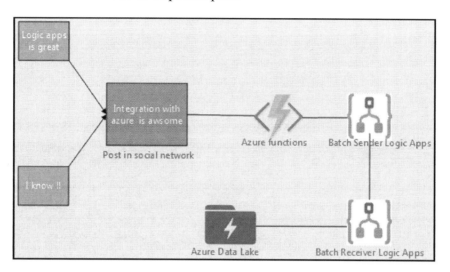

In the last chapter, we covered how to trigger Logic Apps on the Cosmos change feed. We will continue our learning now and build two Logic Apps instances. One is a sender, which will listen for HTTP posts, and another is a receiver, which will control batch processing and send the batch result to Azure Data Lake through the Logic Apps Data Lake Connector:

1. The first step is to define the batch receiver Logic Apps instance. To do this, create a new Logic Apps workflow in the specified resource group.

2. In Logic App workflow designer, search for the batch connector trigger and populate the required batch trigger connector properties such as batch mode, batch name, release condition, message count, batch size, and schedule.

3. Set the batch mode to inline if you have a single release condition. If you have multiple release conditions, set the batch mode to integration account. In an integration account, you can maintain multiple batch conditions that can be used by Logic Apps at runtime.

4. In the batch name property, provide a valid batch name and populate the required release condition. In this case, we have set multiple release conditions based on the message count, the batch size, and the schedule.

5. Add a Data Lake Connector action to the Logic Apps workflow. This connector will upload a document to Azure Data Lake:

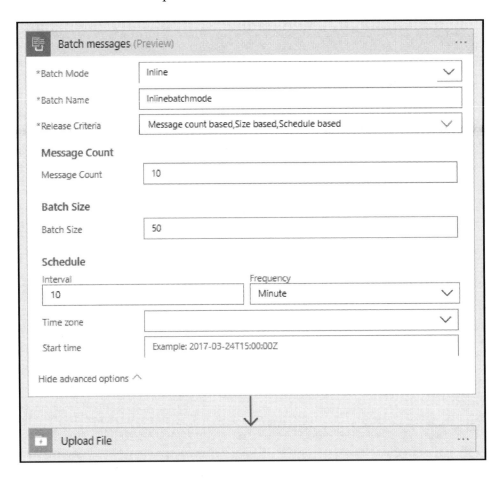

6. The next step is to define a batch receiver Logic App workflow. In the Logic Apps batch sender, use the HTTP request trigger along with the configuration for the batch receiver connector.

7. In the batch receiver connector action configuration, you need to set the message content, the batch name (the receiver Logic App batch name), the partition name, and the message ID, along with the trigger name, as shown in the following screenshot:

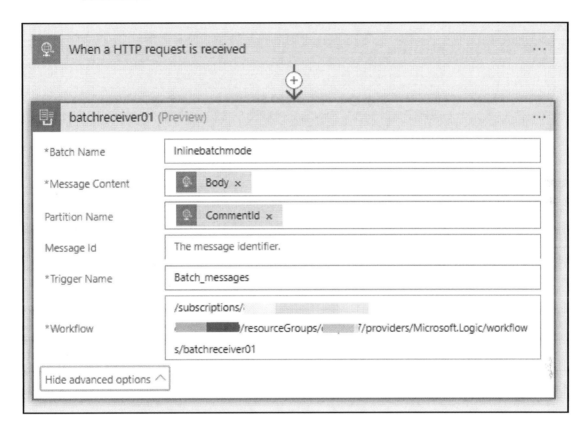

8. The next step is to test the Logic App batch process. To do this, add documents in the Cosmos graph database and use the CosmosDB change feed feature to initiate batch processing:

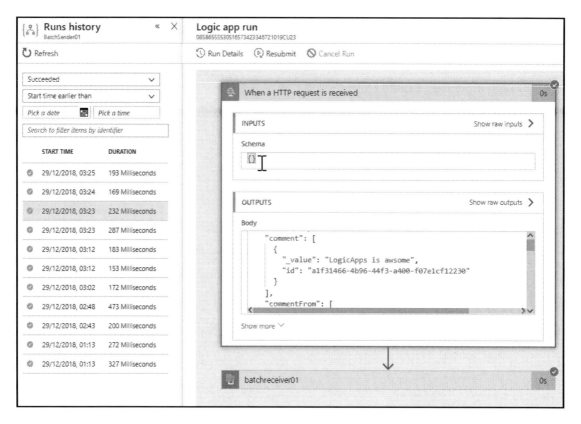

9. Based on the batch receiver configuration for release, Logic Apps will run multiple instances of the change feed until any condition (such as the batch size, the message count, or schedule) is satisfied.

10. In the next step, after the batch exits the process, the batched message will be posted to Azure Data Lake through a standard Data Lake Connector, as follows:

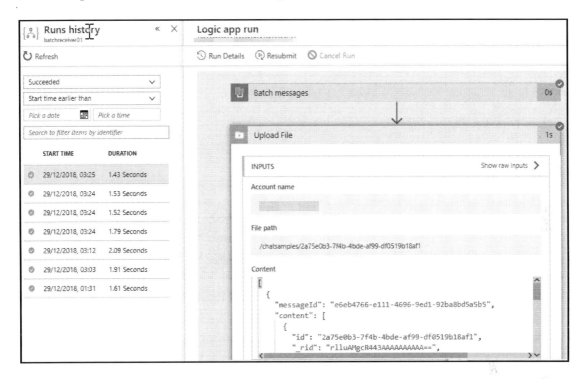

Example 2 – Asynchronous patterns for long-running APIs

Asynchronous communication patterns have important benefits in enterprise solution implementations. In async programming, the model client does not have to maintain an active thread to listen for an appropriate response from the backend system. Instead, the backend system will send a notification to the client when the system is ready to respond.

In Logic Apps, async patterns with APIs are implemented through polling and webhook patterns. In this exercise, we are going to cover both of these patterns so that whenever you are required to invoke long communications through Logic Apps, you can follow these patterns according to the requirements of your enterprise.

There are two asynchronous patterns that we can use in Logic Apps, which are described in the following sections:

- The polling pattern
- The webhook pattern

The polling pattern

When invoking a long process with an HTTP connector, you might have faced issues to do with timeout. This is because the Logic Apps HTTP connector has a default expiry of two minutes and when the backend API does not respond within that time, the HTTP connector will throw a timeout exception. To control this behavior, we can implement a polling pattern through our external endpoint.

To work with the polling pattern in Logic Apps, the backend API should return the HTTP status code 202 (accepted) in the response header, along with a retry interval to the HTTP connector within two minutes. This will allow Logic Apps to poll specific API endpoints for response messages after the retry interval.

To replicate this polling scenario, we have created an HTTP get method in a web API, which will take a name as a request parameter and send an immediate 202 status code, along with the retry time:

```
[HttpGet]
[Route("api/functioncallapi")]
public async Task<HttpResponseMessage>
GetNameValue(HttpRequestMessage req)
    {

        string name = req.GetQueryNameValuePairs()
        .FirstOrDefault(q => string.Compare(q.Key, "name", true) ==
0).Value;
        runningTasks[name] = false;
        new Thread(() =>
        {
            ExecuteDelayedTask(name);

        }).Start();
        HttpResponseMessage responsemessage = new ,
```

```
HttpResponseMessage(HttpStatusCode.Accepted);
        responsemessage.Headers.Add("location",
String.Format("{0}://{1}/api/{2}?name={3}", req.RequestUri.Scheme,
req.RequestUri.Host, "functioncallapi", name));
        responsemessage.Headers.Add("retry-after", "40");
        return responsemessage;
        }
```

This web API function has an internal method called `ExecuteDelayedTask`, which will run on separate threads and has a wait set for five minutes before sending a response back to the caller:

```
private void ExecuteDelayedTask(string name)
{
    Task.Delay(3).Wait();
    dynamic contact = new ExpandoObject();
    contact.Name = name;
    runningTasks[name] = true;
}
```

To test this web API, we have deployed the web API definition to the Azure resource group and used the recurrence trigger, along with the HTTP action, to invoke the long-running process:

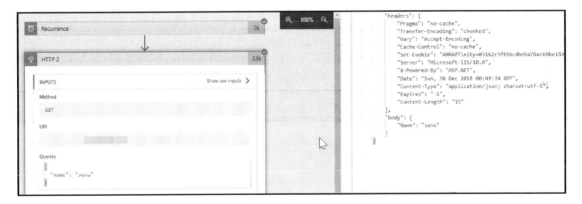

You can find a reference article by Jeff Hollan at the following link: `https://blogs.msdn.microsoft.com/logicapps/2016/02/15/long-running-tasks-in-logic-apps/`. A real-world implementation of polling with the Microsoft Cognitive Services API is available at the following link: `https://medium.com/@abhishekcskumar/logic-apps-large-audio-speech-to-text-batch-transcription-d71e93bbaeec`

The webhook pattern

This is another pattern for running an async long-running process. In this pattern, the caller sends `callbackurl` to the long-running process and, when the process is complete, the sender reverts back to the caller using `callbackurl`.

To demonstrate a simple webhook implementation with Logic Apps, we have created two sets of Logic Apps: one for the caller and one for the sender, which is the long-running process orchestrator. The sender Logic App has an HTTP request trigger with a delay of 5 minutes and an HTTP action to send the response back to the caller workflow:

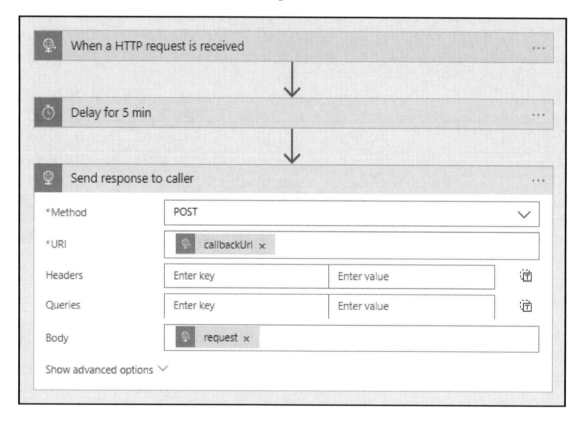

The caller Logic App has a recurrence trigger and an HTTP webhook action that will post the sample data, along with `callbackurl`, to the sender for processing. It will wait for a response from the sender Logic App:

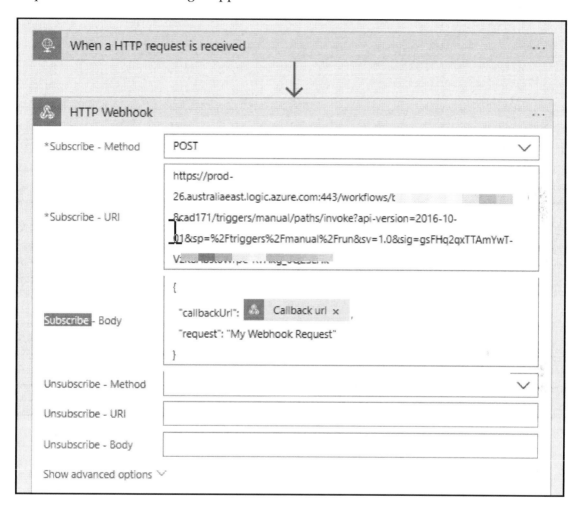

Once the request is received in the sender Logic App, it will wait for 5 minutes and then send a response to the caller workflow through the callback URI:

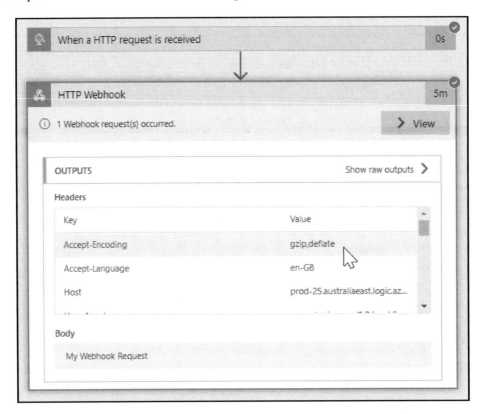

This example has shown how easy it is to set up a webhook pattern in Logic Apps and work with long-running async services. Another great example of this pattern is with durable functions, which you can use along with Logic Apps to implement an enterprise-level stateful workflow. Toon Vanhoutee has written a great blog post that you can refer to for more guidance on Durable Functions with Logic Apps: `https://toonvanhoutte.` `wordpress.com/2018/08/19/perform-long-running-logic-apps-tasks-with-durable-` `functions/`

Example 3 – Messages with API Management, Event Grid, Logic App, and Azure Functions

In this example, we are going to describe how we can broadcast custom messages using API Management, Azure Event Grid, and Logic Apps, with Azure Functions, Logic Apps, and a web app as a listener to the broadcasted messages. The high-level architectural overview of the solution is as follows:

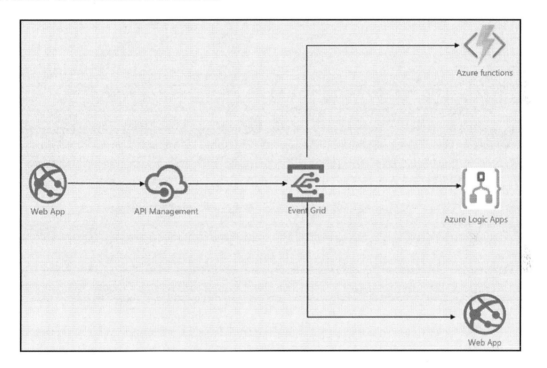

When working with third-party enterprise solutions, it is always advisable to make your integration solution flexible enough to onboard new solutions and patterns. In the broadcast pattern, we used the API Management layer in front of Azure Event Grid to secure the Event Grid backend resource. This process provides sufficient flexibility to modify security properties such as the authentication type, the security key, or the rate policy:

1. For this implementation, the first step is creating a new instance of API Management, or you can use any running API Management with a fixed or consumption plan.

2. If you do not have an Event Grid topic in your subscription, create an Event Grid topic resource:

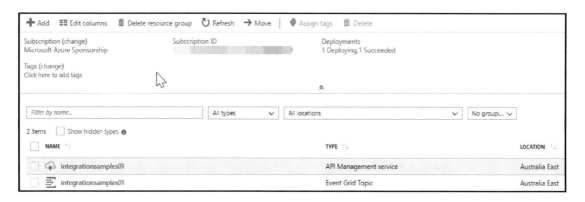

3. Copy the Azure Event Grid topic name and the secret key in the API Management named value pair resource, as shown in the following screenshot. This process will help to prevent any hardcoded Event Grid topic names or secret keys being used in the API Management policy definition. The copied Azure Event Grid topic name and secret key act as global variables and are used across multiple APIs and policy definitions:

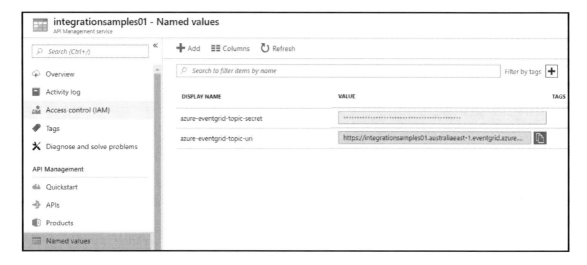

4. To test the endpoint, we need to either import an existing API definition or create a mock API endpoint in API Management. Here, we have added a mock API endpoint in the API Management instance and added policies to set the Event Grid URI along with the secret key for the Event Grid:

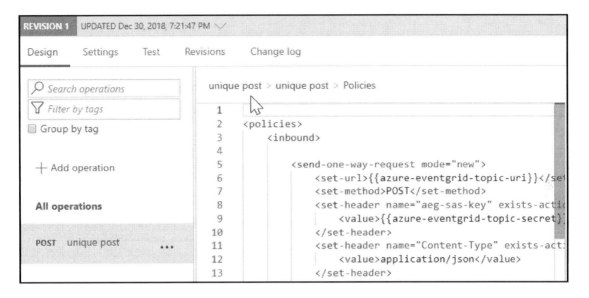

5. The next step is to fire a request with the test console using the API endpoint and API Management key. As we have registered Logic Apps as a webhook to Event Grid, we can see the new event being published to Logic Apps. After that, the events are routed to the CosmosDB, as follows:

6. Azure Functions is another events subscriber that subscribes through the Azure Event Grid subscription. In the following function definition, event details are sent to the Azure Notification Hub in real time:

```
[FunctionName("EventGridEventNotification")]
public static async Task<HttpResponseMessage> Run([HttpTrigger(AuthorizationLevel.Anonymous, "post", Route = null)]HttpRequestMessage req,
{
    string requestContent = await req.Content.ReadAsStringAsync();

    EventGridSubscriber eventGridSubscriber = new EventGridSubscriber();
    EventGridEvent[] eventGridEvents = eventGridSubscriber.DeserializeEventGridEvents(requestContent);

    foreach (EventGridEvent azevents in eventGridEvents)
    {
        if (azevents.Data is SubscriptionValidationEventData)
        {
            var EventData = (SubscriptionValidationEventData)azevents.Data;
            var responseData = new SubscriptionValidationResponse()
            {
                ValidationResponse = EventData.ValidationCode
            };
            return req.CreateResponse(HttpStatusCode.OK, responseData);
        }
        else
        {
            NotificationHubClient hub = NotificationHubClient.CreateClientFromConnectionString(notificationhubconnectionstring, notificationhu
            dynamic socialpost = JsonConvert.SerializeObject(azevents);

            Notification notification = new WindowsNotification(socialpost);
            notification.Headers.Add("X-WNS-Type", "wns/raw");
            var result = await hub.SendNotificationAsync(notification,"sample");
            return req.CreateResponse(HttpStatusCode.OK, result);
        }
    }
}
```

7. For this example, you need to register a Windows device that will listen for the events emitted through Azure Event Grid, though. As this chapter is not about the Notification Hub, we will skip this section, but to find out more about how you can register devices within the Notification Hub, make sure you take a look at the documentation link shared previously.

The Azure Notification Hub is a highly scalable push notification engine that can send events and messages to millions of devices at once. To learn more about the Notification Hub's capabilities, go through the Microsoft documentation at the following link: https://docs.microsoft.com/en-au/azure/notification-hubs/.

We have now discussed how to work with broadcasting patterns with security in mind for enterprise integrations. In the next hands-on lab, we will focus on Service Bus content routing using Logic Apps and Service Bus session management.

Example 4 – Session Management with Logic Apps and Service Bus

When working with Logic Apps as a distributed integration platform, we sometimes need to maintain the order in which messages are received. In integration terms, we call this pattern a sequential convoy.

In this exercise, we will go through the process of creating integration solutions with Azure Logic Apps and Service Bus to get a sequential flow of messages. We will use the session ID property of Service Bus with the Logic Apps Service Bus connector to route the messages to the backend system in the same order as they are received from the client application:

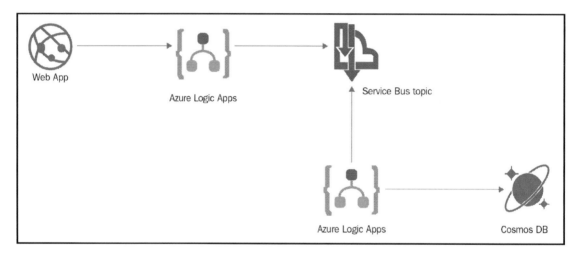

To illustrate this example, we will again take an example of a social media platform in which we are required to build a sequential pattern on a specific posts and comments made by multiple users within a specified time interval:

1. The first step here is to create a Service Bus topic and subscription in the Service Bus namespace resource when creating a subscription for the topic-enabled sessions property, as shown in the following screenshot:

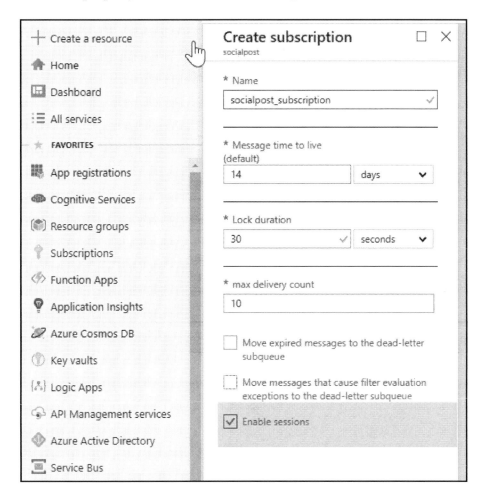

2. In the next step, we will create a Logic Apps instance that will poll the Service Bus topic at regular intervals of time.
3. As depicted in the next workflow, Logic Apps will get the first message from the Service Bus topic through a subscription filter and insert it into CosmosDB.

4. In the next set of actions, Logic Apps will use do-until actions to get all the messages from the Service Bus with the same session ID, as shown in the following process flow screenshot:

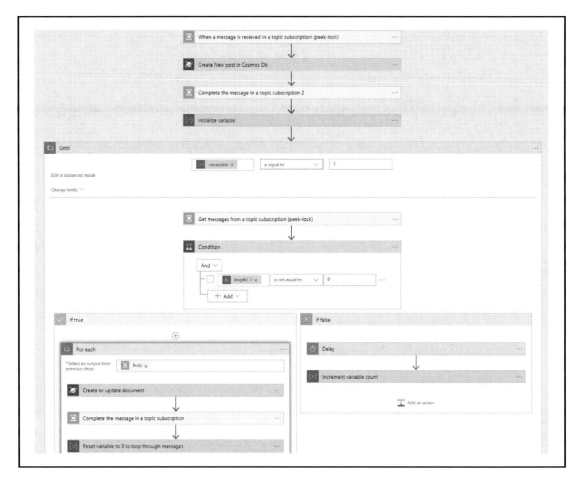

5. In this example, we have used a variable of integer type and initialized it with a value of 0. In the do-until loop, we will get the Service Bus message through Logic Apps' built-in connector and write each message to CosmosDB.

6. The loop process will run until all messages with the same session ID are retrieved and the variable count reaches 5.

There are a few things to keep in mind while working with session management in Logic Apps. These include choosing the right topic name and subscription associated with the topic and changing the session ID from the default value, **None**, to **Next Available**, as shown in the following screenshot:

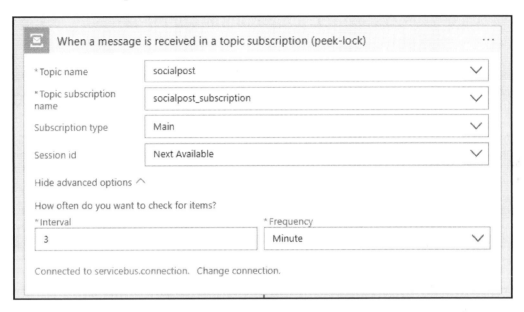

7. To verify that all messages with the same session ID have been picked up by the Logic Apps instance, we can use the `length` function available in Logic Apps. This `length` function will perform a conditional check based on the topic depth. You can write following the conceptional statement in the Logic Apps workflow definition:

```
"expression": {
    "and": [
        {
            "not": {
                "equals": [
                    "@length(body('Get_messages_from_a_topic_subscription_(peek-lock)'))",
                    0
                ]
            }
        }
    ]
},
"type": "If"
},
```

8. Next, we create a publisher logic app that will post messages to a Service Bus topic with the session ID and the related content. Here, we have used a social media website and used the original post ID as the session ID. The associated comments will have the same session ID but different content. The workflow definition of the Logic Apps message sender is shown in the following Logic Apps workflow:

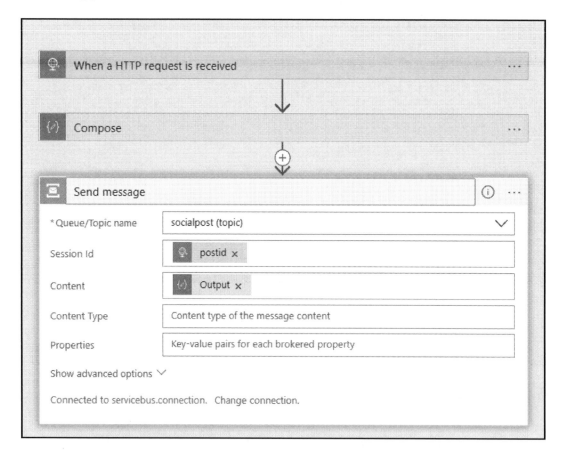

9. In this case, we have to use Postman to invoke the sender logic app's endpoint with the initial post and the related comments with the same session ID and a different request body. The comments will have their own unique identifier for CosmosDB, along with the session information. The overall execution of Logic Apps run is as follows:

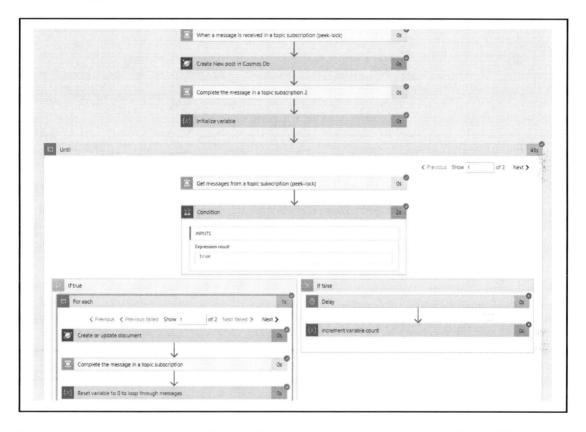

In this exercise, we have worked through session management and an ordered delivery process for Logic Apps. This pattern is useful when you need to maintain order or you need to work through batch processing using a Service Bus and Logic Apps workflow.

Summary

In this chapter, we have covered how to perform exception handling in Logic Apps along with multiple design patterns, such as a sequential message flow and a webhook for event-based architecture patterns. We have also looked at how to carry out simple batching using Logic Apps. In the next chapter, we will cover various other Logic Apps features and demonstrate how you can follow perfect DevOps practice for your enterprise integration solution in the cloud.

9
B2B/EDI Solutions for Enterprise Integration with Azure Logic Apps

In the modern digitized world, the success of any business is predominantly dependent on the digital ecosystem. This means that all the entities involved in a supply chain network must integrate, collaborate, and automate their processes. This is possible only when an organization has a mature and robust B2B integration strategy. A good integration strategy improves order delivery time, makes businesses more responsive to unforeseen events, makes invoice processing faster, reduces operational costs, and improves a business' competitive edge.

Microsoft Azure Integration Services such as Logic Apps, **API Management** (**APIM**), Service Bus, and Event Grid come together to build next-generation integration solutions. Even in this disruptive era of blockchain and artificial intelligence, legacy technologies such as those to do with **Electronic Data Interchange** (**EDI**) (such as EDIFACT, X12, and AS2) are still relevant to businesses. Keeping this in mind, Logic Apps comes with built-in capabilities for just such B2B scenarios.

In this chapter, we will explore the following concepts:

- Understanding Logic Apps' enterprise integration pack
- Creating a sample B2B scenario involving messaging protocols such as EDIFACT and transport protocols such as AS2
- A B2B, Logic Apps-based log analytics solution
- Batching X12 transactions.
- Understanding disaster recovery in B2B Logic Apps

Enterprise integration pack

If you are from a Microsoft BizTalk Server integration background, you will know about the various artifacts needed to build an integration interface. These artifacts include schemas in the XSD file format, XSLT maps, trading partners, and agreements, and X.509 certificates for encryption and the signing of AS2 messages. Logic Apps' enterprise integration pack is a collection of these enterprise capabilities, which you can subscribe to via an integration account:

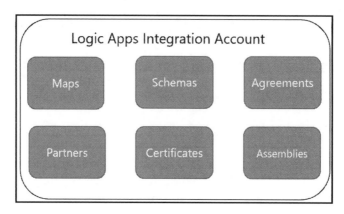

An integration account allows you to build Logic Apps with enterprise B2B capabilities by allowing developers to add various necessary artifacts. The following are the various artifacts that can be added with an integration account:

- **Schemas**: These are standard .xsd files containing the definition of an XML message. If you have BizTalk installed, you can create a BizTalk schema project and add create XSD files visually. You can add these XSD files in an integration account. If you do not have BizTalk installed, you can download Logic Apps Enterprise Integration Tools for Visual Studio 2015, which helps users to create schemas.

- **Maps**: These are XSLT files that transform XML messages from one format to another. Similar to schemas, you can either use a BizTalk transformation project or the integration tools for Visual Studio 2015 to create XSLT files.

- **Agreements**: Business partners need to agree upon some standard rules and protocols to establish B2B communications with each other. These rules will be defined in agreements. These agreements are specific to protocols such as EDIFACT, X12, AS2, and others.

- **Partners**: This is an entity that defines trading partner information. Partner entities will come together in one or more agreements.
- **Certificates**: Since business transactions are sensitive and prone to security breaches, it is important to have a secure AS2 connection. AS2 connections make use of X.509 certificates. Public keys in the .cer format and private certificates in the .pfx format can be uploaded into certificates, and AS2 protocols will use these.
- **Assemblies**: In BizTalk maps, it is common to use helper .NET assemblies. To allow a similar approach in Logic Apps maps (XSLT files), you can upload assemblies into an integration account.

B2B scenario

To understand the capabilities of an integration account, we'll make use of a fictitious company called **ShipAnyWhere**. The **ShipAnyWhere** is a large logistics company that is specialized in commerce and fulfillment solutions for e-commerce businesses around the world. It has got more than 100 distribution centers across more than 30 countries. It provides B2B, e-commerce, and multi-channel fulfillment solutions to its customers using cutting-edge technologies.

It has a trading partner called **Contoso**, who sends X12 orders over AS2. In our scenario, we assume both **Contoso** and **ShipAnyWhere** make use of Logic Apps:

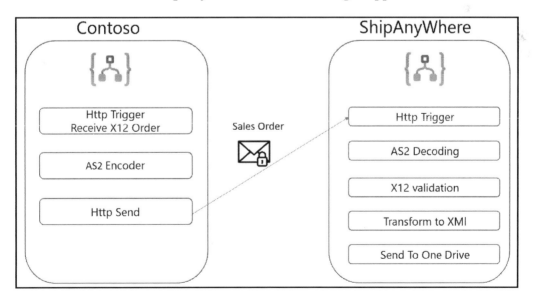

The following are the steps involved in processing order messages from **Contoso** to **ShipAnyWhere**:

1. Contoso generates an X12 order in a logic app. However, for demonstration purposes, we are assuming that the Contoso Logic App receives an EDI X12 order from a postman.

2. In the Contoso Logic App, the X12 order message will be encoded to AS2 using an AS2 encode connector.

3. The encoded message will be sent to the ShipAnyWhere Logic App over HTTP.

4. ShipAnywhere decodes the AS2 message. This means the message will be verified for a signature and then decrypted.

5. An X12 connector validates the decrypted message and converts it to an XML message.

6. The decrypted X12 message will be transformed into an internal XML format, and it will be pushed to a blob location mimicking an end system.

Creating integration accounts

For our scenario, we need two integration accounts. Let's call one `Contoso-SupplyChain` and create it under an Azure resource group called **Contoso-B2B.** Let the second integration account be `ShipAnyWhere-SupplyChain`, and create it under an Azure resource group called **ShipAnyWhere**:

Integration Account   Microsoft

Use the Azure marketplace and create these two integration accounts as described previously:

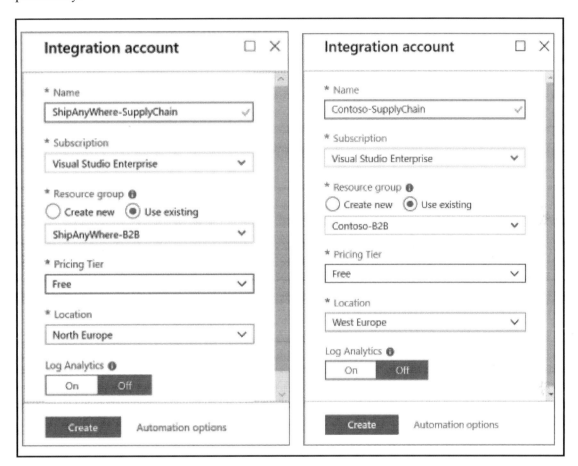

Uploading certificates to Azure Key Vault

For the AS2 transport protocol, both Contoso and ShipAnyWhere must make use of x509 certificates for signing and encryption. In this section, we will see how certificates can be created and uploaded to an integration account.

Creating certificates

For encryption and signing, we need the private and public keys of both Contoso and ShipAnyWhere. Certificates can be created with the `MakeCert` utility (`https://msdn.microsoft.com/en-us/library/windows/desktop/aa386968(v=vs.85).aspx`). I used the following command-line tools to generate the keys:

```
makecert -r -pe -n "CN=www.Contoso.com" -b 01/01/2019 -e 03/23/2036 -eku
1.3.6.1.5.5.7.3.1 -ss my "Contoso.cer" -sr currentuser -sky exchange -sp
"Microsoft RSA SChannel Cryptographic Provider" -sy 12 -a "sha1" -nscp
makecert -r -pe -n "CN=www.ShipAnyWhere.com" -b 01/01/2019 -e 03/23/2036 -
eku 1.3.6.1.5.5.7.3.1 -ss my "ShipAnyWhere.cer" -sr currentuser -sky
exchange -sp "Microsoft RSA SChannel Cryptographic Provider" -sy 12 -a
"sha1" -nscp
```

 Private and public key pairs are already available in the GitHub repository. You can use those files straight away. The password for these private keys is B2B.

Creating a key vault service in each resource group

A key vault service needs to be created in each resource group.

The following screenshot shows how to create a key vault service for Contoso. Logic Apps gets permission to access a key vault using the service principal. In the **Add new** access policy blade, select **Azure Logic Apps** as a service principal:

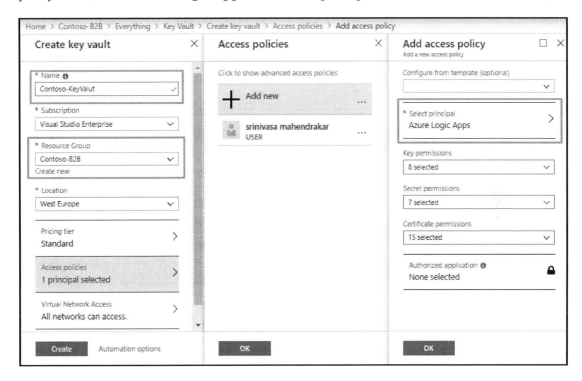

In the **Key permissions** dropdown, ensure that you have selected the permissions shown in the following screenshot. These permissions are necessary for Logic Apps to use the certificate for encryption, decryption, signing, and signature verification:

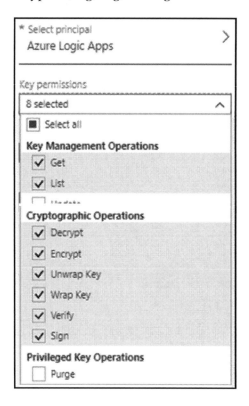

Similarly, create a key vault service named `ShipAnyWhere-KeyVault` in the `ShipAnyWhere-B2B` resource group.

Uploading the private key certificates to the key vaults

Once the key vaults are created, we will have to upload the private keys of **Contoso** and **ShipAnyWhere** to their respective key vaults.

In a key vault, you will have the option to either import a key or generate a new key. Since we have already created a certificate in the previous steps, we will use the **Import** option. In the **File Upload** box, select the `Contoso.pfx` private key file:

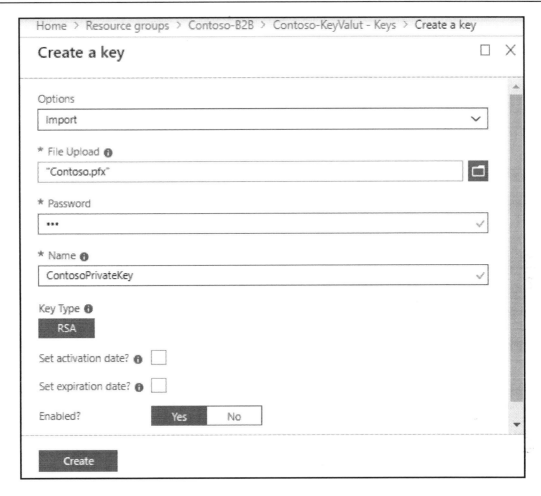

Similarly, upload the `ShipAnyWhere.pfx` file to `ShipAnyWhere-KeyVault`.

Adding certificates to an integration account

In the integration accounts, we will need to add the following different types of certificate:

- The private key certificate (the one uploaded to the key vault) of the host organization
- The public key certificate of the host organization
- The public key certificate of the trading partners

In the **Contoso-SupplyChain** integration account, navigate to **Certificates** and select **Add**:

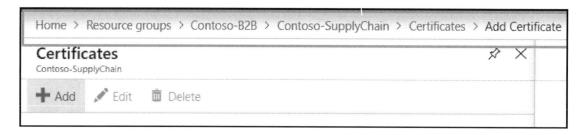

In the **Add Certificate** blade, provide an appropriate **Name**, set the **Certificate Type** to **Private**, upload a public key certificate, and select **ContosoPrivateKey** from **Contoso-KeyVault**:

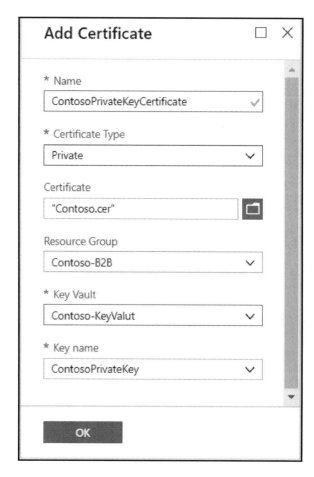

Similarly, add the `Contoso.cer` (host public key certificate) and `ShipAnyWhere.cer` (trading partner public key certificate) public keys to the integration account. In this case, select **Public** as the **Certificate Type**:

Once all these certificates are added, we should see the following list in the **Contoso-SupplyChain** | **Certificates** section:

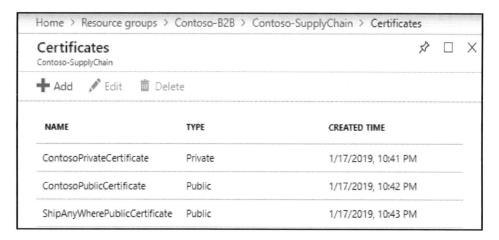

Follow the steps described previously to upload the following certificates to the **ShipAnyWhere-SupplyChain** integration account:

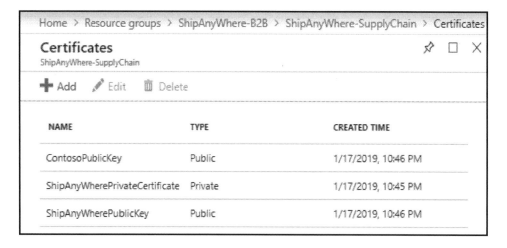

Uploading schemas and maps

In any B2B interface implementation, schemas and maps play a vital role. Schemas ensure that the messages sent from the trading partner stick to a specific EDI standard. Maps help to translate messages from one format to another.

In our scenario, ShipAnyWhere receives an **X12_00401_850** message, so we need the corresponding X12 schema. We also need to convert the X12 format message into an internal purchase order format, so we will have to upload the following two schema files:

 If you have used the BizTalk EDI feature, you will know that BizTalk provides built-in EDI schemas for a range of versions. The same XSD schemas can be used for Logic Apps as well. However, if you do not have BizTalk installed, download Microsoft Azure Logic Apps Enterprise Integration Tools for Visual Studio 2015 2.0 `https://www.microsoft.com/en-us/download/details.aspx?id=53016`. This add-on to Visual Studio helps you to create XSD schemas for various versions of the X12 and EDIFACT standards.

Upload the `Inbound850ToPurchaseOrder.xslt` file to **Maps** in the integration account:

Creating partners in an integration account

Any B2B messages will have sender and receiver IDs in their headers. These IDs, along with some **Qualifier** fields, uniquely identify a trading partner. Any EDI engine should be capable of reading these header values and resolving the corresponding configuration. To help this kind of partner resolution, we have to create a partner entity. These partner entities must be created for both the host and trading partners.

In the **Contoso-SupplyChain** integration account, we have to create two trading partners, named `Contoso` and `ShipAnyWhere`:

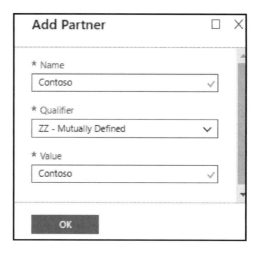

The qualifiers need to be agreed between the trading partners, and they will be used in the EDI messages. The following is our sample EDI header:

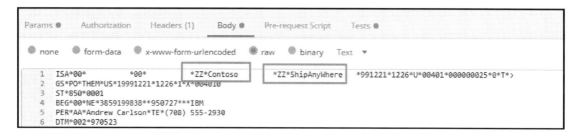

Since we are planning to exchange messages over AS2, we will also need to add AS2Identities for both partners. The following screenshot shows that **Contoso_AS2** is added as an **AS2Identity** for Contoso:

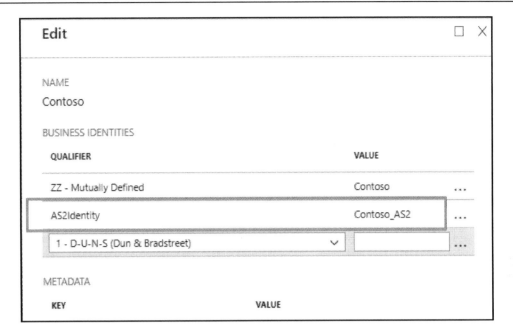

Similarly, add **ShipAnyWhere_AS2** as the **AS2Identity** for **ShipAnyWhere**.

Similar to the previous steps, we need to create two partners, named `Contoso` and `ShipAnyWhere`, in the **ShipAnyWhere-SupplyChain** integration account:

Creating AS2 agreements

When two trading partners exchange messages over the AS2 protocol, they generally agree upon a few configurations of the AS2 protocol. Some of these configurations are detailed here:

- They need to agree upon the AS2 identifiers used in AS2 messages
- They need to agree on whether they are going to sign messages with a cryptographic signature
- They need to agree on whether they are going to encrypt messages
- They need to decide whether they want to send out MDNs after an AS2 message is received
- They need to decide whether MDNs are generated synchronously or asynchronously
- They need to decide whether MDNs will be signed or encrypted

Once these configurations are agreed upon, they need to ensure that the EDI engine enforces them. Integration accounts provide the option to store and enforce them through AS2 agreements.

In our scenario, we need to create AS2 agreements in both integration accounts.

Creating AS2 agreements in Contoso

In the **Contoso_SupplyChain** integration account, select the option to add an integration account:

1. Select **Contoso_ShipAnyWhere_AS2** as the **Name** of the agreement
2. Select **AS2** as the **Agreement type**
3. Since we are creating this agreement in Contoso's integration account, select **Contoso** as **Host Partner**
4. Select **Contoso_AS2** as **Host Identity**
5. Select **ShipAnyWhere_AS2** as **Guest Identity**:

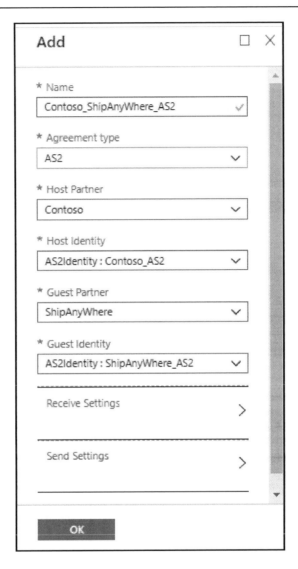

In our scenario, Contoso does not receive AS2 messages. However, it receives MDNs back from ShipAnyWhere. As such, the **Receive Settings** need to be configured as well.

Both Contoso and ShipAnyWhere decided to encrypt and sign the messages they exchange:

- Select ShipAnyWhere's public key certificate as a signing certificate for verifying signatures
- Select **ContosoPrivateKeyCertificate** as the encryption key used to decrypt messages:

Contoso sends messages to ShipAnyWhere. As such, we need to configure the sender-side settings as well:

1. Tick the **Enable message signing** checkbox and select **ContosoPrivateKeyCertificate**:

2. Tick on **Enable message encryption** and select **ShipAnyWherePublicKeyCertificate**:

3. In the **Acknowledgement** settings, select **Request MDN** and **Request signed MDN** options:

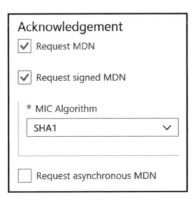

Creating an AS2 agreement for ShipAnyWhere

In the **ShipAnyWhere_SupplyChain** integration account, select the option to add an AS2 agreement:

1. Select **ShipAnyWhere_AS2** as **Host Partner** and **Contoso_AS2** as **Guest Partner**.
2. In the **Receive Settings**, select the option to **Override message properties**. This ensures that the protocol details present in the AS2 message will be overridden from the configurations in the agreement.
3. In the **Receive Settings**, enable the **Message should be signed** option and select the **ContosoPublic** key.
4. In the **Receive Settings**, enable the **Message should be encrypted** option and select **ShipAnyWherePrivateCertificate**.
5. In the receive settings, select the **Send MDN** and **Send Signed MDN** options.

Keep all **Send Settings** as is, without any changes.

Creating an X12 agreement

In B2B messaging, both trading partners need to agree upon variants of the messaging protocols, such as X12 and EDIFACT. The following are a few configurations the trading partners should agree upon:

- The EDI format, such as X12 or EDIFACT
- The version of the protocol standards; for example, X12 has versions ranging from 00100 to 00700
- The EDI sender and receiver IDs used in the EDI messages
- The kind of acknowledgments generated; for example, functional or technical acknowledgments

All these can be defined in X12 or EDIFACT agreements in an integration account.

In our scenario, Contoso is not making use of X12 connectors. As such, we don't have to create an X12 agreement for Contoso. However, on the ShipAnyWhere side, we will create an X12 agreement called **ShipAnyWere_Contoso**:

In the **Receive Settings**, leave all the options as they are by default, except adding the **VERSION**, **TRANSACTION TYPE**, and their corresponding **SCHEMA**, which should be set to **X12_00401_850**, as shown here:

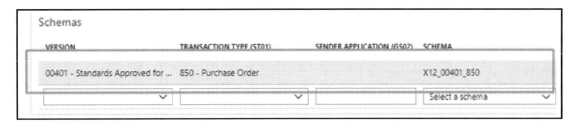

Now we have all the artifacts in our integration account, it's time to create a **ShipAnyWhereOrderProcess** Logic App. The Logic App must perform the following things:

1. Receive an AS2 message over HTTP
2. Verify the signature
3. Decrypt the message
4. Send out the MDN and its status
5. Use an X12 connector to decode the X12 message and convert it into an XML payload
6. Generate acknowledgments
7. Transform the X12 XML payload to a `PurchaseOrder` XML
8. Send the transformed XML to a blob location

In the Azure portal, create a Logic App named `ShipAnyWhereOrderProcess`. Once the Logic App is successfully created, navigate to **Workflow settings** under the **Settings** tab and choose the **ShipAnyWhere-SupplyChain** integration account. Associating an integration account allows the Logic App to access all the artifacts that we created under it:

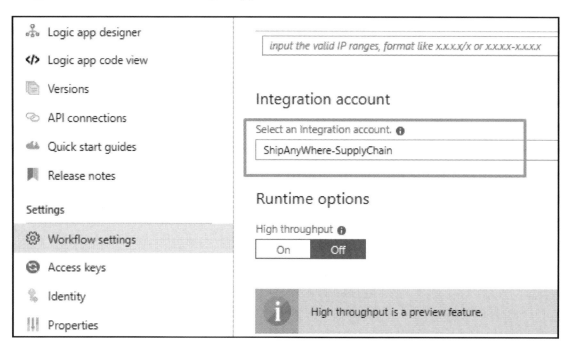

Now we need to define the Logic App with various actions. The Microsoft Logic Apps team has implemented the great option of built-in templates, where you will quickly be able to define a Logic App for a specific scenario. Since, in our case, we are working on the AS2 and X12 protocols, we can easily create one by making use of the **Receive an X12 EDI document over AS2 and transform it to XML** template:

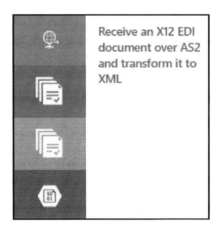

The template allows you to configure the connectors one by one. For AS2 connection configuration, select the name and the **ShipAnyWhere-SupplyChain** integration account, as shown in the following screenshot:

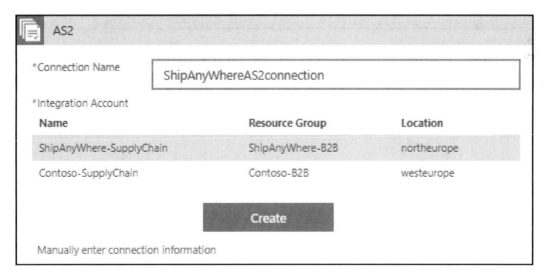

For the X12 connector, provide the appropriate name and select the **ShipAnyWhere-SupplyChain** integration account, as shown in the following screenshot:

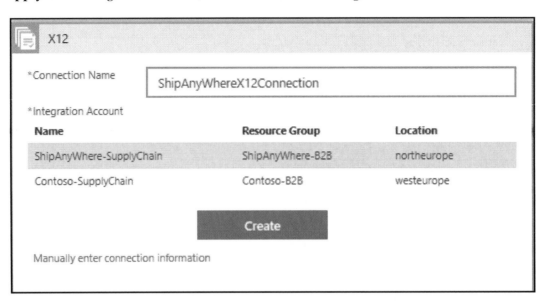

For the blob location, ensure that you have a storage account and provide the account name and access key:

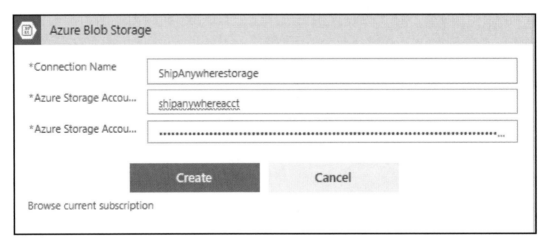

Once all the information is provided, the creation wizard allows you to **Continue**:

Once you click **Continue**, you will have a logic app with most of the connectors already available, with a few pending configurations:

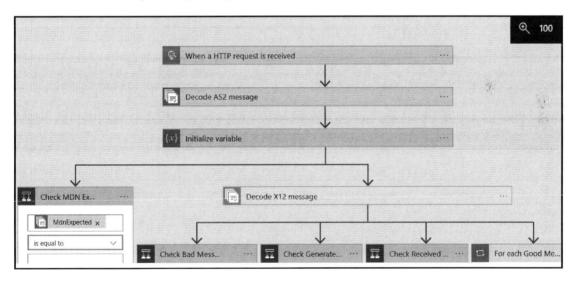

Updating those few pending configurations is done as follows:

1. In the X12 connector, change the X12 flat file message to a decode value with the following expression:

```
base64ToString(body('Decode_AS2_message')?['AS2Message']?['Content'])
```

2. In the transform connector, configure the content with the following expression:

```
xml(base64ToBinary(item()?['Payload']))
```

3. In the transform connector, select the **Inbound850ToPurchaseOrder** as **Map** file:

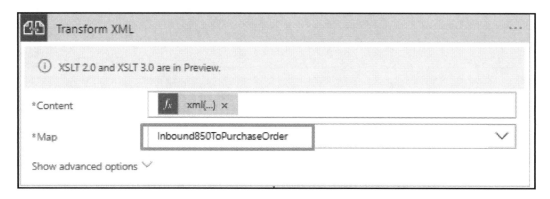

4. For the blob connector, select the options as shown in the following screenshot:

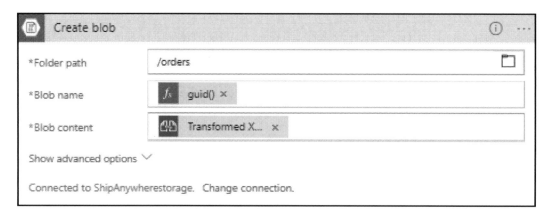

Creating the ContosoSendOrder Logic App

In this section, we are going to create the **ContosoSendOrder** Logic App. Since there are no templates available for HTTP receive and AS2 send, we will have to create them ourselves:

1. Create a Logic App named `ContosoSendOrder`
2. Navigate to **Workflow settings** and select the **Contoso-SupplyChain** integration account
3. In **Definition**, select **HTTP request trigger**
4. Add the **Encode to AS2 message** connector and select the **Contoso-SupplyChain** integration account
5. Configure the **Encode to AS2 message** connector as follows:

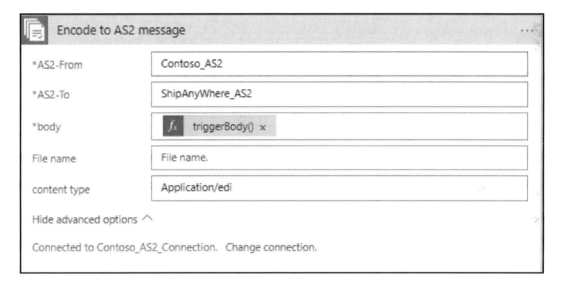

6. Configure the **HTTP** action to **POST** the message to **ShipAnyWhereOrderService**:

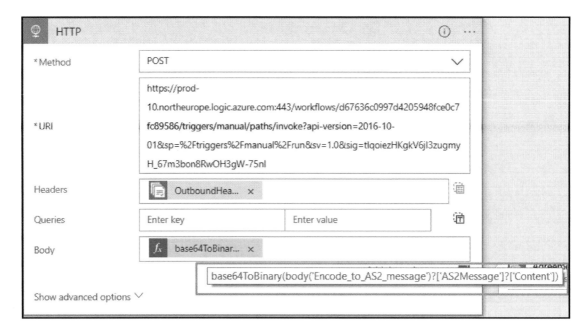

7. Ensure that the body is binary encoded using the following expression:

```
base64ToBinary(body('Encode_to_AS2_message')?['AS2Message']?['Conte
nt'])
```

8. Post the following X12 message to the **ContosoSendOrder** Logic App:

```
ISA*00*          *00*          *ZZ*Contoso        *ZZ*ShipAnyWhere
*991221*1226*U*00401*000000025*0*T*>
GS*PO*THEM*US*19991221*1226*1*X*004010
ST*850*0001
BEG*00*NE*3859199838**950727***IBM
PER*AA*Andrew Carlson*TE*(708) 555-2930
DTM*002*970523
PO1*1*93*BX*145.39**CB*KOW-20392-10
PID*F****Uninterruptible Power System
PER*AA*Camilla Anderson*TE*(708) 555-2011
PO1*2*25*EA*35.68**CB*1093-4927-001
PID*F****High Volume Printer Stand
PER*AA*Miranda Cappelan*TE*(708) 555-1111
PO1*3*4*PC*2002.91**CB*ABX-2001
PID*F****Electronics Cabinet Package (56" High)
```

```
CTT*3
SE*14*0001
GE*1*1
IEA*1*000000025
```

When both Logic Apps are successfully executed, you should have an XML purchase order in ShipAnyWhere's blob location.

Successful execution of the **ContosoSendOrder** Logic App should look as follows:

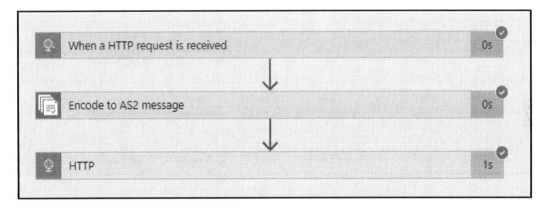

Successful execution of **ShipAnyWhereOrderProcess** is as follows:

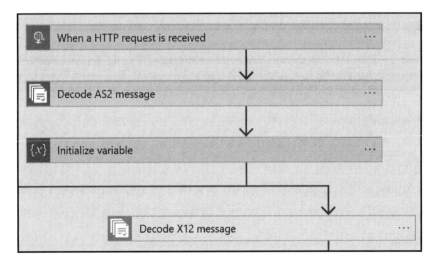

The Logic Apps B2B solution

When creating the samples for this chapter, I faced various issues. The run history was not giving me enough information; I needed to look somewhere for more logs. This will be the case when we work on real-world scenarios.

In the BizTalk server, EDI provides built-in reports on AS2/EDI transactions that are processed, as well as some analytics on those transactions. Any EDI engine should have the capability to provide analytics for their users.

Such needs are common in the EDI world, and so the Logic Apps team introduced the Logic Apps B2B Solution, which allows users to monitor and manage B2B logic flows involving the AS2, X12, and EDIFACT protocols. This solution lets users view and react to message exchanges with trading partners and identify the root causes.

The following are some of the core capabilities of the Logic Apps B2B Solution:

- See all transaction processing by status at a glance
- Use trading partner-specific views to find out which trading partner message exchanges are having issues
- View by protocols such as AS2, EDIFACT, and X12 to easily find where problems are occurring
- Use message-centric views to understand the processing flow of your Logic Apps, including key tracking data items to react quickly to problems
- Search through all tracking data and find any piece of information

The Logic Apps B2B Solution works with integration accounts. I took the following steps to enable this in the **ShipAnyWhere_SupplyChain** integration account.

Creating a workspace and adding the B2B solution

Create a **Log Analytics** workspace called **ShipAnyWhere** under the **ShipAnyWhere-B2B** resource group:

Once the workspace is created, add two solutions as follows:

Associating the Log Analytics workspace with an integration account

Once the workspace is created, we have to associate it with an integration account to log all B2B events:

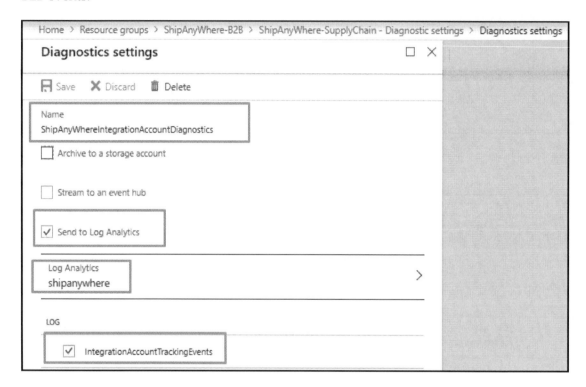

The following are the necessary configurations for the **Diagnostics settings**:

1. Under the **ShipAnyWhere-SupplyChain** integration account's **Diagnostics settings**, select the option to **Add new settings**.
2. Give an appropriate name. I named it **ShipAnyWhereIntegrationAccountDiagnostics**.
3. Select the **Send to Log Analytics** option.
4. Under **Log Analytics**, select the **ShipAnyWhere** workspace.
5. Finally, under the **LOG** section, select **IntegrationAccountTrackingEvents**.

Once you send a few messages, you will be able to see some very useful charts, provided by **Log Analytics**:

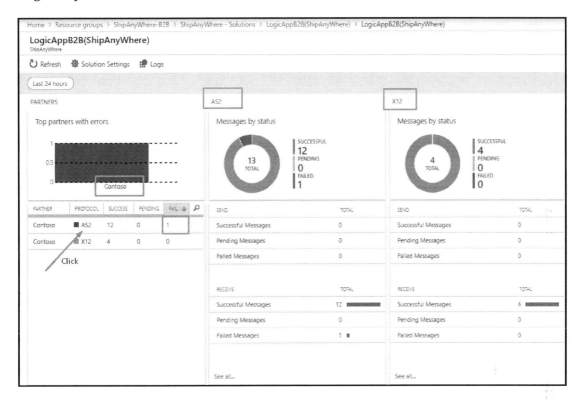

From the preceding charts, you can see that there was a failure in my AS2 flow. When you click on the **AS2 protocol** row, you will see all the AS2 transactions as follows:

If you want to dig deeper into the logs related to the failed transaction, click on the row with the failed status. This opens a lot of log entries:

Handling EDI batches

In B2B scenarios, it is quite common for trading partners to collect all the EDI transactions and send them in a batch either on a time basis or based on some transactions in the batch. Invoice and payment transactions, for instance, are often batched and sent out for nightly batch processing. Logic Apps have batch triggers built in. By combining batch triggers with EDI encoding, we will be able to achieve B2B batching scenarios.

Let's assume that ShipAnyWhere sends batches of orders to Contoso for batch processing. The scenario is depicted here:

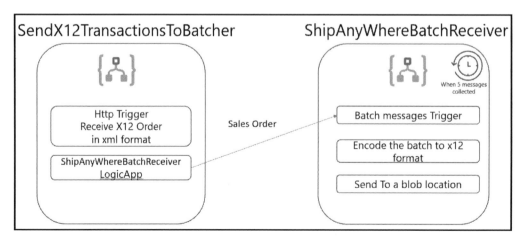

The ShipAnyWhereBatchReceiver Logic App

If we want to collect individual orders for a period of time or wait until n number of transactions have been generated before sending out a batch, we need a batching process. Logic Apps have the built-in capability to create these batch processes by making use of batch message triggers. In our scenario, **ShipAnyWhereBatchReceive** is a batch process that will trigger when it collects five orders and creates an X12 batch, which will be sent to a blob location. The following gives the implementation details of the Logic App:

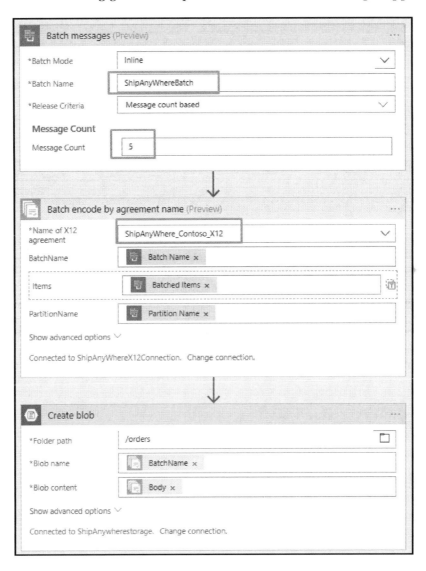

For the Batch encode connector to resolve the X12 schema correctly, we have to configure the **ShipAnyWhere_Contoso x12** agreement's sender settings as follows:

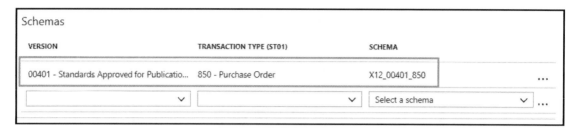

The SendX12TransactionToBatcher Logic App

When we want to send out a batch to our trading partner, there must be logic apps to generate individual transactions. These logic apps, instead of sending the individual transactions immediately to a trading partner, send them to a batch process. As such, these Logic App act as individual transaction ingestors to batch processes. The implementation is as follows:

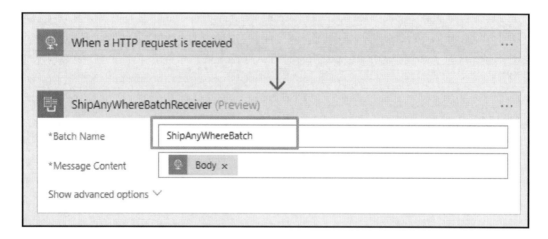

Testing the scenario

Use Postman to send the contents of the sample X12 XML file (`BatchingTest_X12_850_Transaction.xml`) to the **SendX12TransactionToBatcher** Logic App. When you send the message five times, the **ShipAnyWhereBatchReceive** Logic App triggers and releases a batch into the blob location.

B2B disaster recovery

Transactions such as orders, invoices, and shipping notices all involve quite a lot of monetary transactions. Businesses are heavily dependent on the uninterrupted running of their EDI solutions. If for any reason, disaster was to strike and the region in which the B2B solutions are deployed was to go down, business would be halted by the disruption of the transactions. This would be catastrophic for the business. To mitigate the risk of disaster and to ensure business continuity, every EDI provider must provide a disaster recovery plan.

Microsoft's B2B transaction disaster recovery depends on deploying redundant services in different geographical regions. In our scenario, ShipAnyWhere has to implement a disaster recovery plan. They have to deploy all the resources under the ShipAnyWhere-B2B resource group to a new region:

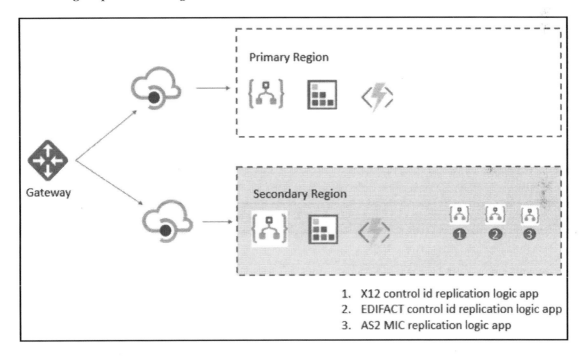

1. X12 control id replication logic app
2. EDIFACT control id replication logic app
3. AS2 MIC replication logic app

X12/EDIFACT control ID replication Logic Apps

Just deploying services such as Logic Apps and your integration account is not going to solve the disaster recovery problem completely – B2B transactions are state-based and each protocol is dependent on some state numbers. In the case of X12, it is an interchange control number. It is important to ensure that when failover happens from one region to another, the control numbers are in sync. This is mainly because most of the trading partner systems will reject duplicate interchange control numbers.

Given all that, in the secondary region, it is important to have a Logic App that looks for interchange control number changes in the primary region and periodically replicates any changes to the secondary region. A typical implementation of such a Logic App looks as follows:

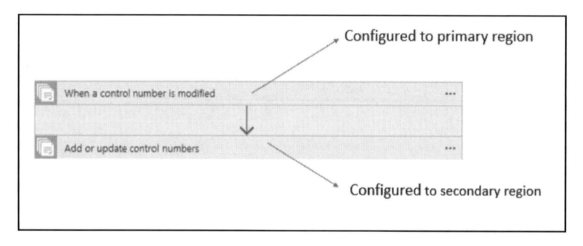

AS2 Message Integrity Check (MIC) replication Logic App

For the AS2 protocol, it is important to replicate the MIC value. A typical implementation of the MIC value is shown here:

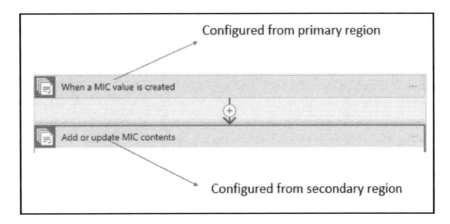

Summary

In this chapter, we learned that creating B2B flows is quite simple when using Logic Apps and an integration account. In the Microsoft integration world, customers are slowly but steadily moving from BizTalk-based on-premises integrations to Logic Apps-based integrations. EDI/AS2-based integrations are the ones that are moving to the cloud the fastest.

10
Hybrid Integration, BizTalk Server 2016 and an On-Premises Data Gateway

This chapter introduces the concept of hybrid integration using an on-premises data gateway and BizTalk 2016's new cloud integration capabilities. It will explain how we can create a bridge between applications running within enterprise firewalls and cloud-hosted services by taking advantage of Logic Apps, on-premises data gateways, and BizTalk's extensive integration capabilities.

We will cover the following topics in this chapter:

- Introduction to hybrid integration
- Why hybrid integration?
- Introduction to the on-premises data gateway
- What's new in Microsoft BizTalk Server 2016
- Integrating a Logic App with an on-premises data gateway
- Integrating a BizTalk server with Logic Apps

Introduction to hybrid integration

For many years, organizations have spent huge amounts building custom applications and infrastructure, such as on-premises services, running within their company firewalls. Most of these custom-build applications hold large amounts of business-centric data. With the shift toward the cloud and the global market, businesses are being required to share data, in one form or another, with customers and partners in a secure manner. Coupled with commitments to their cloud adoption strategies, organizations are also making huge investments in cloud offerings by looking at the benefits of multiple **Software-as-a-Service (SaaS)** products and **Platform-as-a-Service (PaaS)** offerings.

The big challenge these organizations are facing is bridging the gap between on-premises resources sitting behind corporate firewalls and cloud services in a secure manner. To solve this mission-critical issue, hybrid integration is increasingly being applied. In a hybrid cloud infrastructure approach, customers use cloud services to deploy servers and platforms within an extended network connected to their local domain. Hybrid solutions span the cloud (whether it be a public, private, or community cloud) and on-premises resources within the corporate local network. Hybrid integration is the key enabler for an enterprise to be able to use their existing infrastructure and data with SaaS and PaaS offerings on the cloud. Hybrid integration is a robust way of innovating with existing data, taking a competitive advantage and creating a new business model:

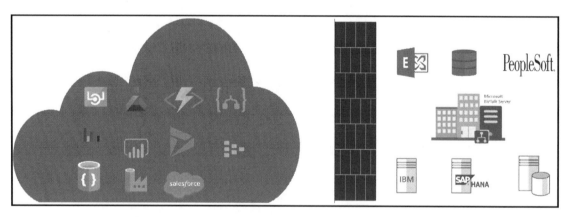

Why hybrid integration?

Data is more important than ever. An organization relies heavily on its existing data for both current market requirements and future innovation. In the journey of digital transformation, applications can span cloud-based and on-premises environments. Hybrid integration provides a perfect middleware solution for enterprises, ensuring that data from on-premises legacy systems can integrate with cloud solutions in a secure manner. This also ensures that businesses can take full advantage of existing infrastructure when driving the business forward.

Hybrid solutions provide many advantages compared to solutions based on running within a corporate firewall. Some of those benefits are discussed here:

- **Maximization of past and existing investment**: Most businesses have invested huge amounts of resources in building custom enterprise applications and storing data that is relevant to their business. For many businesses, data is the key enabler for future innovation, and in most cases, data resides within legacy systems sitting on premises. With the advent of a more competitive market, businesses are taking advantage of cloud applications that can talk securely to on-premises applications to give a new avenue for future growth. Hybrid integration provides a layer over legacy enterprise applications to give optimal access to business-relevant data. Hybrid integration provides benefits in terms of reduced cost, easy maintenance, better connectivity, and more.

- **Standards and regulations**: Organizations cannot move whole applications to the cloud due to regulatory compliance, as some data must remain within the corporate firewall, and cannot be accessed from outside. (These rules particularly apply for the financial and banking sectors.) As such, creating a cloud-only system is not possible, and so hybrid integration is the best possible action.

- **Security and privacy**: Businesses are always concerned about storing sensitive data in the cloud. With hybrid integration, businesses can choose what data can be stored in the cloud and what data should remain within the corporate firewall but still be accessed in a secure way through a hybrid integration layer.

- **Wider audience**: With hybrid integration, businesses can reach a wide range of consumers by enabling customer-facing applications running on the cloud. Most cloud infrastructure can be auto-scaled based on demand, which gives businesses the opportunity to expand in different regions.

Introduction to the on-premises data gateway

An on-premises data gateway acts as a bridge between on-premises data sources behind corporate firewalls and cloud-hosted services such as Logic Apps, Azure Analysis Services, PowerApps, PowerBI, and Microsoft flow. An on-premises data gateway ensures that communication between Azure-hosted services and applications running on premises is secure, while still leveraging the capabilities of the cloud. To use an on-premises data gateway, there are certain infrastructure requirements, which are described in the Microsoft documentation
at `https://docs.microsoft.com/en-us/power-bi/service-gateway-onprem`.

Setting up an on-premises data gateway is a four-step process:

1. **Download and run the on-premises data gateway**: The first step is to download the data gateway setup from Microsoft
   (`https://aka.ms/azureasgatewayon`) and run the setup .exe. This will prompt you to specify the location. Enter the location and accept the terms and conditions, then click on **Install** to install the gateway setup in your local environment.

2. **Register the gateway for secure connection**: In this step, provide the name and recovery key, which will be used to register the gateway with gateway cloud services, and click on **Configure**:

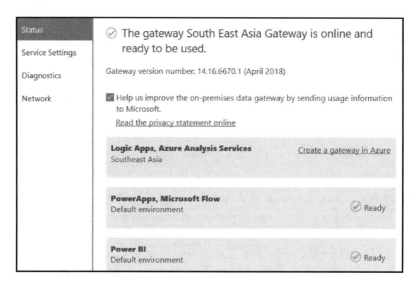

3. **Gateway resource in Azure**: In the next step, you need to create a gateway resource in your Azure subscription. For this, you first need to log in to the Azure portal with the login credentials you used to register the gateway in the previous step and create an on-premises data gateway instance, which you can do via the enterprise integration blade. Once completed, verify the on-premises data gateway instance within the resource group:

4. Connect your servers to your gateway resource: Configure your connections to use the on-premises data gateway. This will allow your servers to be accessed by services such as Logic Apps, Microsoft Flow, and PowerApps.

 If you are looking for detailed documentation about the configuration and setup of an on-premises data gateway, then see the Microsoft documentation
at `https://docs.microsoft.com/en-us/azure/analysis-services/analy sis-services-gateway-install`.

On-premises Data Gateway Architecture

This section will describe the basic architecture of an on-premises data gateway and list the different components that communicate with each other to provide secure messaging between cloud-hosted services and on-premises resources.

When you install and configure your instance of an on-premises data gateway on a server, it creates a gateway that runs under NT SERVICE\PBIEgwService. With initial On-premise data gateway Setup NT SERVICE\PBIEgwService gets log-on-as-service rights on the server and uses port 443 for outbound communicate with other Azure services.

Under the hood, after the installation/configuration of an on-premises data gateway, it is registered with the gateway-cloud service hosted on Azure with Azure Service Bus. The architecture is described in the following diagram:

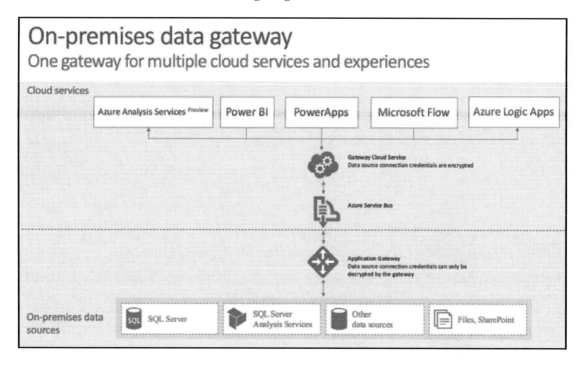

Let's now analyze what happens when queries and data flow through an on-premises data gateway:

1. When a query is created by the cloud service, the cloud service sends the query along with the encrypted credentials for the on-premises data source to the gateway to process.
2. The gateway cloud service will then look into the query and send the request to the Azure Service Bus queue.
3. The on-premises data gateway polls the Azure Service Bus queue for any new service requests.
4. The gateway then gets the query, decrypts the credentials, and connects to the systems with those credentials.

5. The gateway sends the message to the data source for execution.

6. The results are sent from the data source back to the gateway, and then on to the cloud service. The service then uses the results returned from the on-premises data gateway.

Enabling Hybrid Integration with Microsoft BizTalk Server 2016

Microsoft BizTalk Server is a central platform for hybrid integration. For many years, BizTalk Server has served as the mainstream integration platform for customers the world over. With the 2016 release, Microsoft BizTalk Server has come up with a better hybrid cloud integration strategy that has support for Logic Apps, API Management, Service Bus, Power BI, and more.

With Microsoft BizTalk Server 2016 and the integration of Logic Apps into the workflow, enterprises can now easily connect to any number of cloud-hosted services, such as CRM Online, Salesforce, Dynamics AX, and Azure Active Directory. For example, when a new user is added in Azure Active Directory, an enterprise can easily share the user details with applications sitting within the corporate firewall by using a Logic Apps connector.

We will discuss Logic Apps adapters in detail in the coming sections, and we will see how easily we can create a connection with Logic Apps and BizTalk, using the power of both integration offerings to build a hybrid solution.

Traditionally, BizTalk Server is used for the following:

- Enterprise application integration
- B2B
- Business process automation

In the coming sections, we will discuss the options available for making hybrid connections between Azure and on-premises BizTalk Server.

Azure Service Bus Relay

Azure Service Bus Relay is a cloud-based service that allows you to host an endpoint that relays any request to a listener associated with that endpoint. The Service Bus Relay service enables us to build hybrid applications that are exposed in the cloud but hosted locally in your on-premises environment using **Windows Communication Foundation (WCF)**. WCF relay bindings that permit BizTalk as a listening service on the relay point can be combined with WCF adapters to use BizTalk:

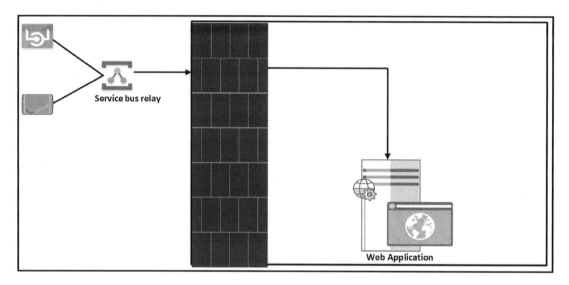

The WCF-WebHttp, WCF-BasicHttp, and NetTCpRealy adapters in BizTalk allow the sending and receiving of messages through Azure Service Bus Relay using BizTalk as the service broker between the on-premises application and the cloud-based application.

For more detail, see the following documentation:
https://docs.microsoft.com/en-gb/azure/service-bus-relay/relay-w
cf-dotnet-get-started.

The Service Bus (SB) – Messaging adapter

The SB-Messaging adapter first shipped with BizTalk 2013 R2 and is used for connecting Azure Service Bus entities. The SB-Messaging adapter can send and receive messages from Service Bus entities such as queues and topics. You can use SB-Messaging adapters to form a bridge between Azure and BizTalk Server, thereby enabling users to create a typical asynchronous hybrid application:

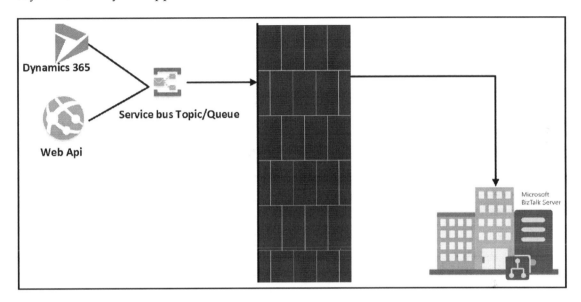

To configure BizTalk to use an SB-Messaging adapter, refer to the following Microsoft documentation:

- How to configure an SB-Messaging Receive Location: https://msdn.microsoft.com/en-us/library/jj572840.aspx
- How to configure an SB-Messaging Send Port: https://msdn.microsoft.com/en-us/library/jj572838.aspx

In this chapter, we will not go into detail about SB-Messaging adapters and Azure Service Bus Relay. There are already multiple articles describing how you can use relays and SB-Messaging adapters with BizTalk. We will now discuss a new way to do hybrid integration with Logic Apps adapters.

The Logic Apps adapter

With the latest release of BizTalk Server 2016, Microsoft introduced Logic Apps adapters, which are used for communicating between BizTalk Server and Logic Apps workflows running on the cloud.

BizTalk's Logic Apps adapter uses an on-premises data gateway to form hybrid connectivity with inbound workflows running on the cloud:

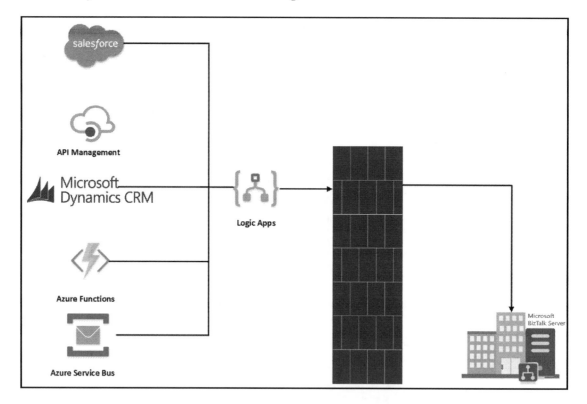

Logic Apps connectivity has made it possible to use multiple connectors in the cloud in conjunction with BizTalk Server. For example, it is now possible to connect to cloud SaaS offerings such as Azure Cognitive Services, Dropbox, and Slack with BizTalk, without any custom coding or having to buy any third-party BizTalk Server adapters.

Comparison matrix

Communication Matrix for Hybrid Integration with BizTalk is listed in following table:

Matrix	Service Bus Relay	SB-Messaging	Logic Apps
Two-way communication	ü	û	ü
IIS independent	û	ü	û
Publish/subscribe	û	ü	ü
One-way communication	ü	ü	ü
Message rate control	û	ü	ü
Transformation	û	û	ü
Security	ü	ü	ü
API Management and Azure function integration	û	û	ü
On-premises data gateway independent	ü	ü	û
Multiple content type support	û	û	ü

Installing and configuring Logic Apps adapters in BizTalk Server 2016

We assume that you have already installed and configured BizTalk Server 2016, along with Visual Studio 2015 and the appropriate version of SQL Server.

The Logic Apps adapter is able to integrate with on-premises line-of-business systems through the BizTalk Connector, both synchronously and asynchronously. We will discuss both messaging patterns in the coming sections.

These are the steps to follow in order to install a Logic Apps adapter:

1. Close any programs you have open. Run the BizTalk Server 2016 installer as Administrator.
2. On the **Start** screen, click **Install Microsoft BizTalk Adapters**:

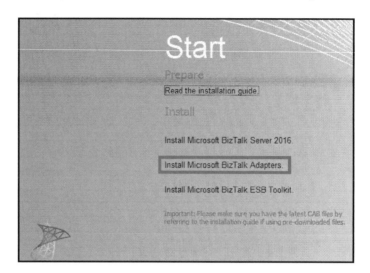

3. On the next **Start** screen, the first step is to install the WCF LOB Adapter SDK. Select **Step 1. Install Microsoft WCF LOB Adapter SDK**:

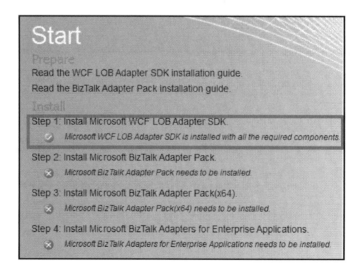

4. On the **Welcome to the Windows Communication Foundation LOB Adapter SDK Setup Wizard** screen, click **Next**.

5. On the **End-User License Agreement** screen, select **I accept the terms in the License Agreement** to accept the license agreement, and click **Next**.

6. In the **Choose Setup Type** screen, select **Complete** as the installation type.

7. On the **Ready to install WCF LOB Adapter SDK** screen, click **Install**.

8. On the **Completed the Windows Communication Foundation LOB Adapter SDK Setup Wizard** screen, click **Finish**.

9. Back at the **Start** screen, the second step is the installation of the Adapter Pack (x86). Select **Step 2. Install Microsoft BizTalk Adapter Pack**:

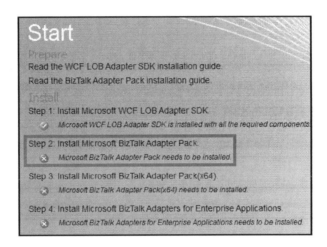

10. On the **Welcome to the Microsoft BizTalk Adapter Pack Setup Wizard** screen, click **Next**.

11. On the **End-User License Agreement** screen, select **I accept the terms in the License Agreement** to accept the license agreement, and click **Next**.

12. On the **Choose Setup Type** screen, set the installation type as **Complete**.

13. On the **Ready to install Microsoft BizTalk Adapter Pack** screen, click **Install**.

14. On the **Customer Experience Improvement Program** screen, choose whether you want to join the customer experience improvement program or not and click **OK**.

15. On the **Completed the Microsoft BizTalk Adapter Pack Setup Wizard** screen, click **Finish**.

16. Back at the **Start** screen, the next step is installing the Microsoft BizTalk Adapter Pack (x64). Note that before you install this pack, you have to install x86 first. Select **Step 3. Install Microsoft BizTalk Adapter Pack(x64)**. An installer for the SDK is launched:

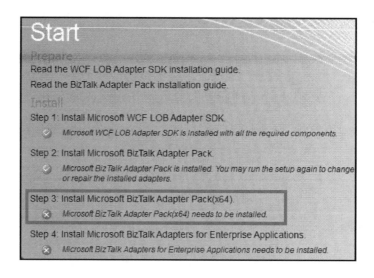

17. On the **Welcome to the Microsoft BizTalk Adapter Pack(x64) Setup Wizard** screen, click **Next**.

18. On the **End-User License Agreement** screen, select **I accept the terms in the License Agreement** to accept the license agreement, and click **Next**.

19. In the **Choose Setup Type** screen, select **Complete** as the installation type.

20. On the **Ready to install Microsoft BizTalk Adapter Pack(x64)** screen, click **Install**.

21. On the **Customer Experience Improvement Program** screen, choose whether you want to join the customer experience improvement program or not and click **OK**.

22. On the **Completed the Microsoft BizTalk Adapter Pack(x64) Setup Wizard** screen, click **Finish**.

Connecting BizTalk Server 2016 with Azure Logic Apps

In this section, we will use a fictitious company, Sunny Electrical, to see how we can get a cognitive analysis done for product feedback. We will be using a WCF-SQL adapter to poll the on-premises SQL Server and retrieve sales data that Logic Apps can use for cognitive analysis:

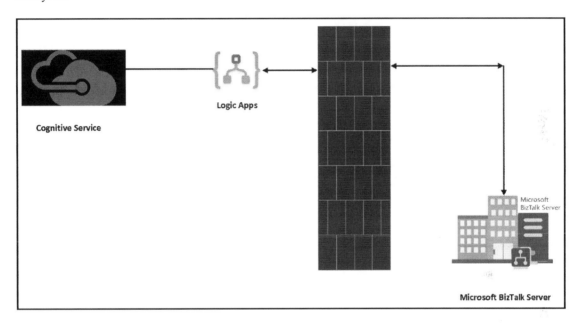

This solution requires the following components to be installed and configured along with Microsoft BizTalk Server 2016:

- Logic Apps adapter
- WCF-SQL adapter

Step 1 – Creating Logic Apps for Cognitive Services

Azure Cognitive Services is very easy to use from within Logic Apps. In the solution, we will show how to use a logic app that does sentiment analysis on sales data. To perform sentiment analysis, we will use the Text Analytics API from Cognitive Services. To do this in the Azure portal, create a Cognitive Services account:

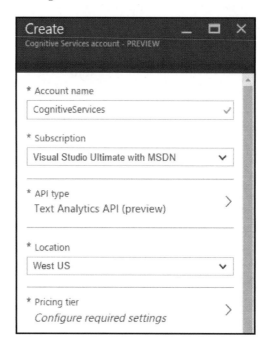

Once a Cognitive Services account has been created in the Azure portal, create a new logic app with a HTTP request response. This logic app will use a sentiment analysis API on the requested data and send the response score to the caller:

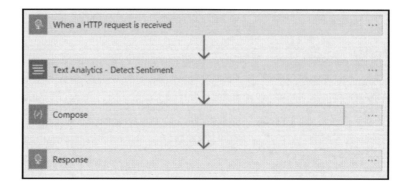

The next step is to create a BizTalk project and request-response Logic App port to make a request call to the cloud-hosted Logic App endpoint.

Step 2 – Typed polling with the WCF adapter

To poll for sales and product feedback data from SQL Server, we will use a WCF-SQL adapter in BizTalk 2016. The adapter supports receiving polling-based messages, where the adapter executes a specified SQL statement, retrieves or updates the data, and provides the result to the BizTalk receive location.

The WCF-SQL adapter supports three types of polling:

- Weakly-typed polling (also called polling)
- Strongly-typed polling (also called typed polling)
- XML polling, using statements or procedures that include a FOR XML clause

For the purposes of this sample, we will be using the sales table of Sunny Electrical's database. The table script is shown here:

```
CREATE TABLE [dbo].[SalesOrderTable](
[SalesId] [int] IDENTITY(1,1) NOT NULL,
[CustomerId] [int] NOT NULL,
[Transationdate] [datetime] NULL,
[ProductName] [varchar](50) NULL,
[IsProcessed] [int] NULL,
[ProductScore] [varchar](50) NULL,
[CustomerProdcutFeedback] [varchar](max) NULL
) ON [PRIMARY] TEXTIMAGE_ON [PRIMARY]
```

To start, create a Visual Studio BizTalk project and use **Add Generated Items** | **Consume Adapter Service** to generate an XML schema for the typed polling, which will return sales data based on the date processed state:

After selecting **sqlBinding** as the adapter, populate **URI Properties** with the server name, database name, and **InboundId**, as shown here:

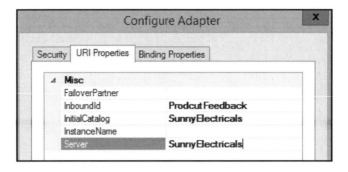

In the **Binding Properties** tab, set the adapter to use typed polling and populate **PollingDataAvailableStatement** with a SQL statement that counts how many records match the polling query. In the **PollingStatement** value, enter a query that will return records from the sales table where the `IsProcessed` flag is 0:

```
select count(*) FROM [SalesOrderTable] where IsProcessed= 0
```

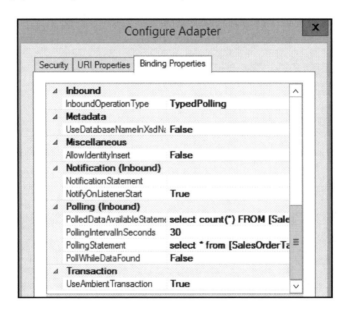

Click **Connect** to make sure that the URI configuration is correct. Select **Service (Inbound Operation)** in the dropdown for the contract type. Choose **TypedPolling** and click **Add** while selecting choose **Generate Unique Schema** type:

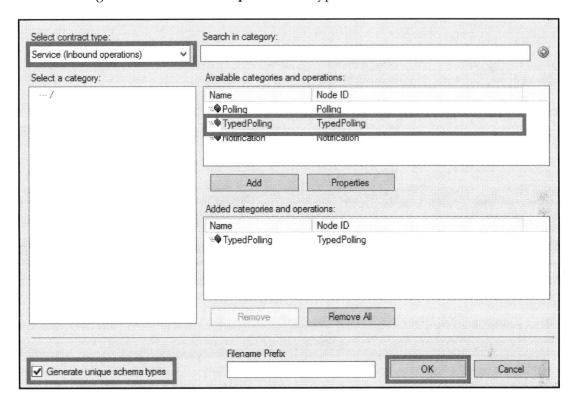

Connecting to a SQL database

Click **Connect** to make sure that the URI configuration is correct. Select **Service** (Inbound Operation) in the dropdown for the contract type. Choose **TypedPolling,** click **Add,** and choose the **Generate Unique Schema** type:

When the wizard is finished, you will end up with one new schema (and one binding file) added to the project:

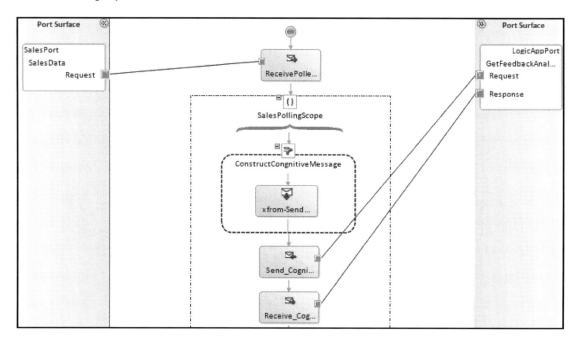

The final step is to split the polling data into separate distinct messages. This can be done by setting the envelope property of the generated schema and the Xpath of the repetitive node. Create an orchestration that will trigger the sales data and call a two-way Logic Apps endpoint to perform customer feedback analysis:

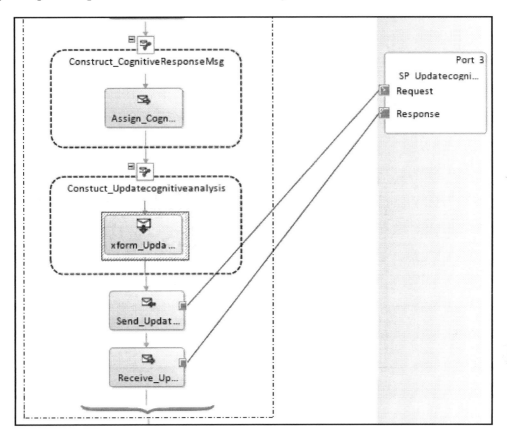

Once Cognitive Analysis data is received for the sales data feedback from Logic Apps, the result will be stored in the sales table with the result from the Cognitive Analysis API:.

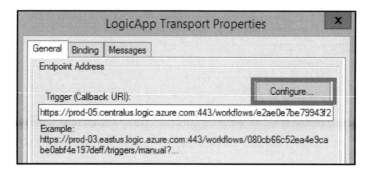

Creating a two-way send port for Logic Apps

From the BizTalk Administrative Console in the newly deployed application, create a new two-way send port for Logic Apps. It will require you to sign in with your Azure subscription. After signing in to Azure, select the appropriate Logic Apps endpoint:

Once the BizTalk orchestration is correctly bound by WCF-SQL and Logic Apps adapters, you can verify the run from the Azure portal and can also see the sentiment analysis update on the sales data:

SalesId	CustomerId	Transationdate	ProductName	IsProcessed	ProductScore	CustomerProd...
1	1	2015-12-11 00:0...	FAN	1	0.9661295	Prodcut is good
2	2	2016-09-11 00:0...	FAN	1	0.9937462	Awsome. but it ...
3	1	2016-08-05 00:0...	AIRCONDITION	1	0.2740484	not good

BIZTALK2016.Sunny...o.SalesOrderTable

Connect Azure Logic App with on-premise BizTalk Server 2016:

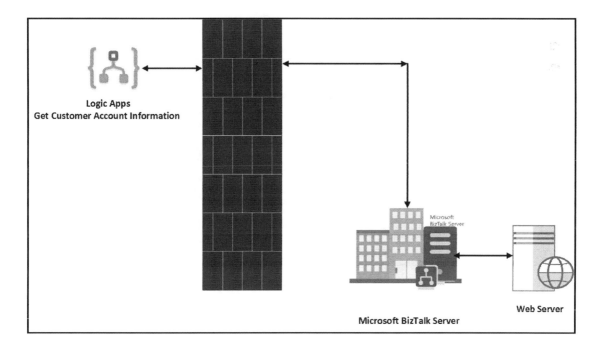

Logic Apps
Get Customer Account Information

Microsoft BizTalk Server

Microsoft
BizTalk Server

Web Server

Connecting Azure Logic Apps with BizTalk Server 2016

In this section, we will discuss how to call an on-premises WCF service from Logic Apps through BizTalk Server 2016. In this scenario, the WCF service will be expected to collect account details for a specific Sunny Electrical customer. We will use the Consume WCF Service Wizard to generate XSD schemas for the WCF service and generate an IIS endpoint for our logic app to trigger:

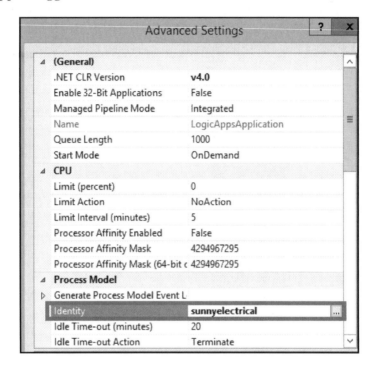

This solution will require the following components that have to be installed and configured along with Microsoft BizTalk Server 2016:

- An on-premises data gateway
- IIS configuration for the Logic Apps adapter
- A WCF-Basic HTTP adapter
- A Logic Apps adapter

We have already discussed in this chapter how to install and configure an on-premises data gateway using your MSDN subscription. We will use the on-premises data gateway along with BizTalk Server 2016 and a Logic App adapter to build the hybrid solution.

IIS configuration for Logic App adapters

We assume that you have already installed and configured an on-premises data gateway on BizTalk Server 2016. If not, you can refer to the preceding section for the installation process to install and configure an on-premises data gateway. Once you are done with the on-premises data gateway, you need to set up and configure the Logic App IIS endpoint connector correctly to access the BizTalk environment from Logic Apps.

The following are the steps you need to follow to configure IIS for your logic app connector:

1. Click the Windows icon and type run to open up the command window. Type inetmgr in the search box and hit *Enter.*

2. Create an application pool by right-clicking **Application Pools** and enter the correct information.

3. In the advanced settings of the newly created application pool, set the **Identity property** to an appropriate user, that is, a member of the BizTalk Administrative group:

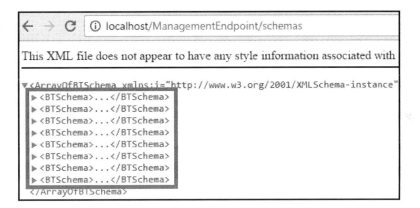

4. Next, right-click **Default Web Site** and click **Add Application**. In the dialog that opens, enter the name for the application as ManagementEndpoint, and for the **Physical Path**, enter the installation path of Logic App ManagementEndpoint. The default path will be C:\Program Files (x86)\Microsoft BizTalk Server 2016\LogicApp Adapter\BizTalkManagementService. Select the **App poll** for the newly created application pool.

5. Once you have configured the web application, click **OK**. To test, open a web browser and enter the following URL: `http://localhost/ManagementEndpoint/schemas`. This will return the list of schemas deployed in the BizTalk Management database:

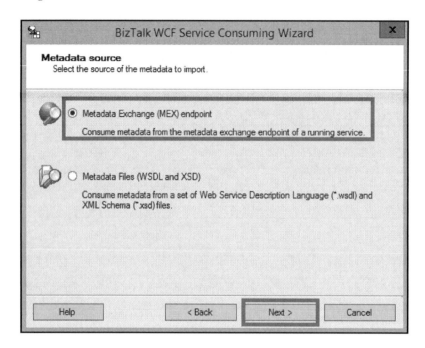

Consuming the WCF service in BizTalk 2016

We move ahead to create a BizTalk solution that will call a WCF service hosted within the corporate network.

Create a Visual Studio BizTalk project and use **Add Generated Items | Consume WCF Service** to generate an XML schema for the WCF service that will return customer account details:

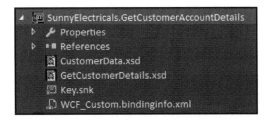

Enter the URL of the on-premises WCF service to generate the WCF data contract that will be used within the orchestration:

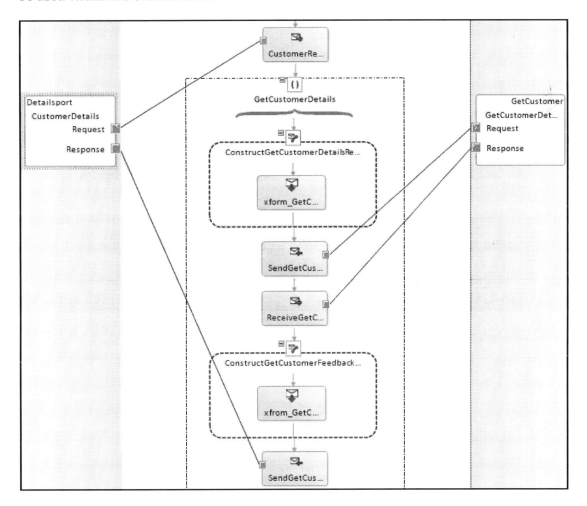

Create a simple orchestration that will receive a **customerId** instance as the request and call the WCF service to get the customer's account details. All the logical ports in the orchestration are configured with specify-later binding. The solution containing the schemas and orchestration is signed with a strong name and deployed to the BizTalk runtime:

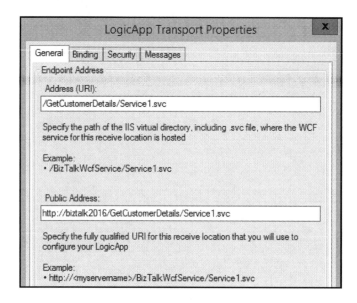

The configuration of the physical send and receive ports is done after the solution is deployed to the BizTalk Administration Console.

To create a web port, import the binding file in the BizTalk solution, which is generated from Add Generate Item. To create a request-response, receive location for Logic Apps, Create application within IIS for **GetCustomerDetails** and set the application poll to that of the **LogicApp Management endpoint**. Set the application path for **GetCustomerDetails** to use `C:\Program Files (x86)\Microsoft BizTalk Server 2016\LogicApp Adapter\BizTalkWcfService`.

In the BizTalk Administration Console, create a request-response port within the **GetCustomerDetails** solution that will run under the Logic Apps adapter handler. The configuration details are shown here:

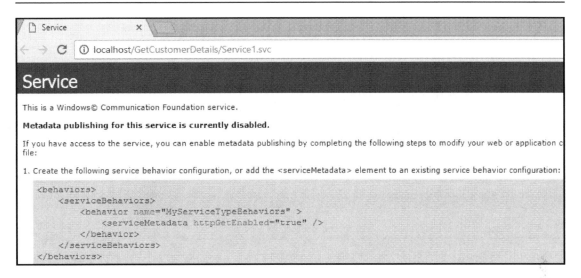

Create a Logic Apps workflow to call the Microsoft BizTalk server endpoint:

1. From the Azure portal, click **New**, then search for the `logic app` and then click **Logic App**.
2. Enter a **Name**, **Subscription**, **Resource Group**, and **Location** for your Logic App and then click **Create**.
3. Create Logic Apps workflow with a HTTP request trigger along with a BizTalk connector in Logic Apps. The overall design is shown as follows:

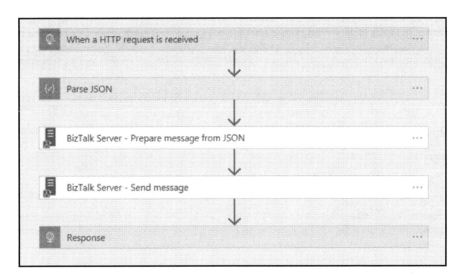

4. To test the Logic Apps, fire the request message through Postman or Fiddler using the HTTP request URI of LogicApps. In the next step, to see the run history navigate to the Logic Apps overview section and then click on run details. This will open the action run, as shown in following screenshot:

	05:53:10	05:53:15	05:53:20	05:53:25	05:53:30	05:53:35	05:53:40	05:53:45
	SUCCEEDED	FAILED	RUNNING	SKIPPED	ABORTED			
	4	-	-	-	-			

ACTION	STATUS	DURATION
Prepare_message_from_JS...	Succeeded	25.28 Seconds
Prepare_message_from_XML	Succeeded	180 Milliseconds
Response	Succeeded	62 Milliseconds
Send_message	Succeeded	8.76 Seconds

Summary

In this chapter, we have explored the capabilities of Logic Apps and how they can be applied to typical hybrid integration scenarios using Logic Apps adapters. Logic Apps provide connectivity to on-premises applications.

We have shown how we can connect on-premises BizTalk to a wide variety of services, such as SQL and WCF services, hosted within corporate networks with no access to the cloud. In the next chapter, we will discuss tooling and monitoring, which can be used within Logic Apps to monitor the cloud integration platform.

11
Intelligence in Integration Using Azure Cognitive Services

In October 2015, Google's **artificial intelligence (AI)** program Alpha Go beat Lee Sedol in the very complex board game Go. It also beat the world number one player Ke Jie in 2017. Voice recognition systems such as Cortana and Amazon Echo are not only able to identify words being spoken, but are also capable of understanding various nuances and semantics of spoken language. Netflix's recommendation engine identifies a user's taste and suggests appropriate programs. Based on millions of historical trips, tech giants such as Uber and Lyft can estimate arrival times accurately. All of these innovations can be directly attributed to major developments in the field of AI and machine learning. This development has been rapid, particularly in recent years. There are three main reasons for this trend:

- The internet boom and cheaply available storage caused a huge increase in digital content creation. This also resulted in the storage of a large amount of historical data, making it available for analysis.
- The availability of cloud-scale computing power.
- The realization (credited to Arthur Samuels in 1959) that instead of teaching computers everything they need to know about our world, it is possible to teach them to learn by themselves.

Certain terms, such as AI, machine learning, and neural networks, are buzzwords that are floating around quite a lot in the tech world. Though they are related, there are subtle differences between them. Let's try to understand these terms in more detail.

AI

AI is a very broad concept that involves machines being able to perform human-like tasks in a way that is considered *smart*. In computer science, AI research is based on the study of intelligent agents. A device is said to be equipped with AI if it learns from its environment and performs actions that increase its probability of successfully achieving its goals. In other words, the term AI is used when a machine imitates the cognitive functions performed by humans, such as learning and problem solving. AI has been around for a long time. Greek mythology contains stories of mechanical men (`http://www.greekmythology.com/Myths/Creatures/Talos/talos.html`) designed to mimic our own behavior. Based on these ideas, there have been many works of fiction in literature and film exploring AI.

As can be seen from the following diagram, AI is a broad concept that covers the concepts of machine learning and neural networks:

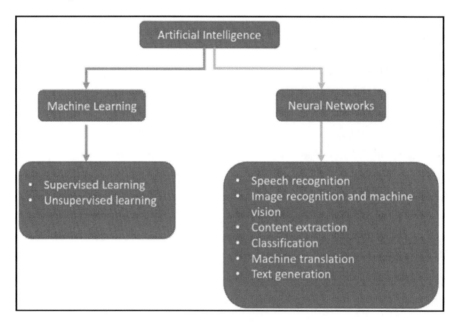

Machine learning

Humans become intelligent only through the learning process. This involves perceiving millions of things through our sensory organs. Similarly, for machines to become intelligent, we need to make them learn by providing a large amount of data, generally, known as big data. They can then be put through a learning process that makes use of various algorithms. This process is called machine learning. There are two different types of learning a machine can be put through:

- **Supervised learning**: In supervised learning, we provide a large dataset to the machine. Each input will be labeled with the expected output. Once the machine processes all the input data, the machine will be able to identify or classify a random input. For example, if we provide various pictures of a person as a dataset, the machine will be able to identify a new image of that person. Google's Face ID and Alexa's voice recognition are examples of supervised learning.
- **Unsupervised learning**: In unsupervised learning, machines are still fed with a large amount of data. However, each dataset is unlabeled. This means that for each data input, the outcome is unknown. The machine should be able to discover different patterns based on the data fed to it. For instance, in supermarkets, every time someone shops, their shopping list could be fed to a machine. Based on the input, the machine could be able to come up with a shopping pattern for the customer. Sometimes, the outcome will be a completely unknown pattern.

Neural network

A neural network is a set of algorithms and mathematical models that try to mimic, approximately, how the human brain works. In a way, neural networks try to teach computers to think and understand the world in the same way a human brain does. They can be taught to recognize images, speech semantics, content extraction, and so on. At a high level, neural networks are based on probability. Based on the data fed to them, they are able to make statements and decisions with a degree of certainty.

Machine learning and digital transformation

Industries are always striving for the competitive advantage and trying to make use of cutting-edge technology to do so. Machine learning is one technology that is transforming organizations in domains such as finance, retail, and healthcare. It can provide the following benefits:

- **Customer satisfaction**: Machine learning can help an organization to decipher the intent and meaning behind emails and delivery notes to prioritize tasks and ensure sustained satisfaction. AI-based chatbots are capable of providing coherent and semantically correct responses. This leads to greater customer satisfaction and provides an economic advantage to organizations.
- **Reacting to market trends**: In the investment banking sector, where reacting to market trends such as volatility is a very crucial part of the business, machine-learning-based systems can recognize trends more efficiently than humans. Most algorithm-based trading platforms make use of machine learning.
- **Calculating risks**: Based on the data available, we might want to calculate risks, such as business risk, credit risk, and so on.
- **Personalized health monitoring**: In healthcare organizations, machine learning can help to analyze historical data and provide personalized care to patients.
- **Recommendation engines**: Machine learning is behind engines that are able to recommend users appropriate products or video content, for example.

Due to all of the benefits that AI and machine learning can bring, organizations are moving quickly to adopt them in their technology stacks.

Microsoft and the democratization of AI

The democratization of machine learning means making machine learning available for everyone, including individuals and businesses. Microsoft is one company that is making this possible, through the following four approaches:

- Microsoft is striving to change how people interact with ambient computing by using AI.
- Microsoft is trying to introduce AI in every application or device that people interact with in their daily lives.
- Microsoft is trying to provide cognitive capabilities to every application developer in the world.
- Microsoft is in the process of building the world's most powerful supercomputer, which will be equipped with AI, open source, and accessed through the cloud so that anyone can tackle the challenges associated with AI.

Microsoft has pledged to carry out this vision for democratizing AI. In the following sections, we will try to understand the capabilities of Microsoft's AI platform and how to use it in our application development, especially in integration scenarios.

The Microsoft AI platform

Microsoft makes use of the Azure platform and a wide variety of tools to provide greater flexibility to organizations to build smart applications. The main offerings of the Microsoft AI platform are Azure AI and Microsoft's comprehensive AI platform.

Azure AI

The Azure AI platform provides built-in services in four different forms. Users can choose the appropriate one, adapt it to their target scenario, and achieve maximum productivity and reliability.

Cognitive Services APIs

Not all organizations and developers will have the capacity, resources, or data science skills and knowledge to implement direct AI. One of Microsoft's goals is to make AI and data science available to all application developers as a service. With this in mind, it provides REST APIs, SDKs, and services that help developers build intelligent applications. With Cognitive Services, developers can add features such as speech, facial, and vision recognition:

The Cognitive Services APIs that Microsoft provides to developers are listed here:

- **Vision APIs**: These APIs provide developers with access to various advanced algorithms for image processing and intelligence. With this service, you can build applications that extract printed or handwritten text, generate thumbnails, analyze an image for classification, and so on. Face recognition, content moderation, emotion detection, and video indexing are some of the advanced capabilities of Vision APIs.
- **Speech APIs:** These APIs provide developers with access to various advanced algorithms for processing speech and converting it to text. The APIs also expose advanced functionalities such as speech translation, speaker voice recognition, and text-to-speech and speech-to-text conversion services.
- **Language APIs:** These APIs provide the option of natural language processing on text content, thereby analyzing the sentiment, language detection, and key phrase extraction. The **Language Understanding Intelligent Service (LUIS)** allows applications to analyze and understand the intention of people's writing.

- **Knowledge APIs**: Netflix tailors their video content to their users' interests. Similarly, some websites, such as `medium.com`, provide personalized articles on their websites. This is made possible by logging the customer's decision to use particular content. Knowledge APIs such as Custom Decision Service understand content in terms of its text, images, videos, and overall sentiment. Knowledge APIs such as QnA Maker provide the option to create a conversational question-and-answer layer on top of the input data.
- **Search APIs:** Microsoft exposes most services from its Bing search platform. The APIs provided by Search APIs include Bing News search, Bing Video search, Bing Web search, Bing Auto-Suggestion, and Bing Image search.

For more information on the Azure Cognitive Services, please refer to the following article: `https://docs.microsoft.com/en-us/azure/cognitive-services/`.

Conversational services

Azure Bot Service allows developers to build intelligent bots that are capable of understanding natural language and can also handle question and answers. A bot allows the users of an application to interact as if they are interacting with a real person behind the chat session. The following screenshot shows the various conversational services:

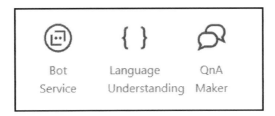

To find out more about Azure Bot Service, refer to the following article: `https://docs.microsoft.com/en-us/azure/bot-service/bot-service-overview-introduction?view=azure-bot-service-4.0`.

Data Science Virtual Machine (DSVM)

Large enterprises often want to implement their own analytics, machine learning, and AI over their own data. The DSVM provides Azure VM images that are pre-configured and tested with popular tools commonly used in the AI industry. These VMs can scale, based on demand, either vertically or horizontally. This ensures that customers pay only for the capacity that they are using. The following screenshot shows some of the tools and operating systems provided by the DSVM:

Learn more about these VMs by taking a look at the following documentation: `https://docs.microsoft.com/en-us/azure/machine-learning/data-science-virtual-machine/overview`.

Comprehensive platform and tools

Azure also provides a comprehensive set of tools, frameworks, and infrastructure that enables businesses to build their own AI services. The different categories of tools and frameworks provided by Azure AI include the following:

- **AI tools**: Microsoft provides comprehensive tools to create AI-based services. The tools that are available at the moment are as follows:
    - Visual Studio Code tools for AI
    - Azure Machine Learning packages
    - Machine Learning Studio
    - AI Toolkit for Azure IoT Edge
    - ML.NET
    - MMLSpark

- **AI framework**: Microsoft's DSVM and deep learning VMs support various learning frameworks to help developers to build AI-based applications. Some of these deep learning frameworks are listed here:
  - TensorFlow
  - ONNX
  - Azure Cognitive Toolkit
  - Caffe2
  - PyTorch
  - MxNet
  - Scikit-learn
  - Chainer
- **AI-related infrastructure**: The infrastructure components provided by Azure to create AI-based solutions are as follows:
  - Azure Databricks
  - Azure Kubernetes Service
  - Azure Cosmos DB
  - Azure SQL Database
  - Azure Batch AI
  - Azure Data Lake Storage
  - DSVM
  - Apache Spark for Azure HDInsight
  - IoT Edge

Intelligence in serverless integration

Returning to the main theme of this book, serverless integration, it is imperative that serverless features such as Logic Apps and Azure Functions make use of AI capabilities to help businesses and their applications use the power of AI. Logic Apps especially has built-in connectors to integrate with Azure Cognitive Services APIs and Power BI to bring intelligence into integration, as well as connecting to other cloud services and **Software-as-a-Service (SaaS)** applications.

The following diagram shows the various categories of Cognitive Services connectors available in Logic Apps:

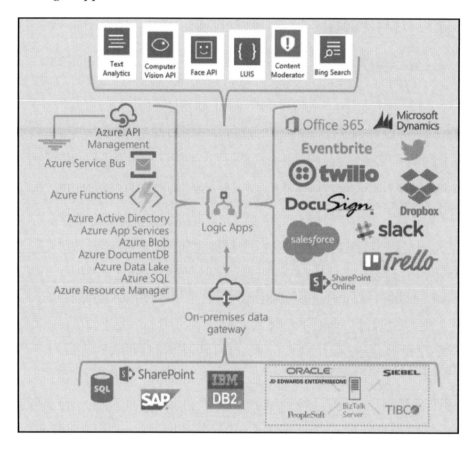

In the following sections, we will explore the Cognitive Services that we can use in logic apps by making use of out-of-the-box connectors.

Computer Vision APIs

As human beings, we use our eyes and our brain to make sense of the various visual scenarios we are exposed to. When we look at an image, we are capable of identifying its contents, making sense of any text in the image, and so on. Traditionally, image processing software was used to perform these tasks. Azure Computer Vision APIs provide developers with advanced algorithms to extract, analyze, and understand content hidden in images.

Computer Vision APIs allow developers to use capabilities such as image tagging, categorizing, face recognition, optical character recognition, and thumbnail creation in their applications.

In serverless scenarios, both Azure Functions and Logic Apps can use these Computer Vision APIs. In Logic Apps, the actions provided by Computer Vision APIs are as follows:

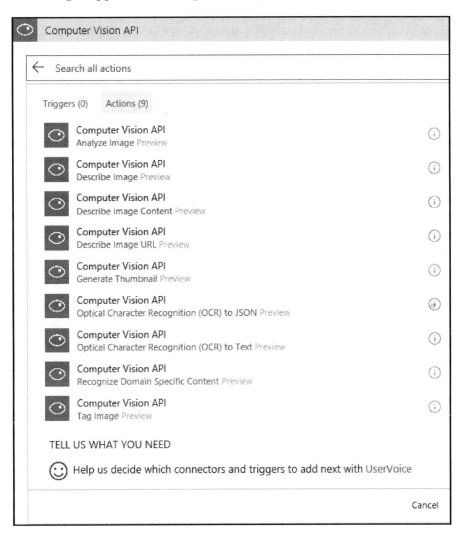

The Analyze Image API

The Analyze Image API extracts various visual features from given image content. The visual features might be categories, tags, description, faces, image type, color, and more. When you call this API, you have the option to specify what feature you are interested in getting out of the picture. For example, consider the following photo:

If we want to tag the picture with the various things present in the picture, we can make use of the Analyze Image API. I am going to send a post request to the following URL:

```
https://northeurope.api.cognitive.microsoft.com/vision/v1.0/analyze?visualF
eatures=Tags&language=en
```

The content posted is a blob URL:

```
{"url":"https://shipanywherestorage1.blob.core.windows.net/visionapisimages
/logistics-company.jpg"}
```

The following are the headers passed to the API call:

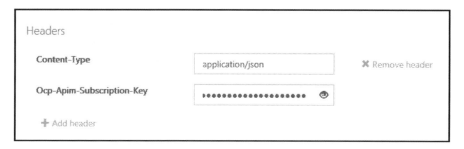

The result from the API is as follows. This clearly lists all the items present in the photo:

```
{ "tags": [{ "name": "sky", "confidence": 0.9999314546585083 }, { "name":
"outdoor", "confidence": 0.99404704570770264 }, { "name": "container",
"confidence": 0.99404704570770264 }, { "name": "truck", "confidence":
0.14557225261547824 }, { "name": "construction", "confidence":
0.090924330727579022 }, { "name": "crane", "confidence":
0.085285348497175867 }], "requestId":
"7a0c9a6f-93d4-447c-9f92-238532084267", "metadata": { "width": 800,
"height": 600, "format": "Jpeg" } }
```

Optical character recognition (OCR) to JSON

Optical character recognition (**OCR**) extracts machine-readable text from an image containing printed or handwritten characters.

Consider an example where a fictional company called **ShipAnyWhere** receives expenses filled by their employees in a paper form, as shown in the following screenshot:

They now need to automate the process of logging the expenses in the database. They are going to use the OCR-to-JSON API to get a JSON file from the image.

A POST request is made to the API as follows:

```
https://northeurope.api.cognitive.microsoft.com/vision/v1.0/ocr?language=un
k&detectOrientation =true
```

The post request has a blob location in the body:

{"url":"**https://shipanywherestorage1.blob.core.windows.net/ocr/Expence.png**"
}

The resulting JSON file from the API is as follows:

```
{ "language": "zh-Hant", "textAngle": 0.0, "orientation": "Left",
"regions": [{ "boundingBox": "75,46,605,351", "lines": [{ "boundingBox":
"75,46,8,49", "words": [{ "boundingBox": "75,46,8,49", "text": "EMPLOYEE"
}] }, { "boundingBox": "496,81,8,5", "words": [{ "boundingBox":
"496,81,8,5", "text": "9" }] }, { "boundingBox": "611,60,11,82", "words":
[{ "boundingBox": "613,60,9,16", "text": "Em" }, { "boundingBox":
"611,86,9,17", "text": "072" }, { "boundingBox": "613,113,9,29", "text":
"Name" }] }, { "boundingBox": "665,62,15,233", "words": [{ "boundingBox":
"665,62,15,22", "text": "Ex" }, { "boundingBox": "665,97,11,44", "text":
"ense" }, { "boundingBox": "665,148,15,147", "text": "Reimbursement" }] },
{ "boundingBox": "496,109,8,77", "words": [{ "boundingBox": "496,109,8,6",
"text": "D" }, { "boundingBox": "496,116,6,3", "text": "⌈" }, {
"boundingBox": "496,120,8,8", "text": "~" }, { "boundingBox":
"496,128,7,19", "text": "e10" }, { "boundingBox": "496,150,8,36", "text":
"London" }] }, { "boundingBox": "578,229,15,161", "words": [{
"boundingBox": "578,229,15,100", "text": "ShipAnyWhere" }, { "boundingBox":
"578,335,14,55", "text": "Logistics" }] }, { "boundingBox":
"613,229,12,168", "words": [{ "boundingBox": "613,229,12,64", "text":
"Srinivasa" }, { "boundingBox": "613,299,12,98", "text": "Mahendrakar" }]
}] }] }
```

OCR has now recognized the lines and words in the expense form. By making use of JSON data capabilities and the transformation capabilities in Logic Apps, we can translate the output into a format that can be fed into the database.

There are other Computer Vision APIs. These are listed in the following table:

API name	Explanation
Describe image	This API gives an appropriate description for an image based on the content tags identified for the image. The description will be associated with a confidence level.
Generate thumbnail	This API analyzes the image, identifies the **region of interest (ROI)**, and performs smart cropping, which can be used to generate thumbnails.
Recognize domain-specific content	This API helps to identify domain-specific images. Currently, the API supports the celebrity and landmark domains.
Tag images	This API helps to tag the image appropriately based on its content.

Face API

Face APIs provide developers with the functionality to train Cognitive Services with sample images. They also provide the ability to recognize a face in a random image that may not be in the sample set.

The APIs that are available in Logic Apps as actions at the time of writing this book are as follows:

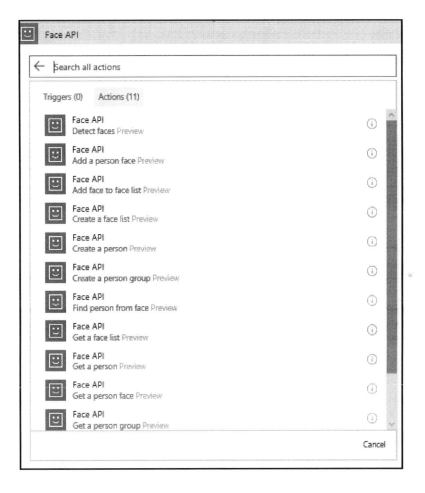

In this section, we will try to understand the functionality of the Face API by training Cognitive Services to identify a person named **Anna**. This involves the following steps:

1. **Create a person group**: First of all, we need to create a person group, which is a container for all the faces that we are going to provide as samples to train the Cognitive Services. Let's call this person group `myfriends`.

2. **Add a person**: We can add one or more people to a person group. Any sample images that we use to train face identification must belong to person entities created under a particular person group.

3. **Register faces**: Once the person is defined, we will have to register the faces of the person that will be used as a sample set for training the Cognitive Services. The following are the face images that we will register as Anna:

4. **Train the person group**: Once all the sample files are registered, we need to train the person group.

5. **Identify a face**: Once the person group is trained, we can try to identify faces in a random image. If the image contains Anna's face, it should detect it. We use the following image for testing our sample:

The following is a console application code that calls the previously mentioned calls using the Face API .NET SDK. I am using the latest SDK version, 2.2, which is a preview version:

```xml
<ItemGroup>
    <PackageReference Include="Microsoft.Azure.CognitiveServices.Vision.Face" Version="2.2.0-preview" />
    <PackageReference Include="Newtonsoft.Json" Version="12.0.1" />
</ItemGroup>
```

The following is the content from the `Program.cs` file:

```csharp
using System;
using Microsoft.Azure.CognitiveServices.Vision.Face.Models;
using Microsoft.Azure.CognitiveServices.Vision.Face;
using System.IO;
using Newtonsoft.Json;
using System.Collections;
using System.Linq;
namespace ShipAnyWhere_FaceAPITest
{
  class Program
  {
      static string _faceAPIKey =
"0be7e081f204437990ad877011103d23";
      const string faceEndpoint =
"https://northeurope.api.cognitive.microsoft.com";
      const string personGroupId = "myfriends";
      const string friendImageDir= @"C:\Git\ShipAnyWhere-
FaceAPITest\Data\PersonGroup\AnnaImages";
      static void Main(string[] args)
        {
            var faceClient = new FaceClient(new
ApiKeyServiceClientCredentials(_faceAPIKey),
                                            new
System.Net.Http.DelegatingHandler[]{});
            faceClient.Endpoint = faceEndpoint;
            //Create a new PersonGroup
            var faceId =
faceClient.PersonGroup.CreateAsync("myfriends","My Friends")
            .GetAwaiter()
            .GetResult();

            //Add a person to person group
            var friendAnna =
faceClient.PersonGroupPerson.CreateAsync(personGroupId, "anna")
            .GetAwaiter()
                            .GetResult();
```

```
    //Register Faces
    foreach(string image in
Directory.GetFiles(friendImageDir, "*.jpg"))
    {
        using(Stream imageStream = File.OpenRead(image))
        {
            faceClient.PersonGroupPerson
                    .AddFaceFromStreamAsync(personGroupId,
friendAnna.PersonId,imageStream)
.GetAwaiter() .GetResult();
        }
    }


    //Train faces
    faceClient.PersonGroup.TrainAsync(personGroupId)
            .GetAwaiter()
            .GetResult();
    //Identify the face
    string testImage = @"C:\Git\ShipAnyWhere-
FaceAPITest\Data\PersonGroup\Family.jpg";
    using (Stream imageStream = File.OpenRead(testImage))
{
    var faces =
faceClient.Face.DetectWithStreamAsync(imageStream,true)
            .GetAwaiter()
            .GetResult();
    var faceids = faces.Select(e=>(Guid)e.FaceId).ToList();
    var identifyResults =
faceClient.Face.IdentifyAsync(faceids,personGroupId)
    .GetAwaiter()
    .GetResult();
    foreach(var result in identifyResults)
{
    if(result.Candidates.Count == 0)
    Console.WriteLine("No one identified");
    else
    {
        var candidateId = result.Candidates[0].PersonId;
        var person =
faceClient.PersonGroupPerson.GetAsync(personGroupId,
candidateId)
        .GetAwaiter().GetResult();
        Console.WriteLine("Identified as {0}", person.Name);
    }
  }
}
```

```
            }
          }
        }
```

When you run the preceding program, you will get the following console output:

```
The thread 27300 has exited with code 0 (0x0).
The thread 34148 has exited with code 0 (0x0).
The thread 12504 has exited with code 0 (0x0).
No one identified
The thread 34452 has exited with code 0 (0x0).
Identified as anna
The thread 27312 has exited with code 0 (0x0).
The thread 13400 has exited with code 0 (0x0).
```

Text Analytics APIs

The Text Analytics APIs allow developers to perform natural language processing on raw text. There are three main functionalities—keyphrase extraction, language detection, and sentiment analysis. The following are the Text Analytics actions available in Logic Apps at the time of writing this book:

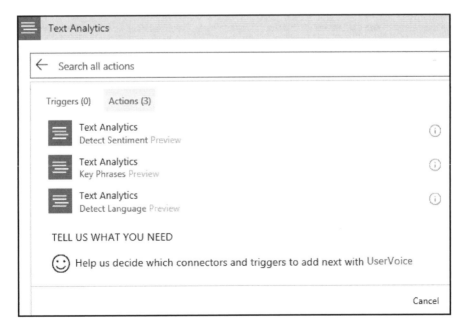

Here are some detailed explanations of these services:

- **Detect sentiment**: The API returns a numerical score between 0 and 1. Scores close to 1 indicate a positive sentiment, while scores close to 0 indicate a negative sentiment. A score of 0.5 indicates a lack of sentiment (for example, a neutral factual statement).

  Take a look at the following input example:

  ```
  {
      "documents": [
      {
         "language":"en",
         "id":"1",
         "text": "This is one of the best technology books i have
  ever read"
      }
      ]
  }
  ```

  The following is the output:

  ```
  {
      "documents":[
       {
         "score":0.92,
         "id": "1"
      }
      ]
  }
  ```

- **Key phrase detection**: The API returns a list of strings denoting the key points in the input text.

  The following is an example input:

  ```
  {
   "documents": [
   {
   "language":"en",
   "id":"1",
   "text": "This is one of the best technology books i have ever
  read"
   }
   ]
  }
  ```

The following is the output:

```
{
    "documents":[
      {
        "id": "1",
        "keyPhrases": ["technology book","read"]
      }
      ],
    "errors":null
}
```

- **Language detection**: The API returns the detected language and a numerical score between 0 and 1. Scores close to 1 indicate a high level of certainty that the identified language is true. A total of 120 languages are supported.

The following is an example input:

```
{
    "documents": [
      {
        "id":"1",
        "text": "Bonour tout le monde"
      },
      {
        "id":"1",
        "text": ":) (:-3"
      }
    ]
}
```

The following is the output:

```
{
    "documents": [
    {
    "id":"1",
    "detectedLanguages":[
    {
    "name":"French",
    "iso6391Name": "fr",
    "score": 1
    }
    ]
    },
    {
    "id":"1",
    "detectedLanguages":[
```

```
{
"name":"(Unknown))",
"iso6391Name": "(Unknown)",
"score": 0
}
]
}
]
}
```

Language understanding APIs

LUIS is a cloud-based service that applies custom machine learning to a user's conversational, natural language text to predict the overall meaning and pull out the relevant information.

A client application for LUIS could be any conversational application that communicates with a user in natural language to complete a task. Examples of client applications include social media applications, chatbots, and speech-enabled desktop applications.

Natural language model

A model begins with a list of general user intentions, called intents, such as `Book Flight` or `Contact Help Desk`. You provide an example text, called an example utterance, for the intents. Then, you mark the significant words or phrases in the utterance, which are called entities. A model includes the following:

- **Intents**: Categories of user intentions (the intended action or result)
- **Entities**: Specific types of data in utterances, such as numbers, emails, or names
- **Example utterances**: Example text that a user enters in the client application

Some examples of utterance and response are shown here:

Example user utterance	Intent	Entities
"Book a flight to **Seattle**?"	BookFlight	Seattle
"When does your store **open**?"	StoreHoursAndLocation	open
"Schedule a meeting at **1pm** with **Bob** in Distribution"	ScheduleMeeting	1pm, Bob

Logic Apps has the following two actions as built-in connectors:

The following are the APIs that are part of LUIS:

API name	Explanation
Get entity by type	For a given entity type, the operation returns the best matching entity model from the LUIS prediction object.
Get prediction	Given some input text, this operation returns a prediction based on a pre-trained model. The prediction object returned can also be used as input for other LUIS actions.

Case study – ShipAnywhere feedback analysis

Consider a fictional logistical company called ShipAnyWhere that specializes in commerce and fulfillment solutions for e-commerce businesses across the world. It has more than 100 distribution centers across more than 30 countries. It provides business-to-business, e-commerce, and multi-channel fulfillment solutions to customers using cutting-edge technologies.

After each delivery, they take feedback from customers. One major component of the feedback is a remark section, where the users are allowed to write their feedback. There are millions of users being served by the organization, and it is important to find the sentiment of these comments and analyze the overall trend of customer happiness.

Currently, all the data is stored in a SQL server. ShipAnyWhere wants their sentiment values to be stored in another SQL server, which will be fed to Power BI. They decide to make use of Logic Apps and its Sentiment Analysis API connectors to analyze the sentiment and publish it to Power BI:

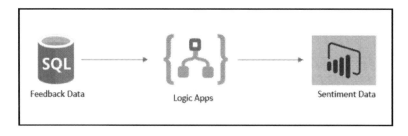

Feedback Data   Logic Apps   Sentiment Data

Provisioning the Text Analytics API service instance

The first step in implementing this kind of solution is to create a Cognitive Services account in the Azure portal. In the Azure portal, select **Text Analytics** from the market place, as shown in the following screenshot:

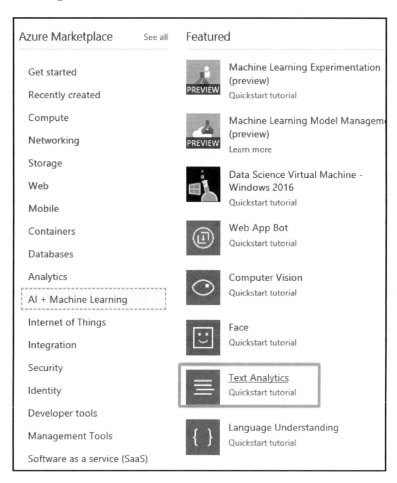

Name the service `ShipAnyWhereTextAnalytics`. Set the **Subscription**, **Location**, and **Pricing tier** appropriately, as shown in the following screenshot:

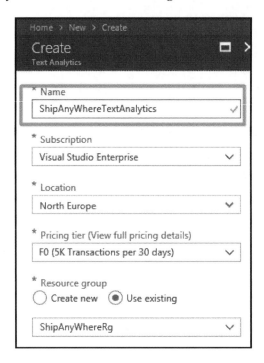

Noting down the connection name and key

To access the Text Analytics API, it is essential that the connection name and the key are noted down. This will be required by the Logic Apps sentiment analyzer connector:

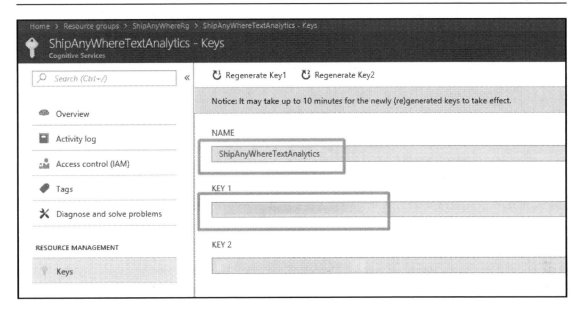

Creating logic apps

The next step is to create a logic app that triggers periodically to check the database table, find all the comments, and report the sentiment.

The following screenshot shows that a **Recurrence** trigger instantiates the logic app, which makes use of a SQL Server connector to retrieve all the rows related to feedback into a JSON file. **Compose** then extracts the feedback comments from the JSON:

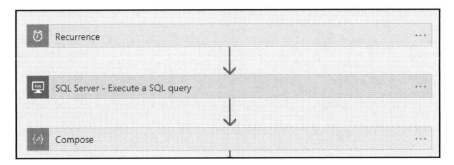

The scope of this section is not to explain the steps in fetching the data; instead, we will focus on the Cognitive Services connector.

Add the **Text Analytics** connector, as shown in the following screenshot:

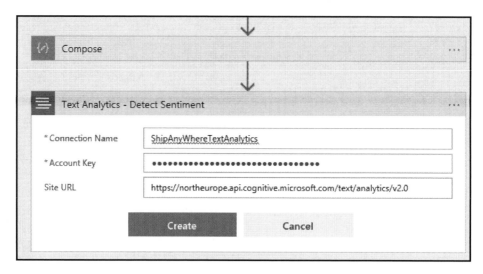

Configure the **Text** and **Language** fields as follows:

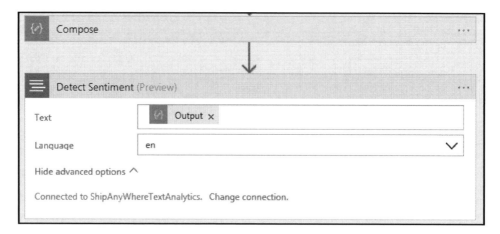

Apart from finding the **sentiment_score**, we also would like to add **keyphrases**. These can be used to plot graphs in Power BI:

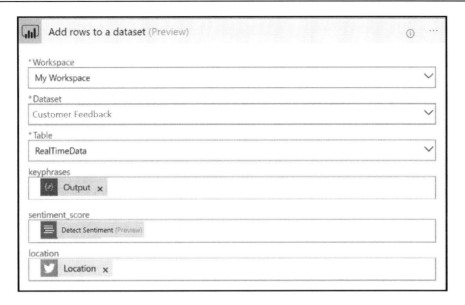

The logic app finally looks as follows:

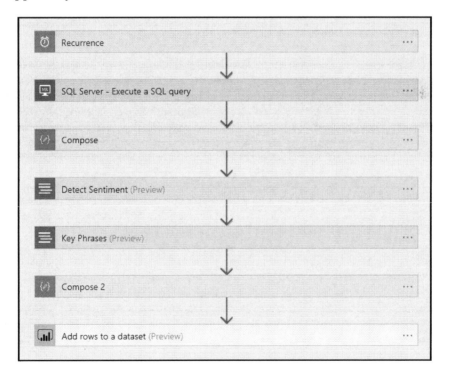

Summary

Microsoft is heading toward making machine learning and AI available to every business. Now application developers can purely focus on their business logic, instead of worrying about deep learning techniques. Serverless integration, particularly in the form of Azure Logic Apps and Azure Functions, will be able to access these APIs to serve complex workflows in various business scenarios.

In the next chapter, we will cover how to utilize DevOps practice for Azure integration services which comprise Logic Apps, API Management, Azure Functions, Service Bus, and Azure Event Grid. We will also cover how to create ARM resource and use them in DevOps pipeline along with source code for continuous integration and deployment of integration solutions.

12
DevOps for Azure Integration

The term DevOps refers to a combination of skills, processes, and product capabilities that enable organizations to achieve the continuous delivery of solutions and services when interacting with end users. DevOps is all about taking the best of software development and IT operations and enabling enterprises to rapidly respond to customer requirements and feedback. Within the DevOps model, development and operations teams are no longer siloed and instead work as a single team to cater to the needs of end users and the business. There are other DevOps models, such as models in which the security and testing teams also merge with the development and operations teams, resulting in a single technology-driven team.

In this chapter, we will cover the following points:

- Benefits of DevOps
- DevOps for integration
- Naming convention for Azure integration services
- DevOps for Azure Functions
- API Management and continuous integration/deployment
- Logic Apps in the DevOps model
- Service Bus and Azure Event Grid
- Monitoring

Benefits of DevOps

Brett Hofer, in one of his posts, *The Art of DevOps: An Introduction to Landscape*, provides some great insight on DevOps:

> *"What are we fighting for here? Ultimately, we're fighting for the absolute best services and features that we can deliver to our customers as quickly as we possibly can, and to eliminate the "War Room" scenario we are all so familiar with."*

The preceding statement gives us a pretty clear interpretation of the benefits of DevOps—it offers value for enterprises and value for customers. Here are some of the key benefits of DevOps:

- DevOps implementation is an agile principle that enables enterprises to remain competitive in the market with optimal time-to-market delivery of products and services. This helps development teams to release changes on the fly with minimal impact to other running services.
- DevOps encourages a culture of collaboration and shared responsibility, improving cooperation between development, business, and operations. In a DevOps environment, overall success does not depend on individual success but rather the responsibility of the team associated with the project.
- With good DevOps practice in place, it is easier for the IT team to detect and fix issues more quickly, thus giving a better user experience to the end user.
- Cross-skilling and self-improvement is another key benefit of DevOps. When a team works together with a single IT goal, it is easy to share knowledge within the team.
- DevOps comes with better automation, which therefore increases the overall productivity of the team.

We have covered here some of the key benefits of DevOps for a business. In the next section, we will cover DevOps for cloud integration and explain how you can utilize the best toolset to automate your integration environment.

DevOps for integration

Being able to deploy integration solutions in a continuous fashion is one of the key requirements of a business. Integration solutions in Azure consist of resources such as Logic Apps, Azure Functions, Service Bus, Event Grid, and Azure API Management.

Making integration agile and meeting business requirements demand that these integration resources are more flexible toward real-time fixes and delivering deployment across multiple regions and multiple environments, such as the production, staging, and user acceptance environments. In this chapter, we will go through each of these resources separately and explain how you can leverage DevOps for Azure to make your environment much more flexible to change.

In Azure, there are several options available for deploying and provisioning resources:

- **Azure portal-based deployment**: Use the classic or the new Azure portal to provision and manage resources individually, and not as a group. You will need to manually set the order of provisioning and deletion of the required resources.
- **Azure PowerShell**: Azure PowerShell provides a more automated way of provisioning resources to ensure they are created in the correct order. Note that some resources may only be created or configured by using PowerShell scripts.
- **Azure Command-Line Interface (CLI) tools**: This provides command-line tools for creating, managing, and deleting services via the command line. These tools are available for Windows, Linux, and OS X. These tools normally interact with Resource Manager APIs and Service Management APIs for the classic portal.
- **Azure Resource Manager (ARM)**: This is available in the new Azure portal. It provides the capability to deploy, update, or delete all resources pertaining to a solution in a single operation. Microsoft's recommendation is to use ARM templates for current and future deployments.
- **Visual Studio**: This allows us to deploy solutions directly from Visual Studio.
- **DevOps for Azure**: This is the cloud-based offering from Microsoft that provides a scalable, reliable, and globally available hosted service to manage your source code. Formally known as Visual Studio Team Services, it provides multiple features for continuous integration and deployment. Some of the features of DevOps for Azure are as follows:
  - **Team Foundation Server (TFS)** and Git as repositories for source control
  - Built-in feature for build and release management to support continuous integration and delivery
  - Tools to test your applications, including manual/exploratory testing, load testing, and continuous testing
  - Customizable dashboards for sharing progress within your organization

There are various other benefits, which we will discuss throughout this chapter while setting up better DevOps practices for integration artifacts. If you do not have a DevOps account, then register for a free account at `https://visualstudio.microsoft.com/team-services/`.

Naming convention of integration artifacts

The use of a consistent, shared naming convention throughout the Azure environment is one of the key points you should follow when building and deploying solutions to the cloud. With a consistent naming convention, it is easy to navigate through and locate your resources in the cloud, and it helps us to build a robust continuous integration and deployment pipeline in Azure.

In this section, we will go through some of the guidelines that can be followed for proper naming standards with integration resources. You can use these recommendations to build your own enterprise-level naming convention. In the following table, we have listed Azure artifacts along with a standard naming pattern:

Entity	Scope	Patterns	Example
Resource group	Resource group	`<service short name>-<environment>-rg`	`enterprisegraph-dev-rg`
Logic Apps	Resource group	`la-<region>-<orgsortname>-<onsourceprocessname>-destination`	`la-ause-contoso-salesorder-sn`
Functions app	Resource group	`func-<orgsortname>-<processname>-<env>`	`func-contoso-propfi-dev`
Functions		`fc_<ontriggername>_<operationname>_<destination>`	`fc_userupdate_getuserdetails_la`
Storage	Resource group	`sa<region><processshortname><env><number>`	`saausecontosodata01`
API Management	Resource group	`{name}.azure-api.net`	`contoso.azure-api.net`
API	Resource group	`API : <service name>-api`	`contosofinance-api`
API connection	Resource group	`<env>.<connectiontype>`	`dev.office365`

Microsoft also came up with a list of patterns and practices that should be followed when you create resources in Microsoft Azure. These recommendations help enterprises to have fine control over billing and resources running on the cloud. For more details on general resource naming conventions, you can look at the Microsoft documentation: `https://docs.microsoft.com/en-us/azure/architecture/best-practices/naming-conventions`.

ARM templates

A typical cloud integration solution normally consists of multiple components, such as Logic Apps, Azure Functions, API Management, SQL Server, and an API app. You will also be able to provision these tools independently through Azure Service Management APIs or PowerShell scripts.

With ARM templates, you can group all these tools collectively and use a declarative-style template written in JSON to execute the deployment of cloud services and the dependencies associated with it. If we use the same template, it allows us to deploy repetitively into various environments across the application's life cycle, which produces the same results with consistency.

The benefits of using ARM templates are as follows:

- We can set up resource locks. This provides the option to prevent the deletion or modification of resources by other users, and more.
- We can view the rolled-up costs of all of the resources for a resource group as they can now be grouped together.
- We can use declarative templates, which can be managed in a source control repository.
- We can set the sequence of provisioning resources by defining the dependencies in the template.
- **Role-Based Access Control (RBAC)** is natively supported.

Pre-built templates are also community-contributed, and you can get started by modifying an existing template that closely resembles your requirements. These templates are available from here: `https://docs.microsoft.com/en-us/azure/azure-resource-manager/resource-group-overview`.

The basic structure of an ARM template is made up of six parameters. The following table describes the elements of the template in more detail:

Element name	Description
`$schema`	This is the location of the JSON schema file and is a mandatory value. The file sets the rules on how the template will be processed. Typically, this value will be set to `https://schema.management.azure.com/schemas/2015-01-01/deploymentTemplate.json` until Microsoft publishes a later version.
`contentVersion`	The version of the template you are authoring can be any value (for example, `1.0.0.0`) and is a mandatory field. Use this to help you keep track of the template version between deployments.
Parameters	Provides the flexibility to collect user input for resource properties prior to starting the deployment.
Variables	Variables are optional. They are used to simplify the template by reusing the same variable throughout the template. The value can be a simple or a complex data type, such as another JSON object. Variable values can also be based on other values.

There are various options available when deploying these templates:

- **Azure portal**: Upload the JSON ARM template into the portal for deployment
- **Azure PowerShell**: You can use a local or external referenced template for deployments using the `New-AzureRMResourceGroupDeployment` cmdlet
- **ARM REST API**: Use the APIs directly to manage the resources
- **Click to deploy**: Provides the capability to deploy templates directly from GitHub
- **Microsoft Visual Studio**: Directly deploys resources and groups from Visual Studio

Creating an ARM template using Visual Studio

Visual Studio 2015 and later versions provide syntax and dependency-checking features as you type. While typing, it also allows you to use the track changes feature through a source control repository. Visual Studio helps you by providing the information necessary to construct a template.

We will now create a template to provision a Service Bus topic and a subscription:

1. Open Visual Studio, add a new Azure Resource Group project, and name it.
2. Once the project is named, you'll see a list of templates. Choose **Blank Template** from the list of options:

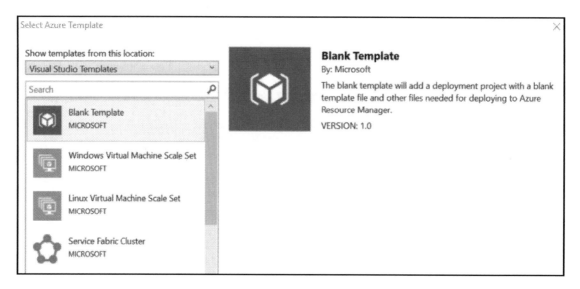

3. This will create a blank ARM definition file, which consists of an ARM schema version and an empty set of parameters, variables, resources, and output:

```
{
  "$schema":
"https://schema.management.azure.com/schemas/2015-01-01/deploymentT
emplate.json#",
  "contentVersion": "1.0.0.0",
  "parameters": {},
  "variables": {},
  "resources": [],
  "outputs": {}
}
```

4. To add an Azure Service Bus namespace resource to the empty ARM template, use the following resource ARM definition in the `definition.json` file:

```
"resources": [
  {
      "name": "[parameters('serviceBusNamespaceName')]",
      "type": "Microsoft.ServiceBus/namespaces",
      "location": "[resourceGroup().location]",
      "apiVersion": "2017-04-01",
      "sku": {
        "name": "Standard",
        "tier": "Standard"
      },
      "dependsOn": [],
      "tags": {
        "displayName": "[parameters('serviceBusNamespaceName')]"
      },
      "properties": {},
  }
]
```

5. To test the basic ARM template for the Service Bus namespace, you can right-click on the template project and click on **Deploy.**

6. This will give you a Visual Studio deployment dialog for manual deployment. Select the correct **Resource group**, **Deployment template**, and **Template parameter file** to deploy the namespace resource within the resource group:

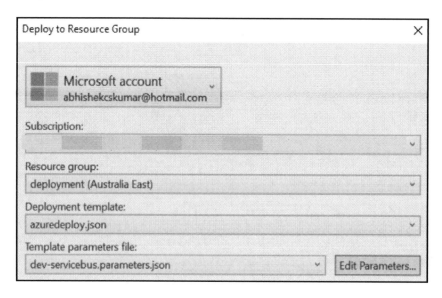

Next, we will add Service Bus queues and a topic to the Service Bus namespace ARM template definition file. This will allow us to create a message container in the Service Bus namespace to perform read and write operations against the queue and Service Bus topic:

```
{
  "apiVersion": "2017-04-01",
  "name": "customerq",
  "type": "Queues",
  "properties": {},
  "dependsOn": [
    "[concat('Microsoft.ServiceBus/namespaces/',
parameters('serviceBusNamespaceName'))]"
  ]
}
```

The preceding code is the definition of a queue with a default property. In enterprise-level applications, you will need to define explicit properties on Service Bus queues and topics. Properties are key/value pairs and need to be placed in the properties section of the Service Bus queue/topic section. It's important to set the `dependsOn` dependency with a proper parent Service Bus namespace resource; otherwise, the deployment will fail at runtime.

Next, we will add a topic and subscription definition within the nested Service Bus namespace definition file. As we know, a Service Bus topic depends on a Service Bus namespace, and each subscription on a topic is dependent on the topic name. The ARM definition should have those dependencies covered as part of a basic definition. Here is the definition for topic creation within the Service Bus namespace:

```
{
   "apiVersion": "2017-04-01",
   "name": "socialconnect",
   "type": "Topics",
   "dependsOn": [
     "[concat('Microsoft.ServiceBus/namespaces/',
parameters('serviceBusNamespaceName'))]"
   ],
   "properties": {},
}
```

The subscription will be a nested resource type within the topic resource. Each subscription has its own definition and ruleset resource associated with appropriate messaging within the Service Bus namespace. The following example shows how you can have a nested resource for a subscription and a subscription ruleset in a topic resource:

```
"resources": [{
    "apiVersion": "2017-04-01",
    "name": "socialconnect_update",
    "type": "Subscriptions",
    "dependsOn": [
      "socialconnect"
    ],
    "properties": {},
    "resources": [{
        "apiVersion": "2017-04-01",
        "name": "socialuser",
        "type": "Rules",
        "dependsOn": [
          "socialconnect_update"
        ],
        "properties": {
          "filterType": "SqlFilter",
          "sqlFilter": {
```

```
            "sqlExpression": "MsgType='socialconnect' and
    Direction='inbound' and Operation='insert' and RecipientId='cosmos'"
            },
            "CorrelationFilter": {}
        }

      }

    ]
  }
]
```

To work with continuous integration and deployment for Service Bus with Azure DevOps, we have hosted the preceding ARM template in the Azure DevOps portal and set the version control type as Git. The Service Bus source code will consist of an ARM definition file that we have developed, along with the parameter file required for different environments:

To work with continuous integration and deployment for Service Bus, we will create, build, and release a pipeline task in DevOps for Service Bus resources:

1. To create a build task in DevOps, click on the **Builds** blade and then select **Azure Repos**:

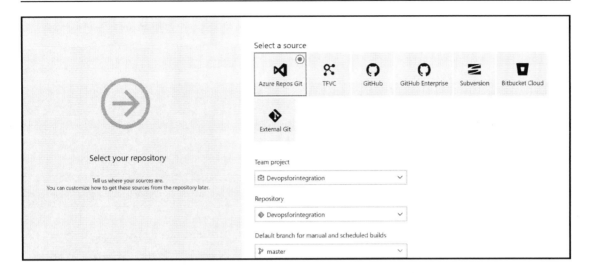

2. On the **Select your repository** page, select **Azure Repos Git**, verify the team
   project, and click on **Continue**. This will open a new build definition page. On
   the build definition page, select **Empty job** from the list of available templates:

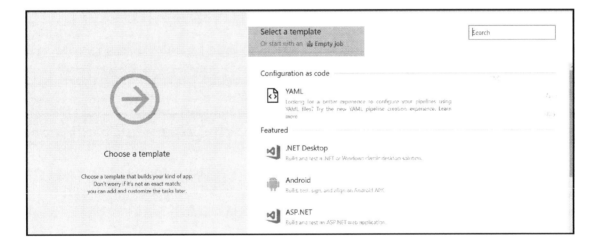

3. On the build pipeline page, give the build task an appropriate name and select **Hosted VS2017** as the **Agent pool:**

4. In the agent job list, add a **Build solution for service bus** task to build the ARM definition solution and a **Publish Artifact** task to publish the build definition for the continuous deployment release pipeline:

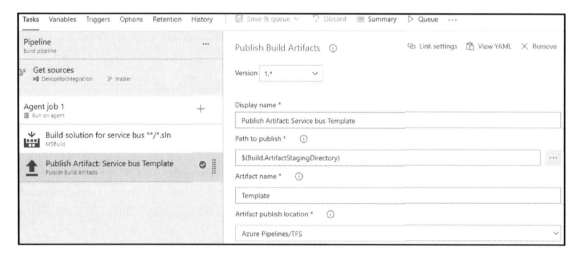

5. In order to enable continuous integration with for local Git version control, navigate to the **Triggers** section of the build definition, check the **Enabled continuous integration** checkbox, and click on **Save:**

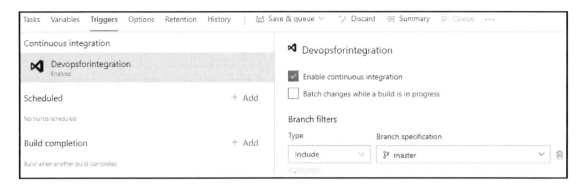

Enabling continuous integration on the source repository will run the build definition against any source repository changes. We recommend you use Git as version control with DevOps. With Git, you can work on a local repository, and once you are satisfied with your local changes, you can push the repository changes to a remote DevOps process to initiate a new build definition:

1. Following is the build task execution of one of the changes made to the ARM definition of Azure Service Bus:

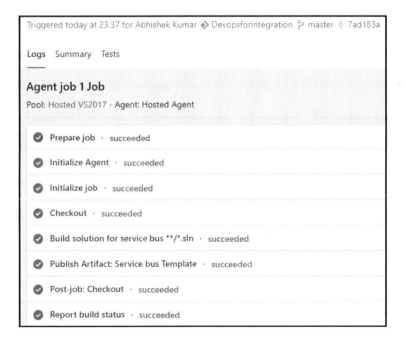

2. To create a release task for Service Bus, click the Service Bus release blade and add a release setup trigger:

3. This will open a new release pipeline definition. From the list of templates, select **Empty job** and then click on **Save**:

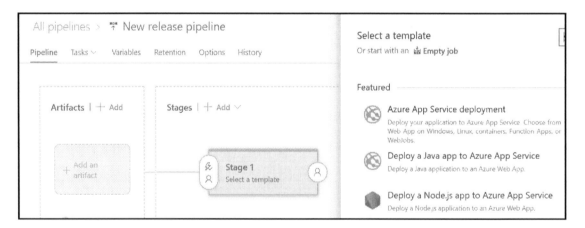

4. Next, change the name of **Stage 1** to Dev and add an ARM task. Populate the stage with the required ARM template file and parameter file and set the deployment mode to **Incremental**:

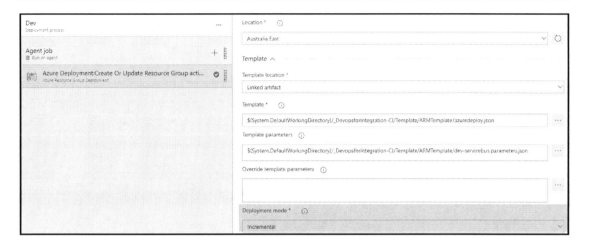

5. Copy the stages into UAT and productions and update the resource group, subscription, and parameter file according to your environment. The following screenshot illustrates the release of Service Bus resources in the DevOps portal:

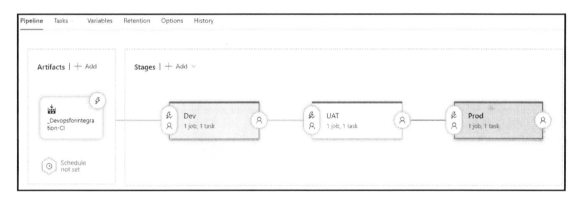

 Each release stage can contain one or more tasks. Here we have used a single task, which is to create or update an Azure resource with the ARM definition file. If you perform full deployment with ARM, you might remove other artifacts in the same resource group, and that is the reason we have chosen incremental deployment.

6. Enabling a continuous deployment trigger with DevOps is simple. Click on the **Artifacts** section in the release trigger, and this will open up the **Continuous deployment trigger** settings. Enable continuous deployment through the **Continuous deployment trigger** in the release pipeline:

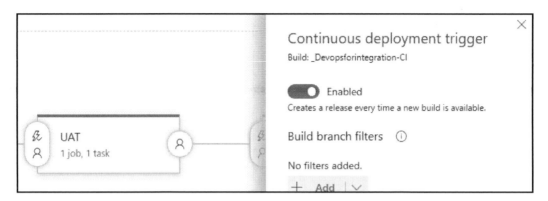

7. The **Continuous deployment trigger** also gives you the option to add filter conditions on the release. You can work with filter conditions when you need to filter multiple build definitions and only release a set of builds to the resource group.

8. In enterprise-wide deployments, it is recommended to add pre-approval or post-approval tasks in the deployment stage section. This will enable the operations team to easily monitor any deployment going through the DevOps pipeline and within Azure tenant:

Azure Event Grid and DevOps

In the previous section, we went through the process of setting up source control for Azure Service Bus and enabled continuous integration and deployment with an ARM template definition and the DevOps portal.

In this section, we will work with Azure Event Grid and walk through the process of creating the automated deployment of a custom Event Grid topic with Azure DevOps.

As we learned in the previous chapter, Azure Event Grid is a fully managed, intelligent, event routing service available within the Microsoft Azure umbrella. With Azure Event Grid, enterprise applications can leverage the event-driven programming model to build reactive interfaces that can be used to connect external or internal enterprise applications. Building a robust continuous integration and deployment pipeline for Azure Event Grid will allow enterprises to build next-generation reactive interfaces for integration.

In this section, we will extend the preceding solution and add an Azure Event Grid resource to the ARM template definition file. We can either add an Event Grid resource to a Service Bus definition file or we can create a separate ARM resource for Azure Event Grid. To separate the resource deployment, let's create another project in the same solution file to hold a definition for Azure Event Grid. The ARM definition of an Azure Event Grid resource is described in the following example:

```
"resources": [{
    "name": "[parameters('eventgridName')]",
    "type": "Microsoft.EventGrid/topics",
    "location": "[resourceGroup().location]",
    "scale": null,
    "apiVersion": "2018-01-01",
    "dependsOn": [],
    "tags": {
      "displayName": "[parameters('eventgridName')]"
    },
    "properties": {}
  }
]
```

The parameter file will contain the Event Grid topic name, and this will be used in the DevOps pipeline to create Azure Event Grid resource in multiple resource groups based on the parameter file:

```json
{
  "$schema":
"https://schema.management.azure.com/schemas/2015-01-01/deploymentParameters.json#",
  "contentVersion": "1.0.0.0",
  "parameters": {
    "eventgridName": {
      "value": "eg-ause-integration-uat"
    }
  }
}
```

The build and release definition of Azure Event Grid follows similar steps to the build and release definition for Service Bus:

1. First, create a build definition for Azure Event Grid with the build task and enable continuous integration on the build trigger blade:

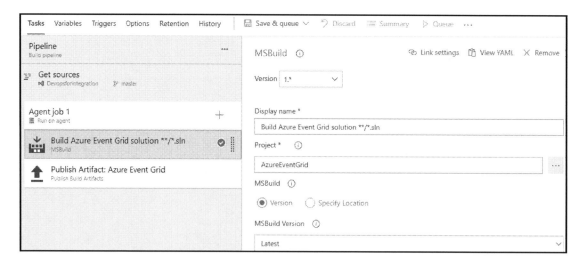

2. In the release task, enable continuous release and select the Event Grid source repository from the list of available release artifacts. Once the build is triggered through check-in or manually, it will run the release pipeline for the Azure Event Grid resource and will update or deploy a new instance of Azure Event Grid:

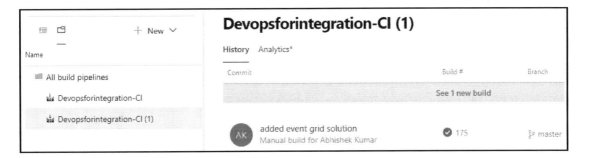

3. In the release pipeline for Azure Event Grid, we will also add a pre-deployment approval process to notify the DevOps team on the specific release of Azure Event Grid. Set pre-deployment approval in the DevOps release pipeline, as shown in the following screenshot:

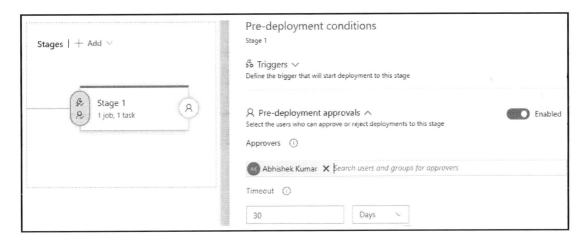

4. In this case, to get the release process triggered, we have modified the Event Grid parameter file in the local Git source repository and committed the change against the central Git repository. This has initiated a continuous build and release task, as follows:

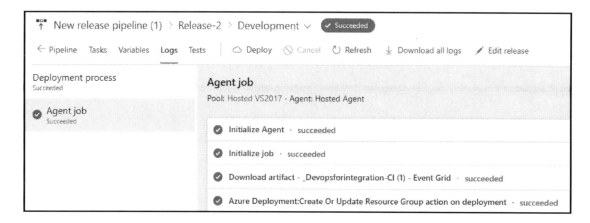

Azure API Management and DevOps with Git version control

In this section, we will focus on Azure API Management and how we can leverage DevOps capabilities to build a continuous release pipeline for API Management. We will work with an ARM template to create and update an API Management instance and demonstrate how we can leverage an ARM template to define products, APIs, and policies within an Azure API Management instance.

We will extend our DevOps solution and add new project for Azure API Management. The project will consist of an ARM definition file and a parameter file, which is used to deploy resources across multiple environments:

1. In the ARM definition file, the first step is to define a resource for API Management with a resource type such as `Microsoft.ApiManagement/service`:

```
{
    "apiVersion": "2017-03-01",
    "name": "[parameters('apimanagementname')]",
    "type": "Microsoft.ApiManagement/service",
    "location": "[resourceGroup().location]",
```

```
    "tags": {},
    "sku": {
      "name": "[parameters('sku')]",
      "capacity": "[parameters('skuCount')]"
    },
    "properties": {
      "publisherEmail": "[parameters('publisherEmail')]",
      "publisherName": "[parameters('publisherName')]"
      "notificationSenderEmail": "apimgmt-
noreply@mail.windowsazure.com"
    }
  }
```

2. To add a global policy, we need to define a nested resource within the Azure API Management instance, which will inherit the dependency from a parent resource:

```
{
    "apiVersion": "2017-03-01",
    "dependsOn": [
  "[concat('Microsoft.ApiManagement/service/',parameters('azureapiman
  agementName')]"

    ]
    "name": "policy",
    "properties": {
      "policyContent": "[parameters('tenanatpolicy')]"
    }
  }
```

3. To define policies in API Management, you can either refer to the preceding chapter on API Management, or you can look into the Microsoft documentation via the following link: https://docs.microsoft.com/en-us/azure/api-management/api-management-policies.

4. Next, we can use the ARM template to import an external API through the OpenAPI definition. Here, we have taken an example of an OpenAPI definition for a pet store:

```
    "resources": [
      {
        "apiVersion": "2017-03-01",
        "type": "apis",
        "name": "sampleswaggerforpetstore",
        "dependsOn": [
    "[concat('/subscriptions/','[subscription().subscriptionId]','/
    resourceGroups/','[resourceGroup().name]','/providers/',
          'Microsoft.ApiManagement/service/',
    parameter('azureapiManagementName'))]"
```

```
            ],
            "properties": {
            "contentFormat": "swagger-link-json",
            "contentValue":
        "http://petstore.swagger.io/v2/swagger.json",
            "path": "examplepetstore"
            }
          }
        ]
```

5. Similarly, you can also add your Logic Apps and Functions (with no OpenAPI definition) endpoint into Azure API Management using the HTTPS protocol:

```
{
 "apiVersion": "2017-03-01",
 "type": "apis",
 "name": "samplellogicapps",
 "dependsOn": [
 "[concat('Microsoft.ApiManagement/service/',
variables('azureapiManagementName'))]"
 ],
 "properties": {
 "serviceUrl": "https://logicappsendpoint",
 "path": "logicapps",
 "protocols": [
 "https"
 ]
 }
}
```

6. To group multiple APIs into single products in the API Management instance, add a products resource to the ARM definition file:

```
{
   "apiVersion": "2017-03-01",
   "type": "products",
   "name": "exampleProduct",
   "dependsOn": [
 "[concat('/subscriptions/','[subscription().subscriptionId]','/
resourceGroups/','[resourceGroup().name]','/providers/','Micros
oft.ApiManagement/service/',
variables('azureapiManagementName'))]"
   ],
   "properties": {
   "displayName": "Sample Product Name",
   "description": "Description for sample product",
     "subscriptionRequired": true,
     "approvalRequired": false,
```

```
          "subscriptionsLimit": 1,
          "state": "published"
        },
        "resources": [
        {
          "apiVersion": "2017-03-01",
          "type": "apis",
          "name": "exampleApi",
          "dependsOn": [
   "[concat('/subscriptions/','[subscription().subscriptionId]','/
   resourceGroups/','[resourceGroup().name]','/providers/','Micros
   oft.ApiManagement/service/',
   variables('azureapiManagementName'))]",
           "[concat('Microsoft.ApiManagement/service/',
   variables('azureapiManagementName'),
   '/apis/sampleswaggerforpetstore')]"
          ]
        }
        ]
   }
```

7. This will allow us to have a single policy defined for a group of APIs along with a single authentication and authorization model for clients to invoke APIs hosted in Azure.

You can find more details on ARM definition for Azure API Management at the following GitHub link, which is managed by Microsoft and community members: `https://github.com/Azure/azure-quickstart-templates/tree/master/201-api-management-create-with-vnet`.

Azure Functions with DevOps

Azure Functions are an integral part of serverless applications, and they are required to build a robust integration platform in the cloud. As discussed in previous chapters, we can code small executables or log running durable functions in Azure Functions and use them within Logic Apps, API Management, or Microsoft Flow using webhooks or HTTP bindings.

Azure Functions also supports many other input and output binding types to connect with multiple platforms. We can also create a custom binding, which can be used to build a serverless integration platform in Azure.

There are various options available to perform continuous integration and deployment for functions, such as running them from a ZIP file, using PowerShell, and setting up a DevOps pipeline directly from the Azure portal. In this section, we will cover automated deployment for Azure Functions using an ARM definition with a compiled assembly through the DevOps pipeline (`https://docs.microsoft.com/en-us/azure/azure-functions/deployment-zip-push`).

To understand the process, follow these steps:

1. Create an Azure Functions project along with associated class libraries to store models and methods with the related dependency injection.
2. Define an ARM template for the function app container to hold function app resource definitions such as the Storage account, application keys, application insights, and the pricing plan:

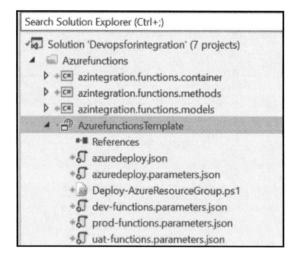

3. In the function app ARM template definition, add the required Functions dependency resources, such as the Storage account, Application Insight account, and the hosting plan (server farms). Here is the definition of Application Insights for the function app:

```
{
  "apiVersion": "2015-05-01",
  "name": "[parameters('appInsightsName')]",
  "type": "microsoft.insights/components",
  "location": "[parameters('appInsightsLocation')]",
  "tags": {
    "[concat('hidden-link:', resourceGroup().id,
'/providers/Microsoft.Web/sites/',
parameters('appInsightsName'))]": "Resource"
  },
  "properties": {
    "ApplicationId": "[parameters('appInsightsName')]"
  }
}
```

Having Application Insights embedded into the function container helps the operations team to monitor the health of each individual function through the Azure portal, and it also helps the development team to get an overview of any runtime issues that might arise during the overall processing of functions.

4. The Storage account is required by the functions app to store the logs' and functions' state information for durable functions. It is good practice to include a Storage account with a proper naming convention within the function's ARM definition template:

```
{
  "type": "Microsoft.Storage/storageAccounts",
  "name": "[variables('storageAccountName')]",
  "apiVersion": "2016-01-01",
  "location": "[resourceGroup().location]",
  "kind": "Storage",
  "sku": {
    "name": "Standard_LRS"
  },
  "dependsOn": []
}
```

5. The last dependency resource for the function app is the compute model (App plan for Function App), as this function app uses the consumption plan to run its Functions. We have defined the ARM resource for the app plan:

```
{
  "type": "Microsoft.Web/serverfarms",
  "apiVersion": "2016-03-01",
  "name": "[variables('hostingPlanName')]",
  "location": "[resourceGroup().location]",
  "properties": {
    "name": "[variables('hostingPlanName')]",
    "computeMode": "Dynamic",
    "sku": "Dynamic"
  }
}
```

6. Now, as we have all the required dependency resources listed for the function app, the next step is to add the ARM definition for the function app with the required dependencies for storage, Application Insights, and the hosting plan:

```
{
  "apiVersion": "2016-08-01",
  "type": "Microsoft.Web/sites",
  "name": "[variables('functionAppName')]",
  "location": "[resourceGroup().location]",
  "kind": "functionapp",
  "scale": null,
  "dependsOn": [
    "[resourceId('Microsoft.Web/serverfarms',
variables('hostingPlanName'))]",
    "[resourceId('Microsoft.Storage/storageAccounts',
variables('storageAccountName'))]",
    "[resourceId('microsoft.insights/components/',
parameters('appInsightsName'))]"
  ],
  "properties": {
    "name": "[variables('functionAppName')]",
    "serverFarmId": "[resourceId('Microsoft.Web/serverfarms',
variables('hostingPlanName'))]",
    "clientAffinityEnabled": false,
    "siteConfig": {
    "appSettings": [
    {
      "name": "AzureWebJobsDashboard",
      "value":
"[concat('DefaultEndpointsProtocol=https;AccountName=',
variables('storageAccountName'), ';AccountKey=',
```

```
listKeys(variables('storageAccountid'),'2015-05-01-
preview').key1)]"
      },
      {
        "name": "AzureWebJobsStorage",
        "value":
"[concat('DefaultEndpointsProtocol=https;AccountName=',
variables('storageAccountName'), ';AccountKey=',
listKeys(variables('storageAccountid'),'2015-05-01-
preview').key1)]"
      },
      {
        "name": "WEBSITE_CONTENTAZUREFILECONNECTIONSTRING",
        "value":
"[concat('DefaultEndpointsProtocol=https;AccountName=',
variables('storageAccountName'), ';AccountKey=',
listKeys(variables('storageAccountid'),'2015-05-01-
preview').key1)]"
      },
      {
        "name": "WEBSITE_CONTENTSHARE",
        "value": "[toLower(variables('functionAppName'))]"
      },
      {
        "name": "FUNCTIONS_EXTENSION_VERSION",
        "value": "~1"
      },
      {
        "name": "WEBSITE_NODE_DEFAULT_VERSION",
        "value": "6.5.0"
      },
      {
        "name": "APPINSIGHTS_INSTRUMENTATIONKEY",
        "value":
"[reference(resourceId('microsoft.insights/components/',
parameters('appInsightsName')),
'2015-05-01').InstrumentationKey]"
      }

    ]
  }
}
```

In the Function's ARM definition, you can add your application secret as a key value in the spp settings section. This will help to limit any manual updates to application settings in different environments.

7. The basic parameter list for our function app is as follows:

```
{
  "$schema":
"https://schema.management.azure.com/schemas/2015-01-01/deploymentP
arameters.json#",
  "contentVersion": "1.0.0.0",
  "parameters": {
    "environment": {
      "value": "dev"
    },
    "appInsightsName": {
      "value": "devfuncappinsights01"
    },
    "appName": {
      "value": "func-integration-dev"
    },
    "functionStorageName": {
      "value": "devsabausefun01"
    },
    "functionApplicationPlanName": {
      "value": "fc-ause-integration-dev"
    },
    "appInsightsLocation": {
      "value": "westus2"
    }
  }
}
```

Azure Function continuous integration and deployment

Once the Function code is checked into DevOps source control, the next step is to build a continuous integration and deployment pipeline using an ARM template and Function definition. To do this, follow these steps:

1. Click on the build definition for the function app in the DevOps portal.

2. Click on **New build definition**, and from the list of available templates, select the **ASP.NET Core** template.

3. Add an additional task in the **ASP.NET Core** template, such as an archive function build definition, and publish the ARM definition for the function app container:

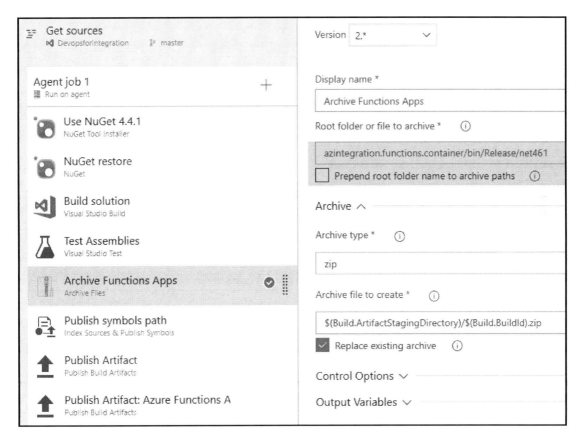

4. To make sure the release is working properly for the function app, change the root path in the archive step to the actual `bin/release/net461` of the function app definition.

5. You also need to uncheck the **Prepend root folder name to archive paths** checkbox. This will will remove any additional root folders to get published for the function app release.

6. Then define your publish artifact path to the staging directory, as shown in the following screenshot:

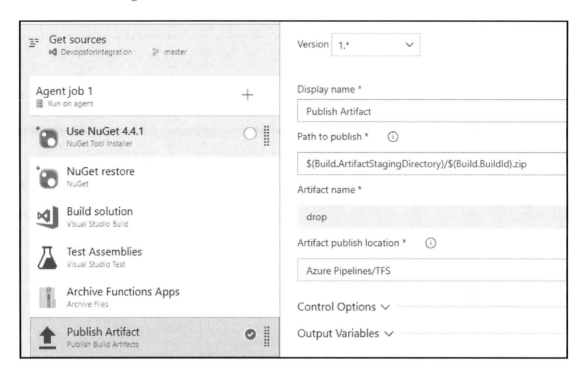

7. We have now enabled continuous integration for our function app from the trigger section of the build task. Once the code has been pushed to the remote repository through source code, we can see that an automated build task is triggered for the functions app. Each of the agent steps will be executed sequentially, and build tasks can either succeed or fail. You can also skip steps, which is not recommended until and unless you have any specific requirements within DevOps:

Agent job 1 Job	Started: 06/01/2019, 19:50:09
Pool: Hosted VS2017 · Agent: Hosted Agent	⋯ 1m 37s

✅ Prepare job · succeeded	< 1s
✅ Initialize job · succeeded	6s
✅ Initialize Agent · succeeded	< 1s
✅ Checkout · succeeded	8s
✅ Use NuGet 4.4.1 · succeeded	< 1s
✅ NuGet restore · succeeded	32s
✅ Build solution · succeeded	32s
✅ Test Assemblies · succeeded 1 warning	1s
✅ Archive Functions Apps · succeeded	1s
✅ Publish Artifact · succeeded	1s
✅ Publish symbols path · succeeded	7s
✅ Publish Artifact: Azure Functions ARM · succeeded	2s
✅ Post-job: Checkout · succeeded	< 1s
✅ Report build status · succeeded	< 1s

8. In the function app release task, we will first enable the continuous deployment trigger through the release process and then add a multiple release agent to the release definition.

9. The next step is to update the resource group with the function container definition and then add the Azure App Service agent task in order to stop, deploy, and start the function app container:

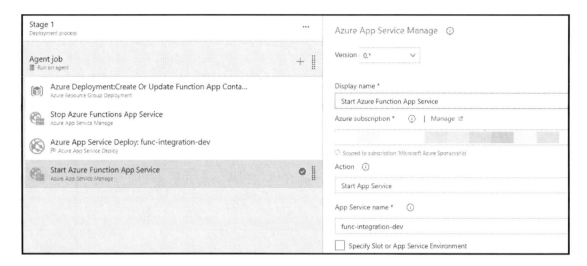

You can also enable slots for the function app using an Azure App Service manage task. For production instances, we suggest enabling slotting for the function container, which will make sure your production instance is never affected by any corrupt releases.

10. At this point, we are done with the initial function app release process. We can repeat the steps to create multiple environments within the same subscription or to other Azure tenants using a service principal (an Azure Active Directory-registered app with the privilege to perform deployment, for instance):

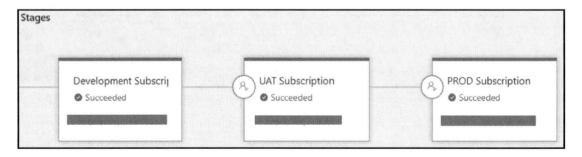

Logic Apps continuous integration and deployment with DevOps

In this section, we will cover continuous integration and deployment for the Logic Apps workflow. The process of deploying the Logic Apps workflow is similar to the process with other Azure resources. There are some basic differences, such as how we can manage API connection resources and the actual naming convention you should adhere to for the API connection. The API connection resource can be managed either through an individual Logic Apps workflow definition or you can have a separate ARM resource to manage Logic Apps API connection properties.

In this section, we will separate the API connection resource from Logic Apps, and we'll try to describe how easily you can enable continuous integration and deployment for Logic Apps and manage API connection resources through a DevOps process:

1. The first step here is to create a blank Azure resource project through Visual Studio Code or Visual Studio 2015 or later:

2. Next, we will add the definition of Logic Apps API connection properties in the ARM template definition file. You can get the basic definition for the API connection through an Azure portal automation script. For example, the Service Bus API connection definition is described here:

```
{
  "type": "Microsoft.Web/connections",
  "apiVersion": "2016-06-01",
  "name": "[parameters('servicebusname')]",
  "location": "[parameters('apiresourcelocation')]",
  "properties": {
    "api": {
      "id": "[concat('/subscriptions/',
subscription().subscriptionId,
'/providers/Microsoft.Web/locations/',
parameters('apiresourcelocation'), '/managedApis/servicebus')]"
    },
```

```
          "displayName": "Azure Servicebus",
          "parameterValues": {
            "connectionString":
        "[parameters('azuresbconnectionstring')]"
          }
        }
      }
```

3. Let's add another API connection resource, such as Cosmos DB, SFTP, Azure Event Grid, or Office 365, and parametrize the required connection properties to enable API connection deployment through the DevOps pipeline:

```
{
  "type": "Microsoft.Web/connections",
  "name": "[parameters('cosmosdbconnectionname')]",
  "apiVersion": "2016-06-01",
  "location": "[parameters('apiresourcelocation')]",
  "scale": null,
  "properties": {
    "displayName": "cosmos database connection",
    "customParameterValues": {},
      "api": {
        "id": "[concat('/subscriptions/',
subscription().subscriptionId,
'/providers/Microsoft.Web/locations/',
parameters('apiresourcelocation'), '/managedApis/documentdb')]"
      }
    }
}
```

4. Like SQL Server API connections, some API connections require authentication properties, which you can add in the parameter section. In the following example, we have added a SQL Server API connection with server details such as the server name, the database name, and user credentials:

```
{
  "type": "Microsoft.Web/connections",
  "apiVersion": "2016-06-01",
  "name": "[parameters('sqlserverconnecitonName')]",
  "location": "[parameters('apiresourcelocation')]",
  "properties": {
    "api": {
      "id": "[concat('/subscriptions/',
subscription().subscriptionId,
'/providers/Microsoft.Web/locations/',
parameters('apiresourcelocation'), '/managedApis/sql')]"
    },
```

```
        "displayName": "SQL Server API Connecton",
        "parameterValues": {
          "server": "[parameters('sqlserverName')]",
          "database": "[parameters('sqldatabaseName')]",
          "username": "[parameters('sqluserid')]",
          "password": "[parameters('sqlpassword')]"
        }
      }
    }
  }
```

5. Once all your connection properties are listed in the ARM definition along with an appropriate parameter listing, test the connection property by manually deploying it through Visual Studio:

To verify that your Logic Apps API connection is deployed successfully, you can log in to the Azure portal and navigate to the resource group that you selected when doing a manual deployment.

- Now that the API connection is a separate resource, you have much more control over the number of API connections created in the Azure resource, and you can also control the API naming convention when you have a distributed team working on a cloud integration framework using a Logic Apps workflow:

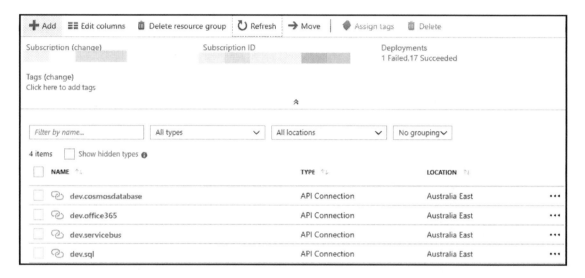

- Next, add the logic API connection resource in DevOps source control and build a continuous integration and deployment pipeline for multiple environments.
- Logic Apps API connection resources are ARM templates, and the build definition for API connection resources will follow the same steps as Service Bus and Event Grid resources.
- To implement DevOps, add a build task and **Publish build artifacts** and enable the trigger for continuous integration:

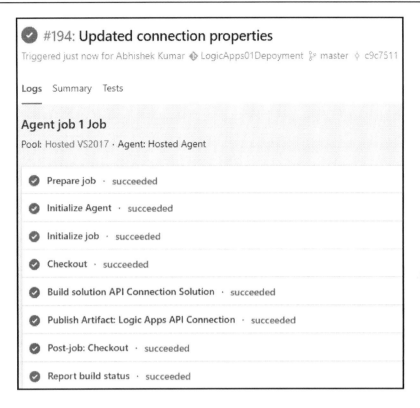

- In the release pipeline for the Logic Apps API connection project, we use a single task to create or update the Azure resource group with the API connection definition.
- The Logic Apps API connection resource project will contain a single API definition file, along with multiple parameter files for different integration environments (UAT, DEV, PROD, and SIT):

The release process can be either triggered manually, scheduled, or enabled through a continuous deployment trigger. In this case, we have used a manual process to create a release to a different environment using the service principal for multiple Azure subscriptions:

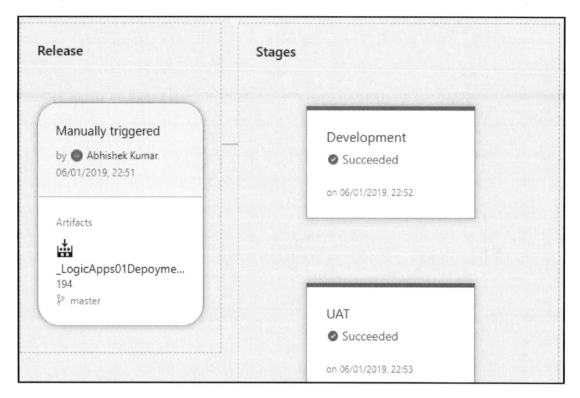

After the deployment of the Logic Apps API connection, it takes time to create an automated deployment process for a Logic Apps workflow because you can create a Logic Apps workflow in different IDE environments, such as Visual Studio 2015 and Visual Studio Code, or through the Azure portal. To automate Logic Apps deployment across multiple environments, it is essential to parameterize the raw Logic Apps workflow definition file, which you can find in the Azure portal or Visual Studio. To get the existing Logic Apps workflow definition file, you can use Visual Studio Cloud Explorer to copy the raw definition file from the Azure portal resource group.

In this example, we will use existing HTTP trigger Logic Apps and import the definition into Visual Studio to perform the required automation steps:

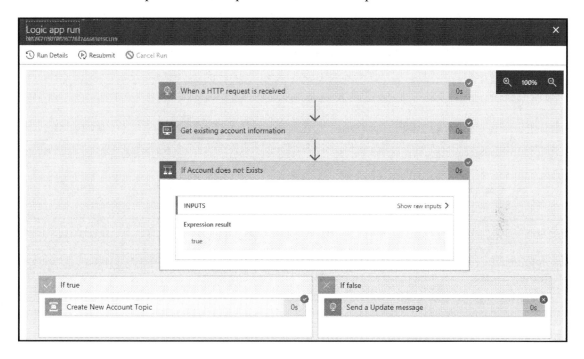

To open the Logic Apps definition file in Visual Studio, you need to authenticate your Visual Studio account against the Azure subscription running Logic Apps. Once the authentication is done, you can open Logic Apps with the Logic Apps editor and download the definition:

The next step is to parameterize the Logic Apps definition file in Visual Studio and update the DevOps source control with the updated Logic Apps workflow definition:

```json
{
  "$schema": "https://schema.management.azure.com/schemas/2015-01-01/deploymentTemplate.json#",
  "contentVersion": "1.0.0.0",
  "parameters": {
    "servicebus_1_Connection_Name": [...],
    "servicebus_1_Connection_DisplayName": [...],
    "servicebus_1_connectionString": [...],
    "sql_1_Connection_Name": [...],
    "sql_1_Connection_DisplayName": [...],
    "sql_1_server": [...],
    "sql_1_database": [...],
    "sql_1_username": [...],
    "sql_1_password": [...],
    "LogicAppLocation": [...]
  },
  "variables": {},
  "resources": [
    {
      "properties": {
        "state": "Enabled",
        "definition": [...],
        "parameters": [...]
      },
      "name": "la-ause-contoso-httpgetaccountinfo-sb",
      "type": "Microsoft.Logic/workflows",
      "location": "[parameters('LogicAppLocation')]",
      "tags": {},
      "apiVersion": "2016-06-01",
      "dependsOn": [...]
    },
```

Once you are done modifying the raw Logic Apps workflow template with the appropriate parameter list, you can push your changes to the DevOps portal, where we can build an automated build and release pipeline. Here is the build definition for Logic Apps:

You can also group multiple Logic Apps definition files within a single ARM template resource. The Logic Apps release will contain one or more resource group tasks, which will deploy Logic Apps into the required resource group and subscription.

Grouping Logic Apps resources into the same definition file, based on business process, allows you to segregate resources and deploy them as individual components. As Logic Apps are built on a microservices model, any changes to certain Logic Apps or groups will not affect the processing of other Logic Apps within the same resource group:

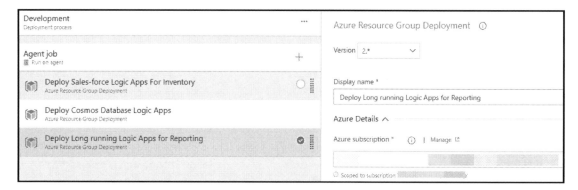

Next, we update the Logic Apps template source code through Visual Studio or Visual Studio Code with the enabled continuous integration/continuous delivery trigger on build and release. We should see the actual Logic Apps resources being deployed through multiple environments (in this case, **Development**, **UAT**, and **Production**):

With that, we have completed this DevOps chapter. If you want to learn the basics of the ARM template, go through the Microsoft documentation at `https://docs.microsoft.com/en-us/azure/azure-resource-manager/resource-group-authoring-templates`. This will help you to work effectively for any resource deployment through the ARM and DevOps processes.

Summary

In this chapter, we have discussed DevOps practices for Azure integration. We have explained why the DevOps process is necessary for modern integration, along with how you can automate Azure integration services using the DevOps pipeline. In the next chapter, we will cover different monitoring options available for Azure integration services, along with different third-party applications that can be used for effective monitoring.

Monitoring for Azure Integration 13

In this chapter, we will discuss the different aspects of cloud monitoring in depth. After we have an understanding of what cloud monitoring entails, we will go on to discuss a few offerings. Besides mentioning a few available products, we will look at how to set up the monitoring of Azure integration components. Along the way, we will discuss some best practices and we will also discuss the cost and benefits of each offering.

In this chapter, we will cover following topics:

- How monitoring benefits an organization's business processes
- What Azure monitoring is and how you can use best-of-breed tools to monitor your Azure artifacts
- Best practices for monitoring, considering features and costs
- How to set up different monitoring options for your solution in Azure

Types of monitoring

It is clear that organizations benefit the most by having smooth-running business processes where all IT resources, internally and externally, work as expected. Unfortunately, that's not how things work in the real world. For IT resources, it is necessary to frequently monitor the health of components that are involved in business processes. Such monitoring can be done in the following ways:

- **Manual**: Monitoring is done manually by administrators
- **Automated**: Software is used for automated tooling and notifications

Manual monitoring

When relying on manual monitoring, administrators or support engineers will frequently have to check the state of different components. For Azure resources, the Azure portal can be used to set up dashboards so the state of any relevant resources can easily be understood.

Manual monitoring is a matter of good discipline and agreements between all involved stakeholders about who is monitoring what, when monitoring must take place, and who must be notified in various scenarios. This may not be so much of a problem during the regular business week, but during holiday seasons, for example, it absolutely needs to be clear who is responsible for what.

For somebody who needs to take care of someone else's monitoring tasks during holidays, it can be quite easy to forget about these tasks, as these tasks will be new and additional to their own usual workload. There is also a huge risk of monitoring tasks not being completely clear or being subject to regular changes. So, tasks will have to be described in a handbook, which needs to be maintained regularly.

Automated monitoring

Automated monitoring can be performed by anything from a scheduled PowerShell script to a mature monitoring solution. Although monitoring solutions require investment both in terms of the budget, learning curve, implementation, and maintenance, they serve a good purpose. When properly implemented, such solutions take away a lot of the cost (and not just financial) of manual monitoring, thereby allowing administrators and support engineers to be more effective as there is less of a demand for them to monitor components manually.

Automated monitoring solutions allow you to be notified of anything before any actual damage to business processes occurs. This is a shift from passive monitoring to proactive monitoring. Automated monitoring puts you in control and will most likely prevent you from receiving embarrassing phone calls or people coming to your desk to tell you that an interface is down.

The challenge with purchasing monitoring solutions, however, is that it can be hard to have a clear understanding of the **Return on Investment** (**ROI**) of purchasing and implementing such monitoring solutions. It will be clear what costs come with purchasing monitoring solutions (such as those for licenses, training, implementation, and support), but it will be harder to calculate what costs are saved by the purchase.

Different types of monitoring

Before we look at how monitoring your Azure solution can benefit your business processes, let's first review what types of monitoring exist. When we have a better understanding of this, we will return to the topic of this section and see how the business processes of an organization are benefited by monitoring.

The following types of monitoring are relevant for monitoring Azure solutions or hybrid solutions:

- Availability monitoring
- Health monitoring
- Performance monitoring
- Threshold monitoring

Let's discuss the characteristics of these types and then identify how each type affects business processes.

Availability monitoring

Availability monitoring becomes relevant when a solution is working as expected from the technical and functional perspectives. This means that all components throughout the solution must be brought back up and running in order to meet the business requirements. Often, the availability of a solution is measured by **Key Performance Indicators (KPIs)**. Here are some examples of KPIs:

- **Overall availability**: This can be measured, quite simply, by taking the planned hours of uptime and comparing them to the actual hours of uptime. Overall availability can be expressed as a percentage. Note that planned maintenance should also be considered when calculating overall availability. Overall availability should be as high as possible.
- **Planned unavailability**: This refers to the amount of time devoted to planned maintenance. Planned maintenance is needed, for example, to bring live changes to a solution. This can be calculated by taking the actual hours of planned maintenance and comparing them to the overall availability. This can also be expressed as a percentage. Planned unavailability should be kept as low as possible.

- **Unplanned unavailability**: Unplanned availability arises when a solution becomes unavailable due to some incident. These incidents can have lots of causes, whether on the Azure platform or in your own IT environment. Unplanned unavailability can be easily measured by taking the hours of unplanned availability and comparing them with overall availability. Unplanned unavailability should be as low as possible.

These are a few basic KPIs you can consider. You will find many more at KPI Library: http://kpilibrary.com/.

To have a clear understanding of what a customer expects of a service provider, contracts can be set up between both parties. Such contracts are called **Service Level Agreements (SLAs)**. Besides providing an understanding of the expectations of the customer, they can also determine what information has to be provided by the service provider to the customer. When setting up such contracts, think of the following:

- **Solution availability**: This can be based upon the KPIs we discussed earlier
- **Performance metrics**: Measure, for example, application performance and error rates
- **Response times**: Measure the average response times of the solution
- **Planned maintenance**: Measure the amount of planned maintenance
- **Usage statistics**: Measure, for example, page views, concurrent use, and demographic use

By adding telemetry to your solution, you can collect a lot of this kind of data.

SLAs are not just about writing down expectations and deliverables; they are also about determining and applying penalties when the conditions of the contract are not met. In such cases, and depending on the importance of the solution, serious damage can be done to the organization, so reasonable penalties and consequences must be agreed upon to protect the organization against such damage.

After deciding on the KPIs and SLAs for your organization, it is equally important to follow up on them. You can set up monitoring products that are designed for that purpose to provide transparent insights as to whether SLAs are being met. The following are globally a couple of examples of such products:

- **BMC:** https://www.bmc.com/
- **Nagios:** https://www.nagios.com/solutions/nagios-sla-reports/

Health monitoring

Another category of monitoring is health monitoring. Your solution may contain a huge number of components. So, it is of great importance to be aware of the state of all these components. Health monitoring involves setting up rules and conditions to determine the health of a solution. If the rules and conditions are not met, proactive reports can be sent to inform stakeholders prior to actual outage occurring. There are many ways to be informed about the health of components, such as the following:

- **Health dashboards**: Such dashboards will contain an overview of the state of the components and whether these components are healthy. Typically, such dashboards are seen at the support desk, allowing support personnel to have quick and up-to-date insights into the well-being of components and systems.
- **Scheduled health reports**: These are frequent emails (or other means of notification) that show the health of components. You can schedule such reports, for example, at 9 A.M. and 4 P.M. every business day, or even more frequently if necessary. These reports provide insights into the current health state of components and systems, irrespective of whether they are healthy or not.

In the end, how you are made aware of the health of your solution depends on the capabilities of your monitoring product.

Performance monitoring

With performance monitoring, you can monitor how well your solution performs under different circumstances. During the development of a solution, there probably won't be a high load on the components, so it makes sense to test how the solution behaves under high load and, it's been once brought to production, to monitor that performance. You could monitor, for example, any of the following:

- Processed transactions
- Transactions per second
- Requests per second
- User satisfaction

You can measure these metrics per component, but also for the entire chain. By segregating per component, it will be possible to identify any bottlenecks. Also, if your solution has to cope with drastically changing workloads, it is good to know that, depending on the Azure component in question, it is easy to scale up there is a heavy load and to scale down when under an average load. In this way, you only pay for resources when you need them, which can be handy if you expect more load on your solution during particular periods of the year.

Another aspect that falls under the category of performance monitoring is user satisfaction. To measure this, you can use Apdex scores (`https://www.apdex.org`). Apdex scores scale from zero (no users satisfied) to 1 (all users satisfied). Performance results are divided into the following categories:

- Satisfied
- Tolerating
- Frustrated

You can find the Apdex score specification here: `http://www.apdex.org/index.php/alliance/specifications/`.

Threshold monitoring

Threshold monitoring allows you to set up state-bound monitoring and send out notifications if an artifact reaches a faulty state. An artifact could be, for example, a Logic App that has been disabled, or an API app with unresponsive endpoints. Of course, we want to prevent artifacts from getting into faulty states, and we have seen that the Azure platform gives us multiple means to provide the best and most affordable way to make our solutions highly available. In the end, it is just a matter of calculating costs versus benefits.

Depending on the importance of your artifacts, you can set up different notification policies and make sure the support team picks up these notifications in a timely fashion. These policies could include any of the following:

- **Delayed notification and low response times**: This concerns low-impact issues that stakeholders will be notified about after at least 1 hour but maybe longer. These are low-priority issues that notifications only need to be issued for within regular office hours.
- **Average notification and response times**: This policy is for medium-impact, medium-priority issues to be notified within an hour and managed during (extended) office hours.

- **Immediate notification and high response times**: This policy is for high-priority issues where immediate action is required. Notification takes place as soon as the issue arises (or very shortly after that) and the issue should be picked up as soon as possible; a 24/7 support window might be needed.

Any flavor between the policies mentioned here is possible and might work well in your scenario. The key thing is that you should keep the level of notification and support in line with your business requirements. In other words, if there is no 24/7 business requirement, it would be a waste of money and resources to set up a 24/7 support team.

Sending notifications of issues or events

Besides deciding what you want to monitor, you also must think about who should receive notifications about any issues or events. When using a monitoring product, email is often the first choice for sending notifications. However, monitoring products exist that enable you to send notifications via products such as Slack, ServiceNow, SMS, and so on. This can be helpful if you want to send these notifications directly to stakeholders or resolution groups.

Typically, IT personnel will receive these notifications first, after which they can take the appropriate actions. To divide the workload and based on the complexity of the issue, different notifications can be sent to different layers of the IT department. You can consider the following division as a starting point:

- **First and second level support**: Receive issues that are repetitive and easy to fix, receive and action health reports
- **Third level support**: Fix complicated issues for which more knowledge of the solution and the business process is necessary

You can also consider involving business people in the support process and send them notifications directly from your monitoring products. As they have the business knowledge of the involved business processes, they will be aware of the consequences if anything goes wrong with an application/interface/solution. This would also take away the need to have the IT department inform business users of incidents.

Moving forward, you can also think of providing business people with read-only access to the Azure Portal, and/or other tooling related to the integrations, for analysis purposes. If the organization has matured enough and there is enough confidence in the tooling, you could even consider giving business people write access to the tooling, so they can fix certain issues themselves without the involvement of the IT department.

Benefits of monitoring

Now that we have seen the different types of monitoring and described a few of their characteristics, let's discuss how organizations benefit from monitoring. For an organization, setting up monitoring for a business process can serve both technical purposes and business purposes. For technical purposes, you can think of topics such as the availability of all the components, which thereby affects the overall availability of the business process. From a business perspective, getting metrics can help to make business decisions. Here are some examples of such metrics:

- **Number of sales during a certain period of the year, in specific regions or of particular product groups**: Useful for marketing campaigns or discounts
- **Overall processing time of a business process**: Useful to improve certain parts of the business process or to check whether KPIs are being met
- **Failure detection**: Useful for alerting if expected messages are not received within a certain timeframe

Improving availability

Whether done manually or automatically, monitoring will lead to higher availability of your solution. This results in fewer breaches in the business process. Especially with automated monitoring, it is very likely that you will discover issues at an early stage, maybe even before any damage can happen to the business process. There are some monitoring solutions that, besides notifying you of issues, have automatic recovery features.

For example, when somebody accidentally disables an Azure Logic App that plays a vital role in your solution, such auto-recovery features will not just tell stakeholders that that Logic App is in the wrong state, it will also try to bring the Logic App back to the enabled state, thereby not just increasing the availability of your solution but also being proactive instead of passive.

Business insights

By monitoring not just the components but also the actual business transactions, you will get a better understanding of the metrics of the overall business process. This allows you to have interesting information, such as the number of business transactions per hour/day/week/month. The more detailed the information is, the more equipped the business department will be when making business decisions.

Usage trends for upscaling and downscaling

Trend analysis is important for understanding how your solution is being used over time. When monitoring for trends, you can identify whether the load on the solution is stable or whether the load is increasing or decreasing over a certain period. This information can be used to decide whether you should upscale or downscale your solution.

Identifying performance bottlenecks

A solution will involve multiple components that are connected to each other. For example, Logic App *A* is triggered by a message from a Service Bus subscription. The Logic App calls Logic Apps *B*, *C*, and *D* to retrieve additional data, before the output of Logic App *A* is transferred to a **Customer Relationship Management (CRM)** system.

By monitoring the performance of the different parts in the solution, you might be able to identify a performance decrease and badly developed Logic Apps that are causing the overall bad performance of the solution. So, based on these performance metrics, you might decide to redesign or redevelop certain parts of your solution.

Azure integration service monitoring

Azure integration services consist of Logic Apps, Azure API Management, Azure Event Grid, and Service Bus. Having better monitoring capabilities adds value to IT and DevOps teams, enabling them to look after the overall health of the integration application. In a coming section, we will discuss monitoring tools and platforms available within Microsoft Azure for monitoring Azure Integration Services. We will also cover Serverless360, a third-party tool, and how you can build Serverless360 into your enterprise integration solution to monitor parts of your Azure integration services.

Azure Logic Apps monitoring with the Azure portal and Azure log analytics

Azure Logic Apps monitoring and tracking can be done through Azure log Analytics and the Azure portal. You can also use event hubs and your Storage account to send integration log data for machine learning and analysis purposes.

You can check the status of Logic Apps, checking things such as the run history, trigger history, status, any performance matrices, and overall workflow performance, through the Azure portal and a configured instance of Azure Log Analytics.

As each Logic App's workflow is a micro component of an integration framework in the cloud, each Logic App requires its own individual monitoring setup, which can be achieved through Logic Apps diagnostics setting. Logic Apps do not provide you with the option to set global tracking at one place, and so you need to follow the steps listed in the following screenshot to enable tracking for your individual Logic Apps:

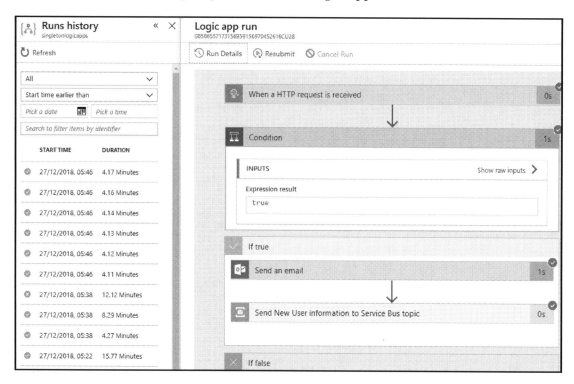

In the Azure portal, click on **Run Details** to find the different states of actions, such as whether an action has failed, succeeded, or skipped. You can also analyze the performance matrix and visualize each action's performance:

09:26:30	09:26:35	09:26:40	09:26:45	09:26:49	09:26:55
Succeeded	Failed	Running	Skipped	Aborted	
4	2	-	-	-	

ACTION	STATUS	DURATION
Business_Logic	Failed	1.05 Seconds
Exception_handling	Succeeded	21.77 Seconds
Filter_array	Succeeded	5 Milliseconds
For_each_failed_message	Succeeded	21.72 Seconds
HTTP	Failed	902 Milliseconds
Post_exception_message	Succeeded	1 Millisecond

For real-time event monitoring of a Logic App's workflow and for richer debugging, we can also set up diagnostics logging. With the proper monitoring setup, you can find and view trigger events, run events, and action events. You can also use this diagnostics data with other services, such as Azure Storage and Azure Event Hubs, for machine learning and analytics purposes.

We can also set up alerts for Logic App run failures. For example, you can configure notification for when any Logic App isn't triggered throughout the entire day, or when there are five concurrent failures on the same Logic App within a specified time interval.

Logic App runs and trigger history

To view a Logic App's overall run history, or its run history for a specified time interval, you can use the Azure portal or Log Analytics. In the Azure portal, you have the option to set start and end times for monitoring.

In the following example, we have listed Logic Apps that have run with a start time earlier than 30th December, 2018:

When working with an enterprise-grade integration solution, one requirement is to find the activity log history. For example, when Logic Apps have been stopped or someone has modified a Logic App's workflow definition, you can find such details within the **Activity log** blade in the Logic App in question. If required, you can send activity logs to Event Hubs for streaming, or you can download activity details as a CSV file:

Logic Apps notifications and alerts

Logic Apps has built-in support for rule-based notification and alerts for key metrics monitoring. In this section, we will cover how you can set up notification systems for Logic Apps based on predefined conditions without using Azure Log Analytics. To set up alerts for a specific Logic App's workflow, follow these steps:

1. In the **Logic Apps** blade menu, under the **Monitoring** section, click on **Alerts**, and then click on **New alert rule**:

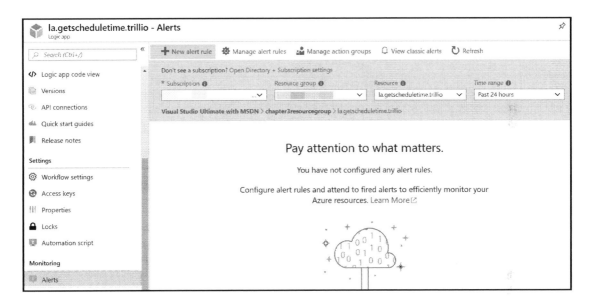

2. In the **Create rule** blade menu, select **Resource** as Logic Apps and then select the Logic App for which you would like to set up an alert feature. Add the required key matrix filter condition, and then you can either create a new action group or use any existing DevOps action group. In **ACTION TYPE**, you can select various ways to send notifications and alerts, such as running a **Webhook, LogicApp, Azure Function, Email/SMS/Push/Voice**, and more:

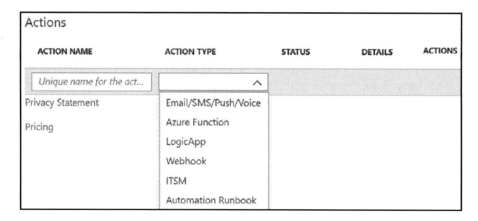

3. In this exercise, we have set alerts via **Email**, with the throttling condition set to **Whenever the Run Failure Percentage is Greater than 10%**. Update the alert details with **Alert Name** and **Alert description** and click on **Create alert rule**:

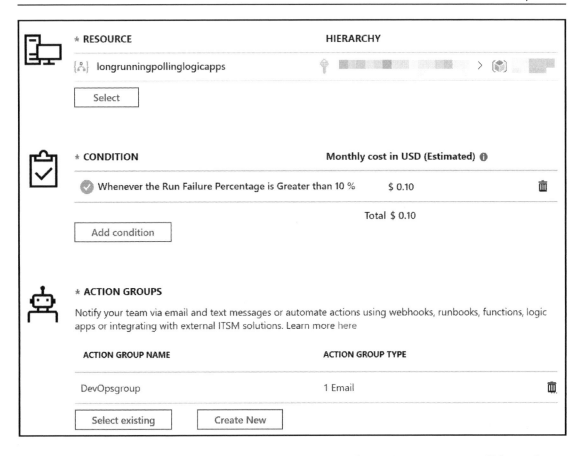

When you choose a Logic App HTTP request trigger as the action type, you will have the option to post the message to teams, send it via Slack, or send an exception message to trigger any other Logic App's workflow.

Azure Log Analytics and Logic Apps

With Azure Log Analytics, you can monitor multiple Logic Apps trigger events, tracked properties, and action events. In this section, we will cover how you can enable Log Analytics and use the OMS blade menu to effectively monitor a Logic App's run history:

1. To get started with Log Analytics, log into the Azure portal, search for `log analytics`, and choose the **Log Analytics** service:

2. Under the **Log Analytics** blade, search for the Log Analytics workspace. To add a Logic Apps management solution to Log Analytics, click on **View solutions**, available through the **Log Analytics Overview** menu blade:

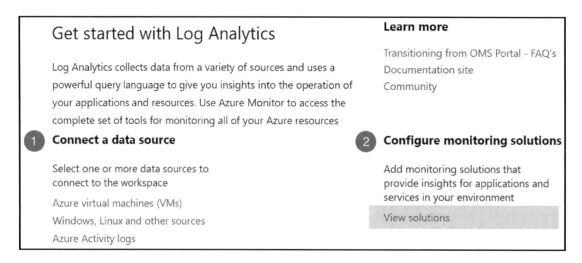

3. On the **Overview** page, click on **Add**, which opens the **Management Solutions** list. From that list, select **Logic Apps Management**. Once that's selected and diagnostics logs are enabled for Logic Apps, we can track a Logic App's run history through **Log Analytics** and the **Logic Apps Management** suite:

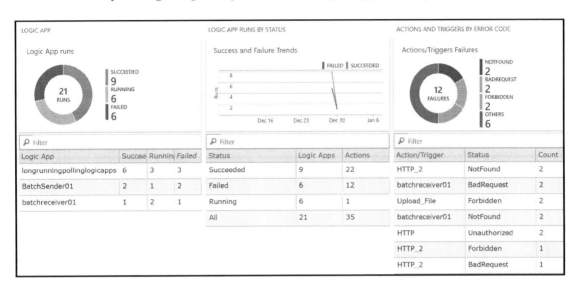

4. To view the entire run history for a specific Logic App or to check its status, select the individual Logic App. This will give you an overview of the individual Logic App's run history in real time:

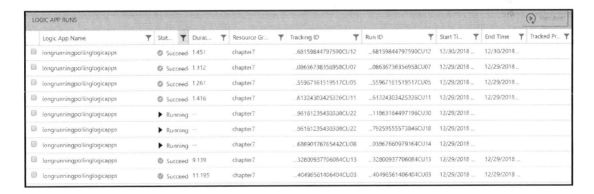

5. **Log Analytics** also gives you the ability to re-run any existing failed or successful Logic App workflow with the Resubmit feature:

6. Enabling the **Log Analytics** feature in Logic Apps can be done either through the Azure portal or with a Logic Apps workflow template. To enable Log Analytics through the Azure portal, navigate to the specific Logic Apps instance and, within the **Monitoring** blade menu, click on **Diagnostics Settings** and on the **Diagnostic Setting** page, and click on **Turn on diagnostics**. Enter the required name in **Diagnostics Settings** and populate the **Send to Log Analytics** section as follows:

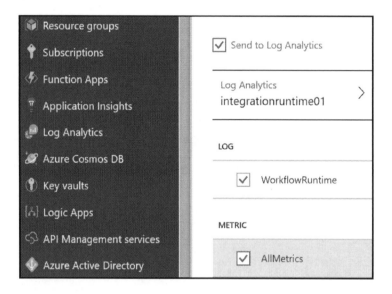

To find out more about the Logic Apps monitoring feature, we suggest you look at the Microsoft documentation (`https://docs.microsoft.com/en-us/azure/logic-apps/logic-apps-monitor-your-logic-apps`).

Azure Functions monitoring with Application Insights

In the previous section, we covered Logic Apps workflow monitoring with the Azure portal and Log Analytics. This section will cover how you can enable Azure Functions monitoring using Application Insights. Azure Functions provide built-in support for Application Insights to monitor an Azure Function's health and performance matrices. In this section, we will show how you can enable the Application Insights feature in your new or existing Functions:

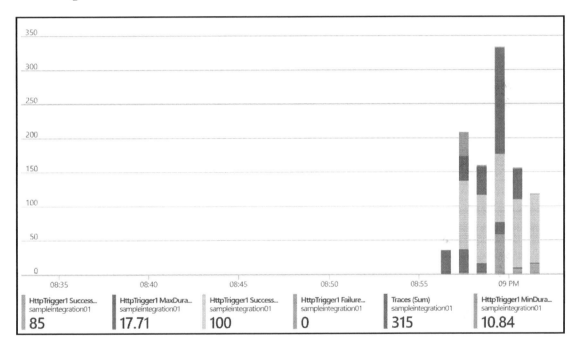

To enable Application Insights monitoring for a new functions app container, you can configure Application Insights while creating the function app resource through the Azure portal or using an ARM template. As we have already covered the ARM template feature in the previous chapter, in this exercise we will show how you can enable Application Insights through the Azure portal.

Application Insights configuration for a new function app

To configure Application Insights for your new function app, do the following:

1. Go to the function app's **Create page** blade menu.
2. Set the Application Insights feature to on.
3. Select an Application Insights location. Choose the region that is closest to your function app's container region and then click on **Create**.

Manually connecting an Application Insights resource to your function app

To manually connect, do the following:

1. Create the Application Insights resource within the resource group and location nearest to your function app
2. Copy the Application Insights instrumentation key from the Application Insights resource
3. In the function app application settings, add a new app setting called `APPINSIGHTS_INSTRUMENTATIONKEY` and as value set to the Application Insights instrumentation key, and click on **Save**

When enabling Application Insights for your function app, it is advisable to disable built-in function logging, which uses Azure Storage. Built-in logging is useful when testing with a low workload in the development phase. To disable it, delete the **AzureWebJobsDashboard** app setting from the Azure Functions application configuration section.

Monitoring functions with Application Insights

After the initial setup of Application Insights for the function app, we can the monitoring logs for individual Functions using the **Monitor** option:

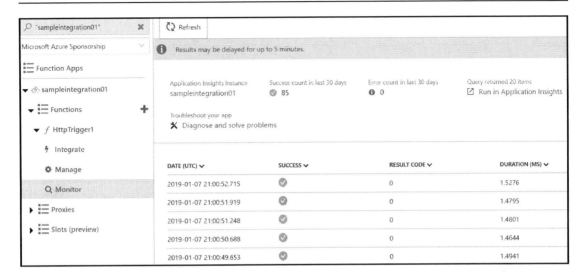

To verify the logs of a particular Function run, you can click on any specific run row and that will bring up logs for the individual run:

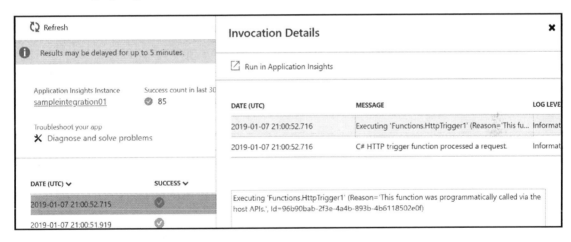

You can also get function app monitoring logs through an Application Insights analytics query. Application Insights is the source of function app health and run logs:

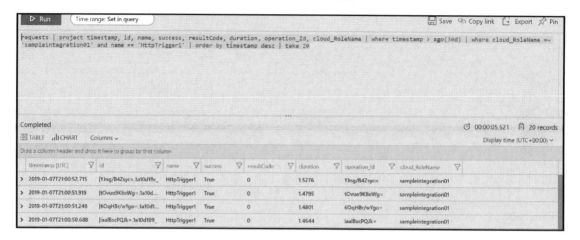

Within your function app, you can directly navigate to the associated Application Insights resource from the Overview section of the function app. You can find the associated performance matrix of each function within the function app:

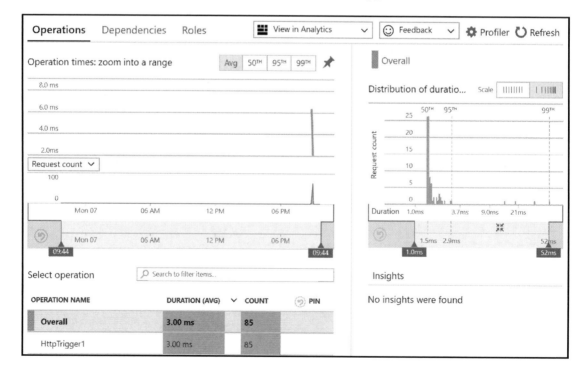

Using Application Insights, you can also easily capture any exception raised during Function execution. This will also enable setting up alerts based on Function failure and server exceptions. Such exceptions could either be due to high resource utilization or broken code within the function app:

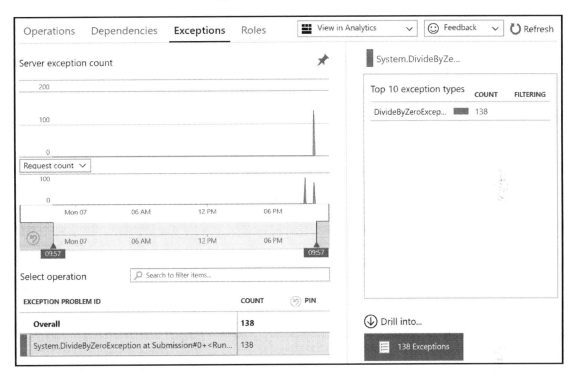

Here we have covered the basic monitoring of a function app using Application Insights. To learn more about how you can query telemetry data from Application Insights, go to the Functions Monitoring section of the Microsoft documentation: `https://docs.microsoft.com/en-us/azure/azure-functions/functions-monitoring`.

Azure API Management monitoring with Application Insights

Like Azure Functions, Azure API Management also enables an enterprise to easily integrate with Azure Application Insights to monitor the Azure API Management platform. In this walkthrough, we will describe the integration of Application Insights with Azure API Management:

1. The first step is to create Azure API Management and Application Insights resources within your specified resource group and location. As we already have Azure API Management and Application Insights resources within our resource group, we will move on to integrate Application Insights with Azure API Management:

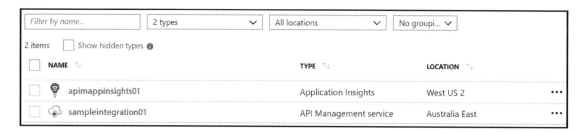

2. The next step is to integrate Application Insights with Azure API Management. To do this, click on **API Management resource**, and in the **Monitoring** blade section, click on **Application Insights**. On the API Management **Application Insights** blade, click on **Add,** select the existing **Application Insights instance**, and give a proper description in the **Description** section, then click on **Create**:

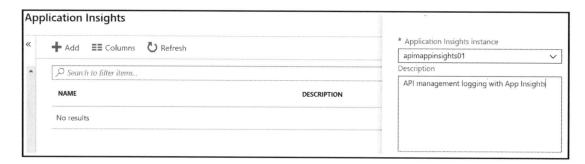

3. This step will update the API Management resource with the Application Insights instrumentation key; now we are ready to enable Application Insights within our API Management resource. To enable global tracing with Application Insights for all APIs, navigate to the **API** menu blade within API Management, click on **All APIs**, and, in the **Settings** tab, **Enable** Application Insights with the appropriate sampling percentage. In this example, we have enabled 85% of logging data. You can also log any additional header properties from the request response header. Click on **Save** to update the global tracking properties:

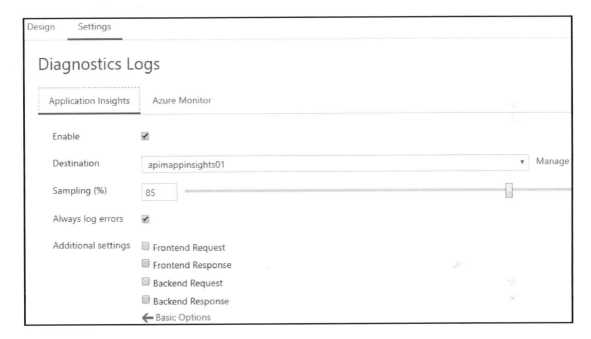

4. To view logs for APIs hosted in API Management, you can now navigate to the Application Insights resource and monitor real-time traffic going through Azure API Management:

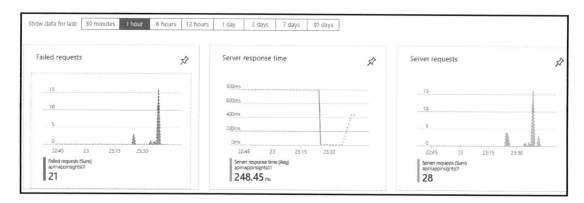

5. Within Application Insights, you can now drill down to the exception to find out more about logged exceptions, so that you can update the appropriate team about specific service behaviors:

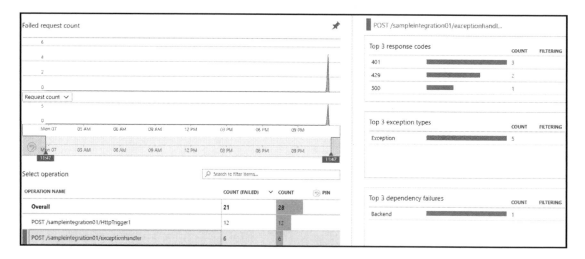

6. You can leverage Application Insights to find API Management application mapping details and the performance matrix for each connection application. To look for API Management in Application Insights, within the **Investigate** menu, click on **Application map**; this will open up the **Application map** page, listing backend systems:

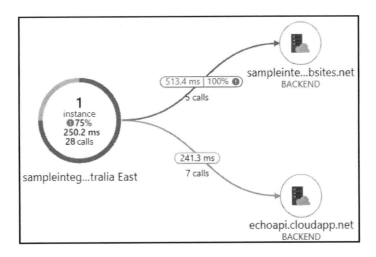

7. API Management also supports API-level tracking. When enabling API-level tracking in Azure API Management, global tracking will be overwritten with individual API tracking properties. To enable API-level tracking, navigate to the specific API in Azure API Management, click on **Settings**, and in **Diagnostics Logs**, enable Application Insights tracking with your custom properties as follows:

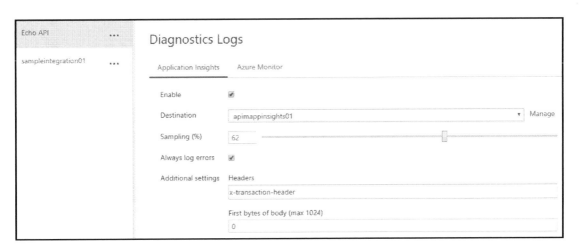

In the next section, we will cover Serverless360, a third-party product, and describe the steps for leveraging Serverless360 to monitor the Service Bus along with other integration artifacts, such as Azure Event Grid and Event Hubs.

Azure Service Bus monitoring with Serverless360

Although we don't want to discuss the product in too much detail here, let's take an overview of the capabilities of Serverless360. The product was first named ServiceBus360. Before capabilities for other Azure technologies were added to the product, it solely contained features to do with the operation and monitoring of Azure Service Bus queues and topics. By also bringing in security features, such as access policies and auditing, scheduled bulk-send message features, and data monitoring features, the product has become a powerful and secure choice for day-to-day use of Azure Service Bus.

The product is still in development, but Serverless360 currently has features that support the following Azure technologies. For each technology, only the most important features are mentioned:

- **Service Bus**: CRUD operations on queues or topics, viewing or resubmitting dead letter messages, purge messages, bulk scheduling (dead letter) messages, state-based monitoring
- **Function apps**: CRUD operations, state-based monitoring, viewing invocation logs
- **Logic Apps**: CRUD operations, running triggers or viewing trigger history, state-based monitoring
- **API apps**: Threshold monitoring
- **Event hubs**: CRUD operations, importing event hubs, creating or deleting consumer groups, state-based monitoring
- **Azure relays**: Managing and importing relays, state-based monitoring

We know by now that a serverless solution can comprise multiple types of many different Azure components. From a monitoring and operating perspective, it is not very efficient to use the Azure portal to operate all these different components, as these components are to be found in many different places in the portal. It would be more effective to treat these components as one application. Because of that, Serverless360 introduced the concept of composite serverless applications, which allows you to group all these different components to the same composite application.

Serverless360 monitoring features

Earlier in this chapter, we saw the different types of monitoring that are relevant for composite serverless solutions. Serverless360 provides features in the following areas:

- **Threshold monitoring**: Used for threshold violation-based monitoring
- **Health monitoring**: Used for health or status checks
- **Data monitoring**: Used for data processing and non-event monitoring

The documentation portal of Serverless360 (`https://docs.serverless360.com/docs/alarms-management#`) tells us more about these types of alarm in Serverless360. The following descriptions are taken from that portal, although the content is adapted to the audience of this book.

Threshold violation alarms

Threshold alarms in Serverless360 can be set to send immediate alerts (or alerts based on configurable persist durations) when the threshold condition of a resource is violated. If required, you can configure the monitoring of threshold violation to occur only during specific times on specific days (say, weekdays between 9:00 A.M. and 6:00 P.M.), which is useful if you want to monitor only during business hours. You can also limit the number of alerts (per violation) that will be sent. This prevents you from being bombarded many times about the same issue and potentially being distracted from more important issues.

Health check alarms

It's a common practice for support people to regularly check the overall health status of the systems they support. For integration solutions, Serverless360 helps to automate that process by allowing you to create a daily health check or status alarm at certain times (for example, Monday to Friday, 11:00 A.M.). When you are creating a health monitoring alert, you can set up the alarm to monitor the health of the integration solution on a periodic basis. You can configure the day/time as per your requirements.

Data monitoring

Your support person might have to regularly watch for successful trigger runs of a particular Logic App, or look out for total billable executions. Serverless360 allows you to set up monitoring based on a set of metrics and be notified when an entity doesn't perform in line with the business SLA. Data monitoring in Serverless360 allows you to set up this kind of process monitoring.

Managing composite serverless applications in Serverless360

Now we understand the different monitoring capabilities of Serverless360. In this part of the chapter, we'll discuss how to set up composite serverless applications in Serverless360. Therefore, we need to perform the following steps:

1. Associate an Azure subscription.
2. Create a composite serverless application.
3. Add Azure serverless components to the application.

After completing these steps, we can start setting up alarms. But first, let's see how to perform the previously mentioned steps.

Associating an Azure subscription

The first task we need to do after starting off with Serverless360 is associate at least one Azure subscription to the product. Depending on the license tier we have, we can add three or more Azure subscriptions. Serverless360 helps you by providing a link to its documentation portal, which describes the process. You can find this documentation here: https://docs.serverless360.com/docs/associating-resources-by-service-principal.

After following the steps mentioned in that article, we will end up with a screen that looks like this:

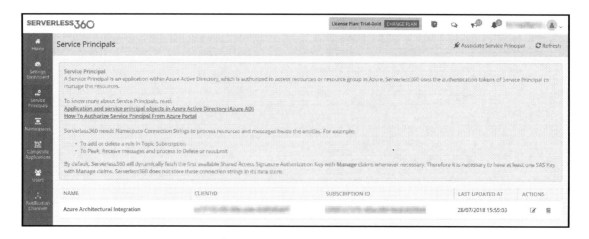

Creating a composite serverless application

Once we have at least one Azure subscription associated with Serverless360, the next step is to create a **Composite Application** in the product. By default, Serverless360 already has an empty **Composite Application** for us, but let's see how to create a composite application ourselves:

1. **Navigate to Composite Applications**: From the service principal screen where we currently are, we navigate to the **Composite Applications** screen. We do this by clicking on the **Composite Applications** button in the left-hand side menu bar.

2. **Create a Composite Application**: The screen that we see next already shows the default application. By clicking the **Create** button, we will create another **Composite Application**:

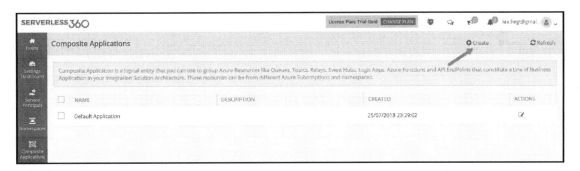

3. **Enter Composite Application details**: The screen contains fields to enter a **Name** and a **Description** for the **Composite Application**. Although only the **Name** field is required, it is recommended to also enter a **Description**, to make the purpose of this **Composite Application** as clear as possible. In our case, we will enter the following for the **Composite Application**:
   - **Name**: ACME Order Processing
   - **Description**: This **Composite Application** is used as a container for all the Azure components for ACME Order Processing:

4. **Save the Composite Application**: The only thing left to do is click the **Add** button to create the **Composite Application**. Once we have done that, we will be redirected to the **Composite Applications** overview screen, and the **Composite Application** we just created will be shown as well:

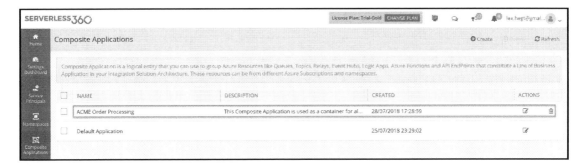

Now that we have created a **Composite Application,** we need to associate Azure serverless components with it. We will discuss this in the next section.

Adding Azure serverless components to the application

To be able to add components to a **Composite Application,** we first must navigate to the **Home** dashboard of **Serverless360**. From there, we can view and manage the **Composite Applications** that have been created. Follow these steps to navigate to that dashboard and add some components to the **Composite Application** that we created in the previous section:

1. **Navigate to the Home dashboard**: Click **Home** in the upper-left corner to navigate to the **Home** dashboard of **Serverless360**:

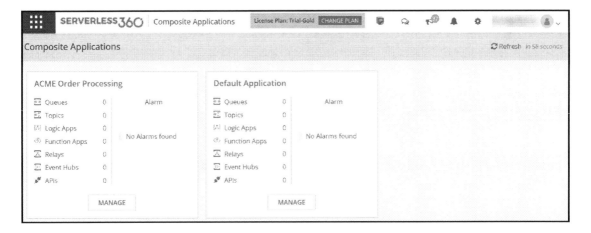

The screen shows both the default application and the one we created ourselves. As we can learn from viewing both containers, no components have been added to the applications and no alarms exist. Each application also has a button named **MANAGE**. By clicking that button, we can add components to the **Composite Application**.

2. **Manage Composite Applications**: Click on the **MANAGE** button for the ACME Order Processing application. This will take us to the following screen:

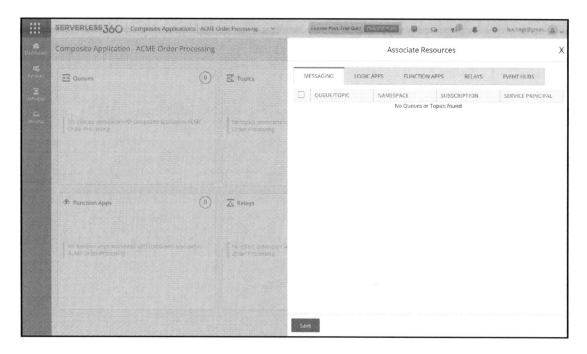

The screen shows the associate resources pane, with an overview screen in the background that has all the different components associated with the ACME Order Processing **Composite Application**.

The **Associate Resources** pane shows five tabs for the different kind of components that we can add to a **Composite Application**. Note that, to be able to associate messaging and relay components to a **Composite Application**, you first need to associate Azure Service Bus and/or Relay namespaces to **Serverless360**. For the remaining component types (Logic Apps, function apps, and Event Hubs), all artifacts from the Azure subscriptions that are associated in **Serverless360** are shown in the subsequent tabs.

3. **Add a few resources to the Composite Application**: Let's add a few Logic Apps to the **Composite Application**. Firstly, we'll click on the **LOGIC APPS** tab:

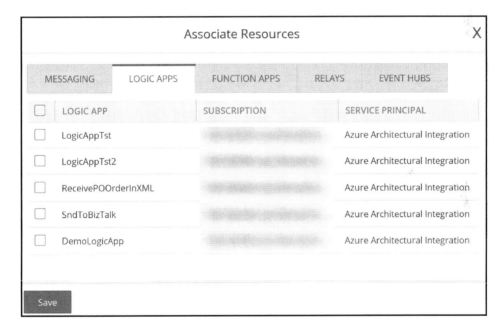

4. Select a few Logic Apps by clicking the checkbox that shows on the left-hand side of each Logic App. Once the Logic Apps are selected, click the **Save** button. We will be redirected to the **Overview** screen, and in the **Logic Apps** frame the recently added Logic Apps will show up:

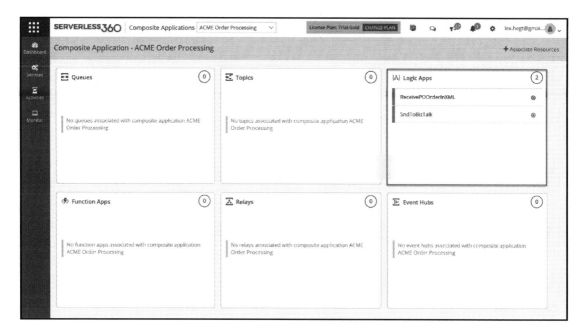

5. From this **Overview** screen, we can access all subsequent sections by clicking on the header of each section. The following screenshot shows what the section looks like for **Logic Apps**:

Here you can, for example, perform the following actions for Logic Apps:

- Disable or enable Logic Apps
- Run triggers
- View trigger properties
- Disassociate the Logic App from the **Composite Application**
- Set up monitoring

Now we have associated some components to a **Composite Application**, we can set up monitoring for these components. This is the subject of the next section.

Setting up monitoring in Serverless360

In Serverless360, an alarm is a logical container in which you configure all kinds of monitoring rules. Once you've done that, you can map artifacts you want to monitor to that alarm. In other words, to create an alarm in Serverless360, we will perform the following steps:

1. **Create an alarm**: Give the alarm a name, configure the type of the alarm and how notifications should be transmitted to stakeholders
2. **Map artifacts to the alarm**: Associate the artifacts that should be monitored with the alarm

Both steps are described in more detail next.

Creating an alarm

In Serverless360, you can create alarms from a couple of different places in the user interface:

- In the **Overview** screen of a **Composite Application**
- Within a **Composite Application**, in the section for a component type (for example, queues, topics, Logic Apps, and so on)

Here we will only describe how to create a threshold alarm. As mentioned before, such alarms can be used to monitor whether the components of your solution are in the expected state.

In the previous section, we left off in the Logic Apps section of our ACME Order Processing application, so let's create an alarm from that section:

1. **Create an alarm**: The blue menu bar on our left-hand side shows **Monitor** as the last menu option. When we hover our mouse over that menu option, we get the following options:

   To create an alarm, we select the **Configure Alarms** option.

2. **Enter the alarm details**: After we have selected the **Configure Alarms** section, a pane shows up where we can enter the details of the alarm. For the following fields, a value can be entered or selected.

3. **Alarm name**: Enter a descriptive name for the alarm. This field is required and a maximum of 50 characters can be entered.

4. **Summary**: The notifications sent by this alarm show this summary. This field is not required and a maximum of 100 characters can be entered.

5. **Choose alarm type**: This dropdown has the following two values:
   - **Threshold**: Set up an alarm for threshold notifications
   - **Health check**: Set up an alarm for status checks at defined times

6. **Disable alarm for maintenance**: By default, an alarm is **Enabled**, but it might be smart to temporarily **Disable** the alarm to prevent receiving false notifications.

In our case, we will create a threshold alarm with the following details:

Field	Value
Alarm name	ACME - Logic Apps
Summary	For monitoring whether the Logic Apps are in the correct state, we use this alarm
Choose alarm type	Threshold
Disable alarm for maintenance	No (which is the default)

After entering the preceding values, we click the **Next** button in the lower-right corner of the pane:

1. **Enter the Threshold Alert details**: As we have decided to create a threshold alarm, the next screen shows fields related to that alarm type. The following fields show up:
   - **Notify when violation ends**: Configure whether you want to receive a notification once the threshold violation is finished and the alarm is healthy again.
   - **If violation persists for**: Here you can configure how many minutes after a violation you want to receive a notification. For important components, you want to receive these notifications earlier than for less important components. A value from 1 to 60 minutes can be selected.

2. **Number of alerts per violation**: This allows you to configure how many notifications you can receive (per violation). This prevents your being bombarded by notifications for the same violation repeatedly, which can lead to you potentially missing more important notifications. A value from 1 to 10 can be selected.

3. **Set alerts on set day and time only**: By using this option, you can monitor only during the configured day and time. This is helpful, for example, when a component is only available on business days.

In our case, let's stick to the default values and click **Next** to proceed to the next screen.

4. **Configure notification channels**: With notification channels, you can configure the means by which you want to receive your notifications. Email is the default notification channel, but you can configure multiple others, such as pager duty, Slack, webhook, OMS, and Microsoft Teams. These notification channels can be configured under **Settings | Notification Channels**. As none of the aforementioned notification channels have been set up so far, we can only configure the email notification channel. Hence, in this pane, only the following fields show up:

   - **Serverless360 email channel**: Set whether you want to use the email notification channel.
   - **Recipient email address**: Email address to which the notifications will be sent. Multiple addresses can be entered, separated by a comma or a semi-colon.

In this case, we'll use following values:

Field	Value
Serverless360 email channel	Yes (switch is green)
Recipient email address	Enter your own email address

5. **Save the alarm**: Now we have configured all the monitoring rules, the only thing left is to save the alarm. Click the blue **Save** button in the lower-left corner of the pane. Once the alarm is saved, the overview screen containing all the alarms for the ACME Order Processing application will show up:

We've now created an alarm, including monitoring rules. With this, we have configured how we will monitor; next, we'll configure what we want to monitor.

Mapping artifacts to the alarm

To configure what we want to monitor, we must map the artifacts we want to monitor to an alarm. After that, we can configure the actual monitoring:

1. **Add artifacts from the Composite Application to the alarm**: In this step, we will map some artifacts to an alarm. To do so, we must navigate to the **Monitoring Dashboard**. From the left-hand side menu, under **Monitor**, we select **Monitoring Dashboard**:

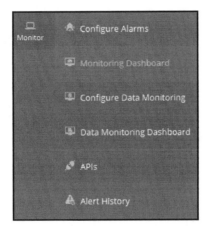

The **Monitoring Dashboard** still looks a bit empty, so let's start by adding some Logic Apps to it by clicking **Add Entities**. From the menu that appears, select **Logic Apps**, after which a pane shows the Logic Apps that we added earlier to the **Composite Application**:

Select both Logic Apps and click **Save**. We are redirected to the monitoring dashboard, which now shows both Logic Apps:

Although both Logic Apps are now added to the alarm, we still need to configure what we want to monitor for. So, that's the next step we will concentrate on.

2. **Configure monitoring**: For all the artifacts we add to an alarm, we can configure what exactly we want to monitor. As, in our scenario, we will be monitoring a few Logic Apps, we can monitor the state of these Logic Apps. Logic Apps can have the following states, which can also be used for monitoring:

- Enabled (default)
- Disabled
- Deleted
- Completed
- Suspended
- Not specified

Configuring which state to monitor for can be done by clicking on a Logic App, after which the **Configure Properties** screen appears. From the following screen, you set up the monitoring of Logic Apps in three steps:

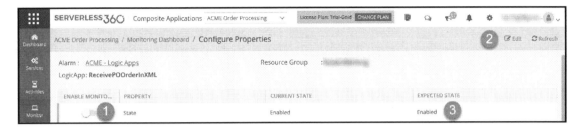

1. **Enable monitoring**: The first step is to enable monitoring for the Logic App. We achieve this by flipping the **Enable Monitoring** switch. After that, the **Edit** button will be enabled.
2. **Click Edit**: Next, we click the **Edit** button to be able to configure the state for which we want to monitor. The **Edit** button becomes replaced by **Save** and **Cancel** buttons.
3. **Configure the expected state**: From the **EXPECTED STATE** dropdown, we configure the state we want to monitor. In most cases, we want a Logic App to be **Enabled**, but there might be very good reasons to have your Logic Apps in a different state.

After we have selected the **EXPECTED STATE (Enabled)**, we click the **Save** button.

This wraps up setting up a threshold alarm for this chapter. If our Logic App is not in the enabled state, we receive a notification in our email inbox. The alarm we created only contains a Logic App, but the alarm can easily be extended with monitors for other component types supported by Serverless360. If you prefer not to use email, you could use another notification channel that Serverless360 supports.

Summary

In this chapter, we discussed monitoring Azure integration services. We have walked through the process of enabling monitoring for Logic Apps, API Management, Azure Functions, and Service Bus. In this chapter, we have also covered how you can use Serverless360 to effectively monitor the messaging layer for your enterprise.

Other Books You May Enjoy

If you enjoyed this book, you may be interested in these other books by Packt:

Azure Serverless Computing Cookbook – Second Edition
Praveen Kumar Sreeram

ISBN: 978-1-78961-526-5

- Integrate Azure Functions with other Azure services
- Understand cloud application development using Azure Functions
- Employ durable functions for developing reliable and durable serverless applications
- Use SendGrid and Twilio services
- Explore code reusability and refactoring in Azure Functions

Serverless computing in Azure with .NET

Sasha Rosenbaum

ISBN: 978-1-78728-839-3

- Understand the best practices of Serverless architecture
- Learn how how to deploy a Text Sentiment Evaluation application in an Azure Serverless environment
- Implement security, identity, and access control
- Take advantage of the speed of deployment in the cloud
- Configure application health monitoring, logging, and alerts

Leave a review - let other readers know what you think

Please share your thoughts on this book with others by leaving a review on the site that you bought it from. If you purchased the book from Amazon, please leave us an honest review on this book's Amazon page. This is vital so that other potential readers can see and use your unbiased opinion to make purchasing decisions, we can understand what our customers think about our products, and our authors can see your feedback on the title that they have worked with Packt to create. It will only take a few minutes of your time, but is valuable to other potential customers, our authors, and Packt. Thank you!

Index

installing 62

28736451R00275

Made in the USA
San Bernardino, CA
08 March 2019